KEY CONCEPTS IN LAW

Palgrave Key Concepts

Palgrave Key Concepts provide an accessible and comprehensive range of subject glossaries at undergraduate level. They are the ideal companion to a standard textbook making them invaluable reading to students throughout their course of study and especially useful as a revision aid.

Key Concepts in Accounting and Finance
Key Concepts in Business Practice
Key Concepts in Criminal Justice and Criminology
Key Concepts in Cultural Studies
Key Concepts in Drama and Performance (second edition)
Key Concepts in e-Commerce
Key Concepts in Human Resource Management
Key Concepts in Information and Communication Technology
Key Concepts in International Business
Key Concepts in Language and Linguistics (second edition)
Key Concepts in Law (second edition)
Key Concepts in Leisure
Key Concepts in Management
Key Concepts in Marketing
Key Concepts in Operations Management
Key Concepts in Philosophy
Key Concepts in Politics
Key Concepts in Public Relations
Key Concepts in Psychology
Key Concepts in Social Research Methods
Key Concepts in Sociology
Key Concepts in Strategic Management
Key Concepts in Tourism

Palgrave Key Concepts: Literature
General Editors: John Peck and Martin Coyle

Key Concepts in Contemporary Literature
Key Concepts in Creative Writing
Key Concepts in Crime Fiction
Key Concepts in Medieval Literature
Key Concepts in Modernist Literature
Key Concepts in Postcolonial Literature
Key Concepts in Renaissance Literature
Key Concepts in Romantic Literature
Key Concepts in Victorian Literature
Literary Terms and Criticism (third edition)

Further titles are in preparation
www.palgravekeyconcepts.com

Palgrave Key Concepts
Series Standing Order
ISBN 1–4039–3210–7
(outside North America only)

You can receive future titles in this series as they are published by placing a standing order. Please contact your bookseller or, in the case of difficulty, write to us at the address below with your name and address, the title of the series and the ISBN quoted above.

Customer Services Department, Macmillan Distribution Ltd
Houndmills, Basingstoke, Hampshire RG21 6XS, England

Key Concepts in Law

2nd Edition

Ian McLeod

palgrave
macmillan

First edition published in 2006
Second edition published in 2010 by
PALGRAVE MACMILLAN

Palgrave Macmillan in the UK is an imprint of Macmillan Publishers Limited, registered in England, company number 785998, of Houndmills, Basingstoke, Hampshire RG21 6XS.

Palgrave Macmillan in the US is a division of St Martin's Press LLC, 175 Fifth Avenue, New York, NY 10010.

Palgrave Macmillan is the global academic imprint of the above companies and has companies and representatives throughout the world.

Palgrave® and Macmillan® are registered trademarks in the United States, the United Kingdom, Europe and other countries.

ISBN 978-0-230-23294-5

This book is printed on paper suitable for recycling and made from fully managed and sustained forest sources. Logging, pulping and manufacturing processes are expected to conform to the environmental regulations of the country of origin.

A catalogue record for this book is available from the British Library.

10   9   8   7   6   5   4   3   2   1
19   18   17   16   15   14   13   12   11   10

Printed and bound in Great Britain by
CPI Antony Rowe, Chippenham and Eastbourne

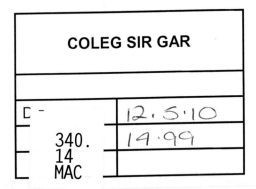

Contents

Preface to the Second Edition

This book is written specifically for readers who are coming to the study of law for the first time. If you fall into this category, one of your first challenges will be to get to grips with the language that lawyers use when talking about their subject. And that is where this book comes in. By explaining many of the words and expressions that lawyers use when talking about their subject, it aims to make the language of the law – and, therefore, the study of the subject itself – much less daunting than it would otherwise be.

I have encountered two main difficulties in writing this book: deciding what to say and then saying it.

In terms of the first difficulty, I hope this book may be useful to students on a wide variety of courses. However, I have taken the typical reader to be someone who is about to embark on, or is in the early stages of, either a Law degree (or another degree with a substantial Law content), or a graduate conversion course (whether it leads to a Postgraduate Diploma in Law or the Common Professional Examination or both). On this basis, I have placed the emphasis very heavily on the subjects which the legal professions' Joint Academic Stage Board has designated as the Foundations of Legal Knowledge (which it amuses me to think of as being FOLK Law). I have, however, strayed beyond the limits of those subjects in a few instances where doing so seemed like a good idea at the time.

In terms of the second difficulty, all I can say is that I have done my best to demystify the subject matter by writing as plainly as the content allows, in order to make the result as intelligible as possible to absolute beginners. With this aim in mind, I have been conscious that dense, dictionary-style definitions generally mean little or nothing to readers who are new to a subject. Accordingly, I have chosen to err on the side of explanation rather than mere definition, except where I have been able to write the definitions so that they really do speak for themselves. Of course, no book of this kind can dot every *i* and cross every *t* in terms of detail, but I hope I have minimised the extent to which I have had to sacrifice accuracy to brevity. On a typographical note, I have used SMALL CAPITALS to indicate cross references on the first appearance in each entry of a word or phrase which requires cross-referencing. However, I have never made a cross-reference where the effect would be simply to return the reader to the entry containing the cross-reference. I have used *italics* for the first appearance of the key word or phrase in each entry, as well as for their traditional role in case names, in Latin and French words and phrases, and for providing emphasis.

Although the modern tendency is to avoid the use of Latin, there is no escaping the fact that the judgments in many older cases (as well as some modern ones) do contain Latin words and phrases. Accordingly, I have included those Latin words and phrases which seem to me to satisfy my basic criterion of being useful to beginners. Moreover, bearing in mind that very few readers of this book will have studied Latin, I have attempted to give guidance on pronunciation. The problem is that lawyers' Latin has no universally accepted pronunciation, although this does have the advantage that you can get away with almost anything, within a fairly wide range of possibilities. Perhaps the best I can do is to pass on the advice which I received over forty years ago: 'when lawyers use Latin they should be using English – therefore they pronounce it as if they are'.

I have tried to satisfy the expectation of gender neutrality by using feminine and masculine forms in alternate letters.

Turning to acknowledgements, I am grateful to Suzie Burywood, Jenni Burnell and Tina Graham of Palgrave Macmillan, and to Ian Kingston, who has, for the fourteenth time in thirteen years put one of my typescripts into publishable form. Durham University generously allowed me to use its library as a visitor, while the staff of Teesside University Library were as helpful as always. I am also grateful to Barrie Goldstone of London Metropolitan University, Annabelle James, Ian Merrett and Dave Powell, all of Teesside University, and a number of readers who wrote to the publishers (who passed their comments on to me, having first anonymised them). Their suggestions have enabled me to avoid more errors, infelicities and undesirable omissions than I care to remember. However, I am happy to comply with the convention that requires me to accept sole responsibility for any deficiencies that remain.

My final acknowledgment must, as ever, be to my wife, Jacqui, for her patient support in general and her editorial assistance in particular.

I have tried to be up to date to 23 August 2009 but I have been able to go beyond this date by dealing with both the existence of the Supreme Court of the United Kingdom and the coming into force of the Treaty of Lisbon 2007 as facts rather than merely as prospects.

Ian McLeod

ABH

See ASSAULT.

Absolute privilege

The word *privilege* means a *special right or immunity*, and is used in many legal contexts. *Absolute privilege* is a defence to an action in DEFAMATION and is available where a statement, which would otherwise be defamatory, is made

- in Parliamentary proceedings, by a member of either House of Parliament;
- in the course of judicial proceedings;
- in fair, accurate and contemporary reports, either in either print or broadcast media;
- by one very high-ranking officer of state (such as a MINISTER OF THE CROWN or a very senior CIVIL SERVANT) to another, but how high-ranking or senior the relevant people must be is unclear.

The *absolute* nature of *absolute privilege* means that, unlike *qualified privilege* (see DEFAMATION), it cannot be defeated in any circumstances.

Absolute title

See REGISTERED LAND.

Abstract of title

When land is being sold, the *seller's* solicitor must satisfy the *buyer's* solicitor (with the *seller* and the *buyer* also being known as the *vendor* and *purchaser*) that she has good title to the land. Historically, an important stage in this process was the preparation, and delivery, of an *abstract of title*, although the modern practice is to prepare, and deliver, an *epitome of title*.

In the case of land with unregistered title (see TITLE TO LAND), an abstract of title contains a summary of the contents of the various deeds and other documents which, taken together, establish the seller's ownership of the land. With the widespread use of photocopying machines, the practice has changed to the use of *epitomes* (rather than *abstracts*) *of title*.

An *epitome of title* consists of a collection of photocopies of all the relevant documents, together with a list of those documents showing how each once constitutes a link in the chain of title. In the case of land with registered title (see REGISTERED LAND), the seller will prepare, and deliver, photocopies of the entries which appear on the register of title, together with a copy of the filed plan which identifies the land; and either an abstract or other evidence relating to matters (such as OVERRIDING INTERESTS) in respect of which the register does not provide conclusive evidence; as well as photocopies or abstracts of any other documents which are noted on the register.

Abuse of a dominant position

The concept of *abuse of a dominant position* is a key part of EU competition law. It raises two questions:

- what is a dominant position?

and, assuming there is a dominant position,

- what counts as an abuse of it?

A dominant position arises where one firm dominates a particular market. The market may be defined by its *substance* or its *geographical* area. Both possibilities may give rise to difficulties in purely practical terms.

For example, a firm which specialises in importing and selling bananas may have a dominant position in that market without having a dominant position in the wider market for fresh fruit. In this case, the question will be whether, in market terms, bananas are interchangeable with other fresh fruit, or whether they form a market on their own.

Similarly, where a firm dominates a particular market within some (but not all) member states, the question is whether or not the dominant position extends to a *substantial part* of the EU market.

Conduct constituting *abuse* of a dominant position includes

- unfair trading conditions such as imposing unfair prices;
- prejudicing consumers by limiting production, markets or technical developments;
- placing some firms at a competitive disadvantage by differentiating between the terms of business offered to them and those offered to their competitors;

- requiring firms to accept obligations which have no connection with the subject-matter of their contracts.

Abuse of power

There is an implied requirement that decision-makers functioning within the public sector shall use in a lawful manner whatever powers the law has conferred upon them. While a detailed knowledge of what is meant by *lawfulness* and *unlawfulness* in this context can only be acquired by studying ADMINISTRATIVE LAW, the underlying principle is that any exercise of power is unlawful if it involves an *abuse of power* (for example, by using the power for an improper purpose, or by failing to exercise a discretion by reference to legally irrelevant considerations).

The Queen's Bench Division of the HIGH COURT controls abuse of power through JUDICIAL REVIEW.

Abuse of process

Where a court is satisfied that allowing a case to continue would cause significant unfairness to one or more of the parties, it may terminate the proceedings on the basis that their continuation would be an *abuse of process* (or, to use a slightly fuller form of the expression, an *abuse of the process of the court*).

Acceptance

See CONTRACT.

Accession

1 Where a treaty exists between two or more states, the process by which additional states become parties (or *accede*) to the treaty is known as *accession* to the treaty.
2 When the King or Queen dies or abdicates, his or her heir accedes to the throne. *Accession* to the throne takes place on the date of the death or abdication, and must be distinguished from the formal act of *coronation* of the new monarch.

A

Accessory

There are four ways of being an accessory to the commission of a CRIME, namely:

- by *aiding* (which means *helping*) the principal offender to commit the offence (for example, by lending her a gun or a car for use in the commission of the offence);
- by *abetting* the principal offender – although the precise meaning of *abetting* is unclear; and it is difficult, if not impossible, to think of a situation which would count as abetting which would not also count as at least one of the other three ways of being an accessory;
- by *counselling* (which means *advising* and/or *encouraging*) the principal offender to commit the offence); and
- by *procuring* (which means *causing*) the principal offender to commit the offence.

In order to be guilty of being an *accessory*, the person doing the *aiding*, *abetting*, *counselling* or *procuring* must do so before the principal offence is committed, although there are also offences of giving various kinds of assistance to offenders after they have committed their offences.

Acquis communautaire

The French phrase *acquis communautaire* (which may be pronounced *ack-ee com-mune-oh-tare*) is sometimes used to describe the whole body of what was previously EUROPEAN COMMUNITY law and is now EUROPEAN UNION law.

See also SOURCES OF EUROPEAN COMMUNITY AND EUROPEAN UNION LAW.

Acquittal

An *acquittal* is the decision of a court that the PROSECUTION has not proved guilt beyond a reasonable doubt.

Before the Criminal Justice Act 2003, acquittal was an absolute bar to any further proceedings in respect of the same charge in all cases. This proposition sometimes appears in the French phrase *autrefois acquit* (which may be pronounced *oh-ter foys a-kwit*), and which simply means that the defendant has been acquitted on another occasion.

Now, however, where there has been an acquittal in respect of a serious offence (included in a list of such offences contained in the 2003 Act) following a trial on INDICTMENT, the prosecution can apply to the COURT OF APPEAL, which must order a retrial if it is satisfied that

- new and compelling evidence has become available; and
- a retrial would be in the interests of justice.

A

Act of God

The expression *Act of God* carries no religious implications, meaning simply a natural event, such as a storm or a flood, which could not be foreseen or prevented.

Act of Parliament

In practice, the GOVERNMENT usually dominates the HOUSE OF COMMONS and the HOUSE OF LORDS seldom frustrates the will of the House of Commons. This combination of factors makes it easy to overlook the fact that neither the Government nor the House of Commons actually *is* PARLIAMENT. The true position is that, subject only to the PARLIAMENT ACTS 1911 AND 1949, a BILL cannot become an *Act of Parliament* unless it has been passed by both the House of Commons and the House of Lords and has received the Royal Assent.

> *See also* CONSOLIDATING ACT; PUBLIC GENERAL ACT; and PRIVATE ACT.

Act of State

The doctrine of *act of state* relates to things done by either the GOVERNMENT or its agents when implementing government policy concerning the United Kingdom's relations with another sovereign state; and which, in the case of things done by agents of the government, the government has either authorised in advance or ratified subsequently.

Acts of state usually involve interference with property rights – for example, setting fire to a barracks in Africa in order to liberate slaves.

A court which is satisfied that a claimant's case arises from an act of state must refuse to allow the case to proceed. Where this happens, the claimant's only course of action will be to seek compensation through political channels, rather than legal ones.

Actual bodily harm

> *See* ASSAULT.

Actual notice

> *See* NOTICE.

Actus reus

In order to establish that a DEFENDANT has committed a CRIME at COMMON LAW the prosecution must prove both the relevant *actus reus* (or guilty *act*)

A

and the relevant MENS REA (or guilty *mind*). (The first word of the phrase *actus reus* is pronounced in the obvious way, while *reus* may be pronounced *ray-us*. The first word of the phrase *mens rea* is pronounced in the obvious way, while *rea* may be pronounced *ray-a*.)

The *actus reus* of an offence is what the defendant does, when viewed from an external point of view (as distinct from his state of mind, which determines whether the *mens rea* is also present). Common examples include appropriating property belonging to another person (which is the *actus reus* of THEFT) and possessing an offensive weapon in a public place.

Adjectival law

See PROCEDURAL LAW.

Adjournment

A court will *adjourn* a case which it is unable to deal with to its conclusion. Adjournments may be for very short periods (for example, for lunch) or for much longer periods. When adjourning, the court must either specify when the hearing will resume, or adjourn indefinitely, with the parties being informed subsequently of the time and date when they must return to court. Adjourning indefinitely is usually called *adjourning sine die*. (The Latin phrase *sine die* is usually pronounced *sy-nee dye* and is translated as *without a day* – which means, of course, *without a day being specified*.) Another way of designating indefinite adjournments is *dtf*, which is short for *date to fix*, meaning *to a date to be fixed*.)

See also BAIL.

A

Adjudication

1 In its broadest sense, *adjudication* means the process of deciding disputes judicially (or in a judge-like) way.

2 In a narrower sense, *adjudication* is a form of ALTERNATIVE DISPUTE RESOLUTION which is a statutory requirement in respect of certain classes of CONTRACT (see, for example, the Housing Grants, Construction and Regeneration Act 1996) and may be agreed by the parties in respect of others. It is normally subject to short time limits and the award (which is made by a person called the *Adjudicator*) is binding unless it is changed by ARBITRATION or an order of the court.

Administrative Court

The *Administrative Court* is a specialist section of the QUEEN'S BENCH DIVISION of the HIGH COURT, dealing with PUBLIC LAW cases. The cases it deals with were previously known as the *Crown Office list*.

Administrative decision-making

Until the 1960s, the court took the view that the remedies which were available by way of what are now called *claims for JUDICIAL REVIEW* would vary according to whether the decision-making process which was being challenged was *administrative, judicial* or *quasi-judicial*. More particularly, the remedy of *certiorari* (a Latin word which may be pronounced *sir-shore-rare-eye* and was the name of the old remedy which has now been replaced with a *quashing order*, whose function is self-evident) was originally available only in the context of *judicial* decision-making. The distinctions between the three categories were as follows.

Administrative decisions were those where the decision-maker was under no legal duty to weigh the evidence or the arguments, or to solve any issue. The means by which she proceeded to make her decision was left entirely to her discretion.

At the other end of the spectrum, *judicial* decisions were those where there was a dispute between two or more parties, who must be given an opportunity to present their cases; and where disputes of fact and law would be resolved respectively by weighing conflicting evidence and conflicting legal arguments, before making a decision by applying the law to the facts. However, the court was originally unable to quash decisions which did not fall into the *judicial* category and accordingly it invented a category which fell midway between the two extremes and to which it gave the name *quasi-judicial*. Decision-making processes in this category involved disputes between two or more parties, and the presentation of opposing cases with regard to the facts. They may, or may not, have involved arguments as to the law; but, even when they did, the result was not determined by the straightforward application of the law to the facts, but by a process characterised by *administrative discretion*. The court then persuaded itself that decision-making processes which fell into the *quasi-judicial* category were sufficiently like those which were truly judicial for the remedy of *certiorari* to be available to quash the decisions which they produced.

The idea of a spectrum of decision-making processes, with purely judicial and purely administrative functions at opposite ends, is still useful. However, the term *quasi-judicial* is now more or less redundant, with the

A

court taking a much more fluid approach to cases falling between the two extremes, and no longer feeling the need for a label to characterise the middle ground.

Administrative Justice and Tribunals Committee

The *Administrative Justice and Tribunals Committee* (AJTC) keeps the system of administrative justice under review. More particularly, it seeks to make the system as accessible, fair and efficient as possible, and to ensure that the courts, tribunals, ombudsmen and alternative dispute resolution, taken as a collective whole, reflect the needs of users.

The AJTC replaces the former *Council on Tribunals*.

Administrative Law

Administrative Law provides the legal framework within which public bodies and public officials perform their functions. There is often a particular emphasis on identifying the limits of their powers and the legal mechanisms which are available to keep them within those limits.

Administrative tribunals

See TRIBUNALS.

Administrator

1 In the law of *succession*, a man who deals with the estate of someone who has died either without leaving a WILL (in other words, who has died *intestate*) or has died leaving a will but has not appointed an *executor*, is known as an *administrator*. (Where the relevant person was a woman, it used to be common to use the terms *administratrix*, *executrix* and *testatrix* rather than *adminstrator*, *executor* and TESTA-TOR, since these are the feminine forms of the words in Latin. However, on the common-sense basis that *administrator*, *executor* and *testator* are now English words (and quite apart from the contemporary expectation of gender-neutral language), all three terms are generally used for both sexes.

In the first situation, the administrator obtains *letters of administration* from the PROBATE REGISTRY, and then distributes the estate in accordance with the rules set out by statute.

A

In the second situation, the administrator obtains *letters of adminis-tration with the will annexed* and then distributes the estate in accordance with the instructions contained in the will.

2 In company law, an *administrator* is a person appointed by the court to administer the affairs of a company which is unlikely to be able to pay its debts. The court must be satisfied that putting the company into administration will be in the best interests of its creditors.

Admissible evidence

See EVIDENCE.

ADR

See ALTERNATIVE DISPUTE RESOLUTION.

Adult

A person becomes an *adult* on reaching the age of 18. An adult is also sometimes described as being a *person of full age*.

Adversarial procedure

For practically all purposes, judicial proceedings in English law are *adversarial*. This means that the parties present their versions of the facts and their submissions as to the relevant law, and the court decides who shall win. It is no part of the courts' responsibilities to perform an *inquisitorial* function by conducting its own inquiry into the facts of the case.

Adverse possession

Adverse possession, which non-lawyers usually call *squatters' rights*, is the means by which a person may acquire what amounts to a kind of title to land which they are occupying unlawfully. In order to establish title by adverse possession, it is necessary to show that the adverse possession has not been maintained by force; has been open (or, in other words, not secretive); and has not been permitted in return for payment. The Latin phrase for these three requirements is *nec vi, nec clam, nec precario* and may be pronounced *neck vee, neck clam, neck preck-ah-ree-oh*.

The basic rules are that

● the occupation must have been for at least 12 years; and

A

- the occupier must have occupied the land as if she were the owner and with the intention of occupying it.

Where title to the land is an unregistered freehold (see ESTATES IN LAND), the true owner's title is extinguished and the possessory owner acquires a *fee simple* estate. This is a new and independent estate, rather than a transfer of the true owner's estate.

Where title to the land is an unregistered leasehold (see LEASE), the possessory owner will still obtain a fee simple and the leasehold will be extinguished. However, as against the owner of the freehold reversion, the 12 year period will not start to run until the date on which the lease would have expired, because until that date the freeholder would not have been entitled to possession of the land.

Where title to the land is registered, there are two important differences. First, the twelve-year period is broken down into two periods of 10 years and 2 years respectively. More particularly, after being in adverse possession for 10 years, the possessory owner may apply to the Land Registry, asking to be registered as the owner. The Registrar will then notify the registered owner, as well as certain other people who are interested in the land (such as those who have lent money on MORTGAGE, using the land as security for their loan).

If the Registrar receives no objection, she will grant the application and register the possessory owner as the owner.

If the Registrar does receive any objections, she must refuse the application unless there are circumstances (including certain boundary disputes) which make it appropriate that the application should be granted.

If the application is refused, but the registered owner does not begin proceedings to recover the land within two years, the possessory owner may apply again to the Registrar, asking to be registered as the owner of the land. On this occasion, the Registrar must grant the application.

However, and this is the second important point of difference from the position where title is unregistered, the possessory owner will gain only the title which the registered owner has lost. In other words, a possessory owner who displaces a registered leaseholder will gain only that leasehold interest, rather than the freehold. Once the lease reaches its expiry date, however, the possessory owner will be in adverse possession as against the freeholder. In other words, time will start to run in respect of the freehold (with the same 10 year and 2 year timetable applying again), and the possessory owner of a leasehold will have to wait rather longer before she acquires the freehold.

Advocate-General

The role of *Advocate-General* in the Court of Justice of the European Communities (more usually known simply as the EUROPEAN COURT OF JUSTICE, or ECJ) has no equivalent in the domestic English legal system.

The role of the Advocate-General is based on that of the French *Commissaire du Gouvernement* in the *Conseil d'État* (the French constitutional court), who is sometimes described as the 'disembodied conscience of the court'. (It might be more accurate to use a phrase such as 'the embodiment of the conscience of the court'; but, despite its inaccuracy, the other phrase is well established.) More particularly, the Advocate-General is under a duty to act impartially and independently, in order to assist the Court by presenting legal arguments leading to reasoned decisions, which the Court may (or may not) choose to adopt.

Although there appears to be some similarity between the role of the Advocate-General and that of an English COUNSEL TO THE COURT, the appearance is misleading for two reasons.

First, an Advocate-General is an integral part of the ECJ and will appear in every case, while it is rare for an English court to have a counsel to the court.

Secondly, the function of the Advocate-General is to give a reasoned opinion as to what she thinks the relevant Community law is, which the judges may simply adopt in a very short judgment. Counsel to the court, on the other hand, appears at the invitation of the court in order to present whatever arguments are possible in support of an important point of view which would otherwise be unrepresented.

A fortiori

The Latin phrase *a fortiori* (which may be pronounced *ay for-she-or-eye*) literally means 'from the stronger case', but may be translated more colloquially as 'all the more so'. For example, 'Any inexperienced student who skims this book is likely to increase her understanding of legal terminology; *a fortiori* if she studies it carefully'.

A

A-G (or AG)

A-G (or *AG*) is the abbreviation for *Attorney-General* – *see* LAW OFFICERS OF THE CROWN.

Agent

In the law of CONTRACT, an *agent* is a person who acts on behalf of another person, who is known as the *principal*. In general terms, an agent who negotiates a contract between her principal and a third party will not acquire any personal liability (or benefit) under the contract. However, where a person falsely claims to be acting as an agent, she will be liable to a third party for *breach of warranty of authority*.

An agent who negotiates a sale of property on behalf of its owner may agree with her principal that she will become personally liable to pay the purchase price if the purchaser defaults. In return for accepting this risk, the agent will usually require to be paid more for her services than she would otherwise receive. An agent who agrees to work on this basis is called a *del credere* agent. (*Del credere* may be pronounced *del cred-air-eh*.)

Agent provocateur

The French phrase *agent provocateur* (which may be pronounced *arje-on pro-voc-a-tur*) describes a person who behaves in such a way that someone else commits an offence which they would not otherwise have committed – for example by offering to buy controlled drugs from someone who would not otherwise have sold them to that person. A person who commits an offence as the result of the activities of an *agent provocateur* will not be able to use those activities in order to establish a defence, but the court does have a discretion to exclude evidence obtained as a result of them. The criteria according to which the court will decide whether to exercise this discretion are (i) whether the offence was already being committed before the *agent provocateur* became involved (in which case, strictly speaking, she is not really an *agent provocateur* at all); (ii) whether the defendant would have committed the offence anyway; and (iii) whether the defendant had a propensity to commit offences of the type for which she is being tried.

An *agent provocateur* will be guilty either of the offence of INCITEMENT (if the defendant had not committed an offence before she became involved), or as an ACCESSORY if the offence was already being committed.

A

Aggravated burglary

See BURGLARY.

Aggravated damages

See DAMAGES.

Aggravated vehicle taking

See CONVEYANCE.

Agreement for a lease

In almost all cases, a LEASE which is a legal estate (see ESTATES IN LAND) can be created only by DEED. However, one of the MAXIMS OF EQUITY states that *equity* (see COMMON LAW) *looks on that as done which ought to be done*, and, therefore, once a specifically enforceable *agreement for a lease* comes into existence, the agreement will be as good as a lease in the eyes of equity. Another equitable maxim, which produces the same effect in relation to an agreement for a lease, states that *equity looks to the intent rather than to the form*. Whichever maxim is applied, the result is that, for many practical purposes, an equitable lease created by an agreement for a lease is as good as a legal lease, although the exceptions are by no means unimportant. For example, where the agreement relates to land with unregistered title, it may be defeated by a *BONA FIDE PURCHASER FOR VALUE WITHOUT NOTICE* of the equitable interest.

An equitable lease created by an agreement for a lease is often called a *Walsh v Lonsdale* lease, after the leading case of that name, reported at (1882) 21 Ch D 9. By statute, such a lease must be in writing if it is for a period of three years or longer.

Alibi

An *alibi* is a defence to a criminal charge in which the defendant pleads that she was somewhere else when the crime was allegedly committed. At one time, the defence was allowed to produce alibi defences (and witnesses to support them) as surprises at the trial. Now, however, advance notice of an alibi defence, and of the witnesses who will support it, must be given to the prosecution.

(The word *alibi* has acquired the status of being a loan-word in English, but in its original Latin it simply means *elsewhere*.)

A

Alternative dispute resolution

Alternative dispute resolution (which is often abbreviated to *ADR*) is a general expression which includes a number of procedures which the parties to a dispute may choose as an alternative to pursuing court proceedings.

The main possibilities are ADJUDICATION, ARBITRATION, COLLABORATIVE LAW, CONCILIATION and MEDIATION.

Amicus curiae

See COUNSEL TO THE COURT.

Annuity

An *annuity* is a sum of money payable annually, usually for the lifetime of the recipient.

Anton Piller Order

See SEARCH ORDER.

Appeal

Proceedings by way of *appeal* almost always involve the *appellant* asking the court which is hearing *appellate* jurisdiction to substitute its own decision for that of the original court or decision-maker. The exception occurs in *appeals by way of case stated*. These appeals are on points of law only. The appellate court receives a statement of the facts as they were either agreed by the parties or found by the original court or decision-maker, together with a statement of the law as the original court or decision-maker understood it to be. The appellate court is then asked whether that understanding of the law and the decision based on it were correct.

Where an appeal by way of case stated is allowed, the appellate court will usually send the case back to the original court or decision-maker for further consideration, but it may, in an open-and-shut case, substitute its own decision.

Appeals, other than appeals by way of case stated, may be on either *matters of fact* or *points of law* or both. The details will depend on the rules governing the kind of appeal in question, which in turn will depend on the identity of the original court or decision-maker and the identity of the appellate court. For example, a defendant who is convicted by a magistrates' court may appeal on the facts to the Crown Court, but must go to the High Court by way of case stated if the appeal is on a point of law.

Many appeals apart from appeals by way of case stated are sometimes described as being *by way of re-hearing*, but this can be misleading. An appeal to the Crown Court against conviction by the magistrates' court will be a true re-hearing, with the witnesses giving their evidence again. However, in most other appeals which are described as being by way of re-hearing, the appellate court will not re-hear the witnesses, but will confine its consideration of the merits of the appeal to the records of the original court or decision-maker. While this may seem to blur the

A

distinction between *appeal* and JUDICIAL REVIEW, there remains the basic point that in an appeal the focus of the appellate court is on the *correctness of the decision*, while in judicial review the focus is on the *legality of the decision-making process*.

Appeals Committee

See HOUSE OF LORDS.

Appellant

See APPEAL.

Appellate

See APPEAL.

Appellate Committee

See HOUSE OF LORDS.

Arbitration

Arbitration is a form of ALTERNATIVE DISPUTE RESOLUTION which arises when the parties to a contract agree that disputes arising from the contract will be resolved by an independent person called an *arbitrator*, rather than by pursuing legal proceedings through the courts. The parties either agree on who is to be the arbitrator, or appoint someone else to make that decision. From a procedural point of view, arbitration is much less formal than court proceedings, and provided an arbitration is conducted fairly, the usual rules of evidence need not be followed.

The 'judgment' of an arbitrator is called an *award*.

Articles of association

The constitution of a company is contained in two documents, namely its *memorandum of association* and its *articles of association* (which are generally referred to simply as its *memorandum* and *articles*).

The *memorandum* specifies

- the company's name and registered office;
- its objects (or, in other words, the things it may lawfully do);
- the amount, if any, of its authorised capital;
- if appropriate, the fact that it has *limited liability* (see LIMITED COMPANY).

A

The *articles* specify matters concerning the internal arrangements and management of the company, such as

- the issue and transfer of shares;
- alteration of share capital;
- company meetings; and
- the appointment and powers of directors.

Assault

Assault may be both a TORT and a CRIME, but the word does not have exactly the same meaning in both contexts.

The *tort* of *assault* is committed where the defendant puts another person in immediate fear of a *battery*. (*Battery*, which is a separate tort, is committed where the defendant applies unlawful force to the body of another person.)

At COMMON LAW, the *crimes* of *assault* and *battery* have the same meanings as they do in tort. However, the offences of assault under ss. 47, 20 and 18 of the Offences Against the Person Act 1861 (which are presented here in ascending order of seriousness) are much more important in practice. They all involve the infliction of some degree of harm, and therefore, by implication at least, they normally include *battery* within the definition of *assault* (but some *aggravated assaults* may be committed by way of silent telephone calls or stalking).

Section 47 of the 1861 Act deals with *assault occasioning actual bodily harm*. For the purposes of this provision, *actual bodily harm* (which is often abbreviated to *ABH*) means any bodily harm unless it is both trifling and transient. In practice, therefore, it usually means injuries such as bruising and minor abrasions, but it is not limited to physical harm and includes psychological harm (such as medically recognised stress). However, a mere emotion (such as fear) is not sufficient.

Section 20 of the 1861 Act deals with *malicious wounding* and the infliction of *grievous bodily harm*. (In this context, *wounding* means *breaking the skin*, and *grievous* simply means *really serious*.) In practice, a broken bone will usually be treated as bringing an assault within the scope of s. 20.

Section 18 of the 1861 Act deals with *wounding* or *causing grievous bodily harm* provided there is an *intention* either to cause grievously bodily harm or to resist or prevent the lawful apprehension or detention of any person.

All the offences mentioned above are more serious (and therefore carry heavier maximum penalties) when they are *racially aggravated*, under s.

A

32 of the Crime and Disorder Act 1998. An offence is racially aggravated if the defendant is motivated by hostility towards members of a racial group, or if, at the time if the offence, she demonstrates racial hostility towards the victim.

Assault by penetration

See RAPE.

Assent

Where property has been inherited under a WILL or on an INTESTACY, an *assent* is the document by which a PERSONAL REPRESENTATIVE transfers the legal estate in the property to the person who is inheriting it.

Assignment

Certain transfers of property are known as *assignments*. For example, if a landlord (L) has granted a LEASE of land to a tenant (T) for 10 years, but T wants to move when the lease still has some time to run, her sale of the unexpired term will, technically, take the form of an assignment to her purchaser, T2. (In fact there will often be a covenant in the lease controlling possible assignments, with a typical requirement being to obtain L's consent.)

Similarly, if at some stage during the lease, L decides that she would rather have money now than possession of the land at the end of the lease, she can assign the *freehold* reversion to L2.

Changing the context, if someone who is owed money wishes to transfer the benefit of the debt to another person (so that the debt becomes payable to that other person), the transfer will be an assignment of the debt.

Assisting the commission of an offence

See ENCOURAGEMENT AND ASSISTANCE TO COMMIT AN OFFENCE.

A

Assumption of risk

A defendant in a TORT case will have a defence if the claimant has voluntarily accepted the risk of suffering the harm which she did in fact suffer and in respect of which she is bringing the action. For example, a passenger who was injured when a light aircraft crashed could not recover damages because she knew, before they took off, that the pilot was drunk.

In the days when lawyers still used Latin routinely, assumption of risk was often known as *volenti non fit injuria* (which may be pronounced *vol-en-tie nohn fit in-jew-ree-a*). The phrase may be very loosely translated as meaning *someone who has voluntarily exposed herself to a risk of injury cannot complain if she is then injured.*

See *also* CONTRIBUTORY NEGLIGENCE.

Attempt

It is a criminal offence to *attempt* to commit a criminal offence which is either an INDICTABLE OFFENCE or an OFFENCE TRIABLE EITHER WAY, even though the attempt is unsuccessful. In order to secure a conviction, the prosecution must show that the defendant did something which was more than merely preparatory to committing the offence.

A defendant who makes a mistake of fact may still be convicted of an attempt, provided she would be guilty of the substantive offence if the facts were as she believed them to be. For example, a defendant who shoots someone who is apparently asleep, with the intention of killing them, is guilty of attempted MURDER even though, unknown to her, the 'victim' had died from a heart attack a few minutes earlier. Where, however, the mistake is one of law, she will not be guilty of attempting to commit an offence. For example, a defendant who attempts to do something, wrongly believing that what she is attempting to do is a criminal offence, cannot be guilty of attempting to commit something which is not, as a matter of law, an offence.

Attorney-General

See LAW OFFICERS OF THE CROWN.

Audi alteram partem

See RIGHT TO A FAIR HEARING.

Automatism

Where a defendant is alleged to have committed a criminal offence which is based on conduct over which she had no control, she may have the defence of *automatism*. In order to establish this defence, she must establish that she was subject to a complete absence of voluntary control, which was caused by an external factor, and that she was not responsible for her condition.

So, for example, she would have the defence of automatism to a charge of dangerous driving if someone threw a brick at her while she was driving with the driver's window fully open, with the result that she was knocked out and lost control of the car. On the other hand, if her loss of control was due to an epileptic fit, the *internal* nature of the cause of her lack of control would mean that she would not have the defence of automatism (but see below for the defence of *insanity*).

Similarly, if her condition was due to self-induced intoxication through alcohol or some other drug taken otherwise than in accordance with medical advice, she would be responsible for her condition and would not, therefore have the defence of automatism.

Although excluding *internal* causes from the definition of automatism may seem unfair, where a defendant's complete absence of voluntary control is due to an internal cause she will often be able to plead *insanity*. In order to establish this defence, she must prove that, at the time of the alleged offence, she was

- suffering from a disease of the mind (which means, in this context, *impairment* of the defendant's faculties of *reasoning, memory* and *understanding*);
- the impairment must be complete (although it may be only temporary), so that, for example, mental confusion or loss of concentration will not be enough; and
- the result must be that either
  - the defendant did not know the nature and quality of her conduct; or
  - if she did know the nature and quality of her conduct, she did not know it was wrong.

Pausing only to note that these principles are often known as the *M'Naghten Rules* (after the leading case of *M'Naghten* [1843-60] All ER Rep 229), it is obvious that the meaning of *insanity* in this context is by no means the same as the medical, or even the everyday, meaning of the word. (*M'Naghten* is pronounced *MacNorton*.)

A

A defendant who pleads insanity is tried in relation to the ACTUS REUS of the offence (because if she did not do whatever is alleged, there is clearly no need to proceed to a consideration of her mental state).

When a plea of insanity succeeds, the defendant will be found *not guilty by reason of insanity* and (despite the fact that she has been acquitted) may be subject to anything from indefinite detention in a special hospital (such as Broadmoor) to an absolute discharge (except where the charge was murder, in which case the judge has no alternative but to order indefinite detention in a special hospital).

Where the defendant claims to be insane at the time of her trial (rather than at the time of the conduct alleged to constitute an offence, which is the situation dealt with above) the court must decide whether she is fit to plead. The issue here will be whether she is unable to give, receive or understand communications relating to the trial. Where the defendant is found to be unfit to plead, the court has a discretion to choose from a variety of orders up to and including indefinite detention in a special hospital.

A

Bail

When someone has been charged with a criminal offence, there are often good reasons why the case cannot proceed on the first occasion it comes before the court. For example, the advocate for the defence may need an adjournment to take instructions from his client and prepare the defence; or the court may not have time to deal with the case on that day. Whatever the reason for being unable to proceed immediately, the court will remand the defendant, either *in custody* or *on bail*.

If the remand is *in custody*, the defendant is detained in prison. If the remand is *on bail*, the defendant agrees to surrender to custody at a time and date which the court will either fix then or notify to him later. In either case, a defendant who fails to surrender at the required time and place commits an offence. As an additional incentive for the defendant to surrender, the court may require someone else (called a *surety*) to agree to forfeit a specified sum of money if he does not comply with his obligation to surrender. (This is called *entering into a recognisance.*)

Even before the defendant appears in court, he may have been granted bail by the police. Police bail is granted in two situations.

The first possibility is that, having interviewed a suspect, the police realise that they have not yet assembled sufficient evidence to support a charge, but are hopeful that they will be able to do so in the near future. Under these circumstances, the police must either let the suspect go, or bail him to appear at a specified police station at a specified time and date.

Alternatively, where the police do have sufficient evidence to support a charge, they may charge the suspect and then either put him before a magistrates' court as soon as reasonably possible, or bail him to appear before a magistrates' court at a specified time and place.

Where proceedings are begun by SUMMONS, the question of bail does not normally arise, and any postponements of court proceedings are usually dealt with by way of ADJOURNMENT, unless the court feels there is reason to suppose that it would be prudent to remand the defendant on bail in order to obtain additional inducements to persuade the defendant to continue to attend court when required to do so.

Bailment

A *bailment* occurs when one person (called the *bailor*) transfers possession (but not ownership) of GOODS to another person (the *bailee*), on the basis that they will be returned to the bailor. The parties may agree that the goods shall be returned on a specified date, or they may leave the date of the return open. If they leave the date open, the bailment is said to be a *bailment at will*, and the bailor may reclaim the goods at any time.

A bailment may be the essential point of the transfer of possession (for example, in a contract for the hire or transport of goods), or it may be incidental to another purpose (for example, where goods are left for repair).

Where the bailor has agreed to pay the bailee for services in relation to the goods – again, for example, where goods are left for repair – the bailee has a *lien* (which may be pronounced *lee-un*) over the goods. In other words, he will have the right to retain the goods until he has been paid for his services.

Barristers

See SOLICITORS.

Battery

See ASSAULT.

Beneficial owner

Where one person is the owner of property at COMMON LAW and another is the owner in equity (see, again, COMMON LAW) the former is called the *legal owner* and the latter is called the *beneficial owner*. Alternative form of words which mean the same as *beneficial owner* are *equitable owner* and *owner in equity*.

B

Beneficiary

A *beneficiary* is either someone who inherits under (or in other words *benefits from*) a WILL or an INTESTACY; or someone who benefits under a TRUST.

Bequest

A *bequest* is a gift of PERSONAL PROPERTY under a WILL. In practice, the word is often used interchangeably with *legacy*.

Bias

The *rule against bias* is one of the two traditional rules of *natural justice* (or PROCEDURAL FAIRNESS), the other being the RIGHT TO A FAIR HEARING.

Bias exists where a fair-minded and informed observer, being aware of all the facts of the situation, would conclude that there was a *real possibility* that the decision-maker was prejudiced, either consciously or unconsciously.

The Court of Appeal has said it could not conceive of any circumstances in which a valid objection could be based on a decision-maker's religion, ethnic or national origin, gender, age, class, means, or sexual orientation. Nor would it be likely that a valid objection could be based on a decision-maker's social, educational, service or employment background or history, nor that of any member of his family; his previous political associations, or membership of sporting, social or charitable bodies; freemasonry; previous judicial decisions; extra-judicial utterances (for example in textbooks or lectures); previous professional representation of one or more of the parties to the present case; nor membership of the same Inn of Court, circuit or Law Society. On the other hand, however, a valid objection based on bias could well be based on personal friendship between the decision-maker and one of the parties to the case; the decision-maker's outspoken rejection of a relevant person's credibility on a previous occasion; or statements of the decision-maker's personal opinions in such terms as to cast doubt on his judicial objectivity.

Bill

When proposed legislation is introduced into PARLIAMENT it is known as a *Bill*. It does not become an ACT OF PARLIAMENT until it has completed all stages of the Parliamentary procedure and has gained the Royal Assent. The Royal Assent is given in the form of LETTERS PATENT under the GREAT SEAL, signed personally by the Queen (who in practice does not, however, see the Bill itself). The fact that this has happened is announced to both Houses of Parliament.

B

Bill of Rights 1689

Although the *Bill of Rights 1689* is a document of fundamental importance to the British constitution, it is not a bill of rights in the modern sense of that expression (namely a document stating and protecting a range of basic human rights and freedoms); but rather a definitive settlement of the conflict between the Crown and Parliament that had characterised the decades leading up to its enactment.

After King James II abandoned the throne and fled the country in 1688, an informal group, consisting of peers, former members of the House of Commons (which had not met since 1685) and leading citizens of the City of London, invited William of Orange to summon a Convention. The Convention met, declared the throne to be vacant, and invited William and his wife Mary to occupy it jointly. The invitation was, however, conditional on William and Mary accepting the terms of a document which was called the *Declaration of Right*. Once William and Mary had accepted the invitation to take the throne, the Convention passed the Crown and Parliament Act 1689, declaring itself to be a properly constituted Parliament. The newly constituted Parliament then enacted the *Bill of Rights 1689*, which re-stated the terms of the *Declaration of Right* of the previous year. The existence of two documents, having the same content but being created in successive years, sometimes causes confusion. More particularly, the date of the *Bill of Rights* is given variously as 1688, 1689 and even (by the indecisive) as 1688–89. However, when it is remembered that the title of the earlier document was the *Declaration of Right* and the title of the later one was the *Bill of Rights*, no confusion should arise, and the date of the *Bill of Rights* can always be confidently given as 1689.

The most important terms of the Bill of Rights (in modernised spelling) are as follows.

'(1)   That the pretended power of suspending* of laws or the execution of laws by regal authority without consent of Parliament is illegal.

'(2)   That the pretended power of dispensing* with laws or the execution of laws by regal authority as it hath been assumed and exercised of late is illegal.

[*The distinction between *suspending* and *dispensing* was that the former had the effect of preventing the operation of a law generally, whereas the latter took the form of dispensing with the application of the law in relation to specified individuals.]

...

'(4)   That the levying of money for or to the use of the crown by pretence of prerogative without grant of Parliament for longer time or in other manner than the same is or shall be granted is illegal.

...

'(6) That the raising or keeping of a standing army within the kingdom in time of peace unless it be with the consent of Parliament is against the law ...

...

'(8) That election of members of Parliament ought to be free.

'(9) That the freedom of speech and debates or proceedings in Parliament ought not to be impeached or questioned in any court or place out of Parliament.

'(10) That excessive bail ought not to be required nor excessive fines imposed nor cruel and unusual punishments inflicted.

'(11) That jurors ought to be duly impannelled and returned ...

...

'(13) And that for redress of all grievances and for the amending, strengthening and preserving of the laws Parliaments ought to be held frequently.'

Binding over

A person may be *bound over* to keep the peace, or to be of good behaviour, under the Justices of the Peace Act 1361 or the Magistrates' Courts Act 1980. (Despite the fact that the 1361 Act is plainly a statute, many people refer to bind overs made under it as COMMON LAW *bind overs*. This misnaming is so well-established that there is no point in challenging it.)

Someone who is bound over agrees to keep the peace, or to be of good behaviour, for a specified period (typically, 12 months) and enters into a recognisance to pay a specified sum of money (perhaps £200) if he fails to do so. If he is brought back before the court within the specified period, he may be ordered to pay the specified sum of money, as well as being dealt with in respect of the matter for which he has been brought back to court. Strictly speaking, nobody can be compelled to agree to be bound over, but anyone who refuses to be bound over may be sent to prison until they do agree.

Binding over is intended to prevent trouble in the future, which is why it is often called *preventative justice*. It is neither a conviction nor a sentence.

Binding precedent

The doctrine of *binding precedent* deals with the way in which one court may be bound by a decision of another court in a previous case. The basic position is that all courts bind all lower courts and some courts also bind themselves.

The principles of self-bindingness may be summarised as follows.

The HIGH COURT binds itself when dealing with an APPEAL, but not when dealing with either cases at FIRST INSTANCE or claims for JUDICIAL REVIEW.

Generally speaking, the Civil Division of the COURT OF APPEAL binds itself. The principal exceptions to this self-bindingness may be summarised by saying that the court need not follow one of its own previous decisions

- where there are two conflicting decisions (when it must choose between them for the obvious reason that it cannot follow both);
- the HOUSE OF LORDS has made a later decision which does not expressly overrule a decision of the Court of Appeal but which the Court of Appeal nevertheless feels is of such a nature that its own decision can no longer stand; and
- the court is satisfied that one of its own decisions is PER INCURIAM.

The Criminal Division of the Court of Appeal has sometimes said that it is less self-binding than the Civil Division because it is dealing with the liberty of the subject, but the current position is that

- the court will not usually look behind one of its own previous decisions, although it does retain a residual discretion to decide that a previous decision is not binding where there are grounds for believing that it was wrongly decided;
- the discretion to depart from a previous decision is not to be exercised lightly, and in deciding whether to exercise that discretion, the constitution of the court will be a relevant consideration; and, finally
- while there may be a case for following a previous wrong decision where the effect of departure would be to convict a defendant who would otherwise be acquitted, this principle does not apply where the previous decision would provide the defendant with a merely technical defence.

The House of Lords is normally bound by its own decisions but will depart from them when it appears to the House that it would be right to do so. This is most likely to occur where the House is satisfied that

- the earlier decision was wrong in principle (especially if the principle in question was a *constitutional* principle), and its continued application would cause injustice; or

B

- social or commercial circumstances have changed since the earlier decision was made.

But, on the other hand, the House is particularly reluctant to depart from its own decisions

- where departure would retrospectively disturb contracts, settlements of property and fiscal arrangements; and (perhaps) in criminal cases.

The Judicial Committee of the Privy Council is not bound by its own previous decisions, nor by those of the House of Lords or the Supreme Court (although, in practice, it will normally follow such decisions). Similarly, its decisions are not, strictly speaking, binding on any other court (although, in practice, its decisions are generally treated as being so strongly persuasive that they do not fall far short of being binding).

Even where the relationship between the courts is such that bindingness may be expected to apply, the whole of the earlier decision will not always be binding. More particularly, it is necessary to distinguish between the concepts of *ratio decidendi* and *obiter dictum*, because only the former are binding. (The Latin phrase *ratio decidendi* may be pronounced *ray-shee-oh day-sye-den dye*, and is translated literally as *the reason for the decision*. The phrase *obiter dictum*, which again is Latin, may be pronounced *oh-bit-er dic-tum* and is translated literally as *a saying by the way*.)

The *ratio decidendi* (which becomes either *ratios decidendi* or *rationes –* pronounced *ray-shee-oh-nays – decidendi* in the plural) is any statement of law which is based on the *material facts of the case* and the *decision based on those facts*. Any other statement of law is merely an *obiter dictum*. Two consequences flow from the proposition that an *obiter dictum* is, strictly speaking, an aside, rather than being an essential part of the court's reasoning.

First, the advocates may well argue less fully those points of law which they see as being less likely to govern the actual decision in the case than they argue those points which lie at the heart of the dispute and on which, therefore, the court is likely to base the *ratio decidendi*.

Secondly, even if the advocates argue all the law very fully, the court may still give less careful consideration to those statements which it makes by way of *obiter dicta*, knowing that they will have no more than persuasive authority in later cases.

When viewed in this way it becomes obvious why, in many cases, the *ratio* will have greater weight, in terms of its legal authority, than a mere *dictum* will have. However, it is equally obvious that, if the law on which

B

an *obiter dictum* is based has been fully argued by the advocates *and* carefully considered by the court, its weight as an authority in later cases will be very great. Indeed, it may be so strongly persuasive as to be more or less binding.

Blackmail

Although in everyday usage the word *blackmail* tends to be used only to describe the situation in which one person demands money from another in return for keeping quiet about something which the other person does not wish to become public knowledge, as a matter of law blackmail is committed by the making of an unwarranted demand, with menaces, for the purpose of achieving financial gain (either for the person making the demand or for someone else) or causing financial loss (to the person to whom the demand is made).

Body corporate

See CORPORATION.

Bona fide purchaser for value without notice

See PURCHASER.

Bona vacantia

The Latin phrase *bona vacantia* (which may be pronounced in the obvious way and which may be translated literally as *empty goods*) means property which has (or appears to have) no owner. (Despite the fact that the word *bona* in the Latin phrase seems to restrict the concept to GOODS, in English law it plainly embraces all property including realty – see REAL PROPERTY.)

One of the most common examples of *bona vacantia* arises on INTESTACY (or, in other words, where someone dies leaving property which they have not disposed of by WILL).

Ownership of *bona vacantia* passes to the Crown, which often uses the property for charitable purposes.

See also CHARITY and CHARITABLE TRUSTS.

Breach of confidence

The tort of *breach of confidence* is committed by a person who, having received confidential information in circumstances which impose an obligation to respect that confidence, discloses the information. Unless an injunction is being sought, there is no need to show that the disclosure is to the disadvantage of the person to whom it relates.

Breach of the peace

At COMMON LAW, there is a *breach of the peace* where there is behaviour which harms, or is likely to harm, a person, or which puts him in fear of harm to himself, or to his property, provided the property is present at the time.

Breach of statutory duty

One question which repeatedly troubles the courts is simply this: 'is a person liable in damages for harm caused by his failure to perform a duty which is imposed upon him by statute?'

Some statutes which impose duties avoid the problem by stating expressly that such liability does (or does not) arise, but a regrettably large number do not do so, leaving the court with no option but to fall back on the common law test of 'did Parliament impose the duty for the benefit of the public at large, or only for a section of the public?'. If the former, someone who is harmed by a failure to perform the duty will not be able to obtain damages; but if the latter, damages may be available. By way of application of this test, a company which operated a greyhound racing stadium and which was under a statutory duty to provide facilities for bookmakers, failed to make space available for one particular book-maker. Was the duty imposed for the benefit of the public at large (to ensure that they had access to betting facilities when attending race meetings) or for the benefit of bookmakers (to ensure they had the opportunity to ply their trade)? The House of Lords decided it was for the benefit of the public at large; and, therefore, a bookmaker who had not been allocated space at the stadium had no right of action in damages.

Liability for *breach of statutory duty* may arise from a breach of EUROPEAN COMMUNITY law or from a breach of a CONVENTION RIGHT under the HUMAN RIGHTS ACT 1998.

B

Breach of trust

A trustee who fails to comply with the terms of the TRUST, or to act in accordance with the principles of equity (see COMMON LAW), may be held to be in *breach of trust*. He may be held personally liable to the beneficiaries under the trust, but a court which would have authorised the trustee's action if he had asked it do so in advance, will not make the trustee personally liable after the event.

Breach of warranty of authority

See AGENT.

Brief

Although in the argot of the criminal underworld the word *brief* means a lawyer (as in 'I would have got off if my brief had been any good'), on the formal side of legal usage a brief is the written instructions which SOLICITORS give to BARRISTERS.

Burden of proof

The courts within the English legal system almost always work on the basis of ADVERSARIAL PROCEDURE, which means that a great deal of importance attaches to the question of which party has to prove what, since the court is asking not 'what happened?' but 'what has been proved to have happened?'.

Unfortunately, the meaning of the key terminology which is used in this context is not always abundantly clear, but the underlying ideas are relatively straightforward.

First, the *true burden of proof* (namely the burden of proving something which, if not proved, results in the party bearing the burden failing) is often called the *legal burden of proof*. This burden must (except where one party is required to disprove a claim put forward by another party) be discharged

- by the person who alleges the relevant fact (or facts) to be true (but for an exception see the example of self-defence in relation to MURDER (below)); and
- to the appropriate standard (which means *beyond reasonable doubt* in criminal cases and *on the balance of probabilities* in civil ones).

Secondly, there is the burden of putting something into play. Although this is often called the *evidential burden of proof*, it is not really a burden of proof at all, but merely a burden of establishing that there is sufficient evidence to raise a particular issue, after which the burden of proof in relation to that issue falls on the party who bears the legal burden of proof in the case as a whole.

The clearest example of the interrelationship between the two concepts comes in relation to self-defence on a charge of murder. The burden on the prosecution is to prove beyond reasonable doubt both that the accused killed the victim with malice aforethought (see MURDER); and (*provided the defendant has put the matter into play*) that he did not do so in self-defence. So if the accused does not raise the issue of self-defence, that issue will simply not be before the court; but to say that the defence has the burden of introducing it as an issue (if it wishes to do so) is not accurately described as a *burden of proof* of any kind.

It is important to note the distinction between *burden of proof* and STANDARD OF PROOF.

Burglary

Although *burglary* is an offence (see CRIME), among the things which the prosecution must prove is that the defendant committed the TORT of TRESPASS. More particularly, burglary may be committed by either

- entering a building or part of a building, as a TRESPASSER with intent to
  - steal, or do unlawful damage to, anything which is there; or
  - inflict grievous bodily harm on anyone who is there;

or

- having entered a building or part of a building as a trespasser,
- stealing or attempting to steal anything which is there; or
- inflicting or attempting to inflict grievous bodily harm on anyone who is there.

The more serious offence of *aggravated burglary* is committed where, at the time of the burglary, the defendant has with him either a firearm, an imitation firearm, a weapon of offence or explosives. A *weapon of offence* is defined as being any article which either

- has been made or adapted to be used for causing injury to, or incapacitating, a person; or
- the defendant intends to use for the purpose of causing injury to, or incapacitating, a person.

B

Byelaw

A *byelaw* is a form of DELEGATED LEGISLATION which is usually described as being *a law of local application*. (The *bye* part of the word dates from Viking times and is a form of the Old Scandinavian word meaning *a settlement*. It survives, in a slightly reduced form, as a common ending for English place-names such as Whitby.) Although byelaws usually apply only in a single geographical area, they may apply to each piece of land of a particular type (such as land used for airports, railways or military purposes), in whatever part of the country it is located.

Byelaws are most commonly made by local authorities and contains provisions *for the good rule and government* of their areas.

B

Cabinet

The *cabinet* is a group of senior GOVERNMENT ministers (see MINISTER OF THE CROWN) which formulates government policy (although in practice there may be an inner group – sometimes informally called the *kitchen cabinet* – which effectively performs this function, with the whole Cabinet merely adopting the decisions of that group). Each Minister will be responsible for one of the great Departments of State, such as the Treasury and the Home Office.

Curiously, the Cabinet has no legal basis. One consequence of this is that there are no legal requirements as to its composition, but the Ministerial and Other Salaries Act 1975 does restrict to 21 the number of ministers who may be paid as SECRETARIES OF STATE.

As a general principle, cabinet ministers may be members of either the House of Commons or the House of Lords. In practice, however, the vast majority sit in the Commons, and there is a CONSTITUTIONAL CONVENTION which requires that the Prime Minister and the Chancellor of the Exchequer must do so.

Capacity

A person has the *capacity* to do something if, *as a matter of law*, she is *capable* of doing it. The word *capacity*, in this sense, is most frequently used in relation to *contract* (in which context it is necessary to consider not only the COMMON LAW principles but also the Mental Capacity Act 2005) and *crime*.

The general principle of *contractual capacity* is that any ADULT, being of sound mind, has the capacity to enter into any lawful contract. On the other hand, *minors* (who are defined as being under the age of 18) lack contractual capacity (and so any contracts they apparently enter into are void, as a matter of law, unless they are either contracts for *necessaries* or *beneficial contracts of employment*.

The test of whether something is *necessary* involves an assessment, on all the facts of each case, of the individual minor's social and material status. So, for example, the child of a multi-millionaire film star may reasonably expect a higher standard of living than the child of a university lecturer; and, therefore, something such as a car might be regarded as necessary in the one case, and as a luxury in the other.

A contract for more or less any sort of job will be a *beneficial contract of service*. However, in this context, a wide meaning is given to the idea of a contract of service, which will include, for example, a contract with a publisher to publish a book, even though this would more usually be classified as a contract for services (see VICARIOUS LIABILITY).

The Mental Capacity Act 2005 provides a legal framework for decision-making on behalf of people over the age of 16 who lack the mental capacity to make their own decisions. In relation to the law of contract, therefore, the common law principles applicable to people aged 16 to 18 (as discussed in the previous paragraphs) are overridden in the case of individuals to whom the Act applies.

The Act provides that an adult is presumed to have capacity to make her own decisions and that this presumption can be rebutted only in the case of an individual (a) the functioning of whose mind or brain is impaired or disturbed (either permanently or temporarily); and (b) who is unable to (i) understand, retain and use or weigh information as part of the process of making a decision; and (ii) communicate the decision made (whether by talking, sign language or other means). A person is not to be treated as unable to make a decision (a) unless all practicable steps to help her to do so have been taken and have failed; or (b) because she makes unwise decisions. The Act makes it clear that a decision as to capacity must be made in relation to a particular decision and at a particular time (so, at any given time, a person may have capacity to make some decisions and lack capacity to make others, or may lack the capacity to make a particular decision on one day but have capacity to make it on another).

The general principles of *criminal capacity* is that anyone aged 14 or over is capable of committing any offence, while anyone below the age of 10 is incapable of committing any offence. Before the Crime and Disorder Act 1998, there was a presumption that a child aged 10 to 14 lacked criminal capacity (or, to use the Latin phrase which was still current, was *doli incapax*, which may be pronounced *doh-lee in-cap-ax*), but it was open to the prosecution to rebut this presumption (and therefore leave the child liable to be convicted) by showing that the child in question knew the difference between right and wrong. The relevant provision of the 1998 Act expressly abolished this presumption but the House of Lords has held that the true effect of the provision was to abolish not only the presumption but also the whole concept of *doli incapax* in relation to children aged 10

to 14. In other words, the three age bands of (a) under 10; (b) 10 to 14; and (c) 14 and upwards have been reduced to two by eliminating the middle one and reducing the starting point of what was the third one to 10.
See also AUTOMATISM.

Case stated
See APPEAL.

Cause of action

Someone who wishes to sue someone else must identify a *cause of action*, or in other words, identify some fact or facts which the law recognises as giving rise to a right to sue.

Central government

The phrase *central government* is used to mean either the GOVERNMENT (or the EXECUTIVE) itself, or the CIVIL SERVICE or both. It is often contrasted with LOCAL GOVERNMENT.

Certiorari
See QUASHING ORDER.

CFI
See EUROPEAN COURT OF JUSTICE.

Chancery Division

The *Chancery Division* of the HIGH COURT has *jurisdiction* at FIRST INSTANCE in a very wide range of cases involving property matters, as well as bankruptcy and company law. It also has a very limited appellate (see APPEAL) jurisdiction in relation to COUNTY COURTS, from which almost all appeals go to the Civil Division of the COURT OF APPEAL.

Charge

In *criminal law* (see CRIME), a *charge* is an allegation of an offence.

In *property* law (see REAL PROPERTY), a *charge* is a means of taking security when lending money. A lender who wishes to take security for the money she is lending may take a charge over properties belonging to the borrower. If the borrower defaults on repaying the loan the lender may obtain a court order requiring the property to be sold and for the money she is owed to be paid to her out of the proceeds of sale. Unlike a MORT-GAGE, a charge does not give the lender any interest in the property itself, but only in the proceeds of sale.

Charitable trusts

From the beginning of the 17th century until the Charities Act 2006, there were two essential characteristics of *charitable trusts*. The first requirement was that their purposes had to come under one of four headings, namely the relief of poverty; the advancement of education; the advancement of religion; and purposes beneficial to the community. The second requirement was that the purposes of the trusts had to be for the public benefit. (This requirement was, of course, already explicit in the case of trusts coming under the fourth heading, but specifying it as a separate requirement put the matter beyond doubt in relation to the other three headings as well.)

The 2006 Act introduced a more wide-ranging approach by preserving the first three of the old headings before replacing the fourth heading with nine new, more specific, ones, together with a further three additional, and more general, ones. It also preserved the test of public benefit but reversed the pre-existing burden of proof by providing that there is no presumption that the purposes covered by the headings listed above are for the public benefit. In practical terms, this means that it is for the person who is arguing for the charitable status of a specific purpose to establish that, in all the circumstances of the case, the purpose does serve the public benefit.

The nine new specific headings are the advancement of health or the saving of lives; the advancement of citizenship or community development; the advancement of the arts, culture, heritage or science; the advancement of amateur sport; the advancement of human rights, conflict resolution or reconciliation or the promotion of religious or racial harmony or equality and diversity; the advancement of environmental protection or improvement; the relief of those in need by reason of youth, age, ill-health, disability, financial hardship or other disadvantage; the advancement of animal welfare; and the promotion of the efficiency of the armed forces of the Crown, or of the efficiency of the police, fire and rescue services or ambulance services.

The first of the further three additional, and more general, headings covers any purposes which are not included under any of the headings listed above but which are nevertheless recognised as charitable purposes under the pre-Act charity law (including, specifically, s 1 of the Recreational Charities Act 1958).

The second additional heading covers any purposes that may reasonably be regarded as analogous to, or within the spirit of, any of the purposes covered by either any of the headings listed above or the first additional heading.

The third additional heading consists of any purposes that may reasonably be regarded as analogous to, or within the spirit of, any purposes falling within the second category.

As already noted above, the 2006 Act provides that in order to be charitable, a purpose must not only be covered by one of the headings listed above, but must also be for the public benefit.

It is obvious from the terms of the headings listed that charitable trusts need not specify individually identifiable beneficiaries. So, for example, a trust for the advancement of education in Africa would clearly be charitable. Equally clearly, however, the absence of individually identifiable beneficiaries may cause difficulty if enforcement of the trust becomes necessary. In order to cope with this difficulty, the functions of the Attorney-General (see LAW OFFICERS OF THE CROWN) include the enforcement of charitable trusts.

Charities

Many *charities* function through CHARITABLE TRUSTS, with the members of their governing bodies being the trustees. However, some charities function in different ways with, for example, some public schools and some universities operating as companies while also enjoying charitable status.

For the criteria which a TRUST must satisfy in order to be a *charitable trust*, see CHARITABLE TRUST.

For an organisation which does not function through a charitable trust to enjoy charitable status, it must be

- established for purposes which are exclusively charitable (in the same sense as that in which the word *charitable* is used in the context of CHARITABLE TRUSTS); and
- subject to the jurisdiction of the HIGH COURT with respect to charities.

The requirement of being subject to the jurisdiction of the High Court does not relate to any unique or exclusive jurisdiction: any significant jurisdiction is sufficient.

C

Irrespective of the way in which they function, charities benefit from significant concessions in relation to their liability to pay certain taxes. An important consequence of this is that many cases in which the courts have to decide whether a particular activity is charitable are, in reality, disputes about liability to pay specific taxes. Inevitably, therefore, some judges' perceptions of the merits of cases such as these are conditioned more by their perceptions of whether the relevant tax concessions are justifiable than by the desirability of developing a coherent body of law relating to what is, and is not, charitable.

Charity Commission

The *Charity Commission* is responsible for registering and regulating CHARITIES.

Charter of Fundamental Rights of the European Union

The *Charter of Fundamental Rights of the European Union* sets out the whole range of civil, political, economic and social rights of European citizens and anyone else who is resident in the EU. These rights are divided into six sections, dealing with dignity, freedoms, equality, solidarity, citizens' rights, and justice. They are based on the fundamental rights and freedoms recognised by the EUROPEAN CONVENTION ON HUMAN RIGHTS; the constitutional traditions of the member state; the Council of Europe's Social Charter; the Community Charter of Fundamental Social Rights of Workers; and other international conventions to which the European Union or the member states are parties.

The TREATY OF LISBON 2007 provides for the charter to become part of EU law.

C

Charterparty

A *charterparty* is a contract for the hire of a ship. It may be for a fixed period (in which case it is a *time charterparty*) or for a particular voyage (in which case it is a *voyage charterparty*). Under the most common type of charterparty (a *simple charterparty*) the owner of the ship retains possession and control, but uses the ship for the purposes of the hirer. However, there is also the possibility of a *charter by demise*, in which case the owner will transfer possession and control of the ship to the hirer, thus making the arrangement much more like a LEASE of land.

Chattel

A *chattel* is any tangible property other than REAL PROPERTY. The requirement that the property must be *tangible* means that CHOSES IN ACTION are not chattels. Because LEASES combine some of the characteristics of PERSONAL PROPERTY with some of the characteristics of real property, they are sometimes called *chattels real*.

Chattel real

See CHATTEL.

Child destruction

Because the law of abortion deals only with the unborn, and the offences of murder, manslaughter and infanticide deal only with those who have been born, it was thought that a specific offence was necessary in order to protect those who might be killed while in the process of being born. The result was the Infant Life (Preservation) Act 1929, although the offence of *child destruction* which that Act created went some way beyond meeting the perceived need which had given rise to the Act.

More particularly, a person commits the offence of child destruction if she, with intent to destroy the life of a child capable of being born alive, wilfully causes a child to die before it has an existence independent of its mother. The prosecution must prove that the act which caused the death was not done in good faith for the purpose only of preserving the life of the mother.

A child is not born until it is completely outside its mother's body. In order to cope with uncertainties as to proof of this, it is common practice to charge child destruction and murder as alternatives, leaving it to the jury to decide its own view of the detailed facts.

Chose in action

The French word *chose* (which is pronounced *shows* and has become a loan word in English) means *thing*, and therefore the phrase *chose in action* means a *thing in action*. In other words, a *chose in action* is the right to recover (by legal *action*) money or other property. For example, a debt is a chose in action, which can be assigned by the creditor to a third party. By way of contrast with a *chose in action*, a *chose in possession* is any CHATTEL which is capable of being physically *possessed*.

Chose in possession

See CHOSE IN ACTION.

CIF

Cif contracts are particularly common in relation to sales of goods in the world of international trade, where *cif* stands for *cost, insurance and freight*. This means that the price which the buyer pays will cover not only the goods themselves but also the cost of their transport to her and the cost of insuring them in transit.

Cif contracts may be contrasted with *fob* contracts, where *fob* stands for *free on board*. An fob contract means that the price which the buyer pays covers only the goods themselves and the cost of loading them onto the ship (or other form of transport) which will take them to the agreed destination. The buyer is responsible for the cost of transporting and insuring the goods while they are in transit, in addition to the price she has paid for the goods. Although the buyer bears the cost of insurance and transport in both cases, under a *cif* contract she delegates to the seller the trouble of arranging these matters, while under an *fob* contract she has the advantage of being able to negotiate their price and terms.

Circuit judge

A circuit judge sits as a judge of the CROWN COURT and the COUNTY COURT.

Civil law

The phrase *civil law* has two meanings. Within the context of English law it is used to mean anything which is not criminal law (see CRIME). Within a wider context, however, it is used to distinguish the COMMON LAW (which originated in England) from those systems of law (including those which operate in the whole of Western Europe) which can trace their origins back to Roman law, with the latter being known as *civil law* systems. Interestingly, the Scottish legal system is a hybrid of the *civil* and *common law* traditions.

Civil partnership

Partners in same-sex relationships may register their *civil partnership*. The ceremony is similar to that for a register office wedding, but the concept of marriage in English law still requires one of the parties to be a man and the other a woman. It is, therefore, wrong to refer to a registered *civil partnership* as a *gay marriage*. Nevertheless, in relation to property and taxation, a registered civil partnership does give rise to rights which reflect very closely those which subsist between a married couple. Similarly, dissolving a civil partnership has practically the same effect as a divorce.

Civil Procedure Rules

The *Civil Procedure Rules* (or *CPR*) 1998 were made under the Civil Procedure Act 1997, as replacements for the former RULES OF THE SUPREME COURT (or RSC) and the County Court Rules (or CCR). They govern the procedure in almost all civil cases in the COUNTY COURTS, the HIGH COURT and the COURT OF APPEAL.

Civil servant

The staff of central government departments are *civil servants*. For some purposes, such as the conditions of service under which they work, it is important to distinguish *civil servants* from LOCAL GOVERNMENT officers. It is impracticable to list all central government departments, but they include the Treasury, the Foreign Office, the Home Office, the Department for Environment, Food and Rural Affairs and the Department for Education and Skills.

Civil service

The phrase *civil service* is used to mean the whole administrative machinery of CENTRAL GOVERNMENT.

Claimant

C

The person who begins CIVIL LAW proceedings is usually called the *claimant*. However, in some situations, other terminology is used. For example,

- a person seeking a divorce is a *petitioner*;
- a person seeking a LICENCE is an *applicant*; and
- a person who begins civil law proceedings in a MAGISTRATES' COURT is usually called a COMPLAINANT (although, somewhat confusingly, the word *complainant* is also sometimes used to indicate the victim of a CRIME.)

Codicil

A *codicil* is a document which changes the terms of a WILL. It must be made with the same formalities as a will.

Although it is a good idea to file a codicil with the will to which it relates wherever it is possible to do so, the codicil need not be attached to the will. (In purely practical terms, it is bad practice to attach *any* other document to a will, because if it is ever removed it will almost always leave some marks on the will, thus giving rise to a suspicion that perhaps there is a codicil in existence which has varied the terms of the will.)

Codifying Act

See CONSOLIDATING ACT.

Collaborative law

Collaborative law is a technique of dispute resolution used in family law. Its principal features are that

- the parties instruct their own solicitors who are skilled in the technique;
- the parties agree that they will not take their dispute to court;
- the parties also agree to work as members of a team and to be honest, open and prompt when disclosing information;
- other experts may join the team;
- the aim is to resolve the dispute in face-to-face meetings, in which the parties will be in charge but will be supported by their solicitors who will give appropriate advice and guidance;
- the agreement not to go to court is non-binding, so if collaborative law fails to achieve a mutually acceptable result the parties can still go to court, but if this happens they must instruct fresh solicitors to handle the legal proceedings.

Collateral contract

A *collateral contract* is a CONTRACT which is incidental to another contract.

For example, suppose that X employs Y to paint the outside of a building belonging to X, and also that X tells Y to use a particular kind of paint because Z, the manufacturer of the paint, has assured X that the paint will last for 20 years. Accordingly Y buys and uses the paint. Now suppose that the paint lasts for only two years, so X's building needs repainting much sooner than she expected. On the face of it, X cannot sue Z, because the contract for the sale of the paint was made between Y and Z, and therefore the doctrine of PRIVITY OF CONTRACT means that X has no CAUSE OF ACTION. However, the courts can avoid this technical objection to giving Y a remedy against Z, by saying that *Y has a collateral contract with Z*. In terms of the technicalities of contract law, X can be said to have given *consideration* for this collateral contract by instructing Y to use the paint manufactured by Z.

This may seem a rather artificial way of avoiding what would otherwise be an injustice caused by the doctrine of privity of contract; and indeed it is. However, the Contracts (Rights of Third Parties) Act 1999 (see PRIVITY OF CONTRACT) has very largely reduced the need for the courts to rely on collateral contracts such as this.

Commercial Court

The *Commercial Court* is a specialised section of the Queen's Bench Division (QBD) of the HIGH COURT, dealing with cases which have been entered on a special commercial list. As its name suggests, the Commercial Court deals with disputes involving the law and practice of the commercial world (such as cases involving banking, insurance and CHARTERPARTIES) and is staffed by judges of the QBD who have particular experience of such matters.

Committal for sentence

See MAGISTRATES' COURT.

Common duty of care

See OCCUPIERS' LIABILITY.

Common foreign and security policy

See EUROPEAN UNION.

C

Commonhold

From the Law of Property Act 1925 until the Commonhold and Leasehold Reform Act 2002, land could be held only as a freehold (see ESTATES IN LAND) or a leasehold (see LEASE). Both these estates still exist (with freehold land being, theoretically at any rate, held from the Crown, and leasehold land being held from a *lessor* (with the term *landlord* still being widely used irrespective of the sex of the person involved). However, since the 2002 Act there is a new way of holding a freehold, namely from a *Commonhold Association*.

Although the *commonhold* concept is not limited to flats, it is particularly useful where they are involved. For the sake of simplicity, therefore, this entry will explain the operation of commonhold in that context. The law relating to COVENANTS which are not contained in contracts is clearly to the effect that the burden of positive covenants does not run with the land. Therefore, it would be difficult for a freehold owner of a block of flats to sell each flat as a freehold, because the covenants which she would take from each of her purchasers (requiring them, for example, to keep their part of the building in good repair, and therefore being positive) could not be enforced against anyone to whom they subsequently sold their flats.

As a result of this, flats were almost always sold as leaseholds, with the lessor (or her successors-in-title) retaining ownership of the freehold. Because leasehold interests developed as contractual rights rather than interests in land (and are, therefore, *chattels real* – see CHATTEL – rather than fully-fledged REAL PROPERTY) a purchaser from a leaseholder is, in effect, taking an ASSIGNMENT of a CONTRACT. It follows from this that there is no problem in holding the purchaser bound by the terms of the contract which is being assigned to her. However, leasehold ownership has other problems, not the least of which is the fact that there is always another owner (the freeholder) in the background.

The scheme under the 2002 Act is that a landlord creates a Commonhold Association (CA) and draws up a Commonhold Community Statement (CCS). Both the CA and the CCS are then registered at the Land Registry. The CA owns the freehold while the CCS sets out the rights and obligations in respect of the building as a whole. Purchasers of individual flats automatically become members of the CA; and, of course, because both the CA and the CCS are registered, the purchaser of every individual flat has full knowledge of the relevant rights and obligations.

Typically, the owner of each flat is responsible for maintaining her own property, while the CA is responsible for maintaining the common parts, such as the entrance hallway, the stairs, and the lifts (if any). Moreover, and crucially, the positive obligations of both the CA and the individual owners are enforceable by and against each other. Essentially, therefore, commonhold is simply a new way of owning a freehold, which will be held from the CA rather than from the Crown, and from which individual freeholds can be created.

Common law

The phrase *common law* has a variety of meanings, with the correct one depending on the context in which it is being used.

When *common law* is contrasted with *statute law* (which is made by PAR-LIAMENT) and DELEGATED LEGISLATION (which is made by people to whom Parliament has delegated the power to make certain types of law on certain subjects), it means *that part of the law which is contained in the decisions of the courts*. (Since it is an important part of the status of *law* that it must be *binding*, it is worth noticing that the bindingness of the common law flows from the doctrine of BINDING PRECEDENT.)

When *common law* is contrasted with *equity*, a little legal history is necessary in order to explain the distinction.

Historically, the common law originated in the King's courts, whose judges travelled round the country, hearing cases as they went. In the course of their travels they found local variations of the law which seemed sensible and those which did not. By extending the sensible variations (so that they became *common to the country as a whole*) and losing the others along the way, the judges created what became known as the common law. However, the early common law became very inflexible and an alternative body of rules, known as *equity*, developed alongside the common law.

More particularly, equity originated from the King's practice of making exceptions to the way the common law would apply in individual cases wherever it was necessary to do so in order to avoid injustice. (For example, in some circumstances where someone was in breach of contract, equity would compel her to perform her contractual obligation, rather than merely ordering her to pay damages, which is all the common law would order her to do. This remedy is known as SPECIFIC PERFORMANCE.) As time went by, the King started to delegate this function to the Lord Chancellor, and, later still, equity came to be administered by the Lord Chancellor's own court, which was known as the Court of Chancery.

Because equity developed as an exceptional JURISDICTION alongside the mainstream jurisdiction of the King's courts with their stock-in-trade of the common law, the distinction between equity and the common law inevitably led to conflicts between the two systems. These conflicts were resolved by adopting the principle that *where equity and the law conflict, equity prevails*. (Note that in this maxim, the word 'law' is used as shorthand for 'common law'.)

Since the Judicature Acts of 1873–75, both the common law and equity have been administered by the same courts. However, this jurisdictional

C

change did nothing to avoid conflict between the two systems, so it was still necessary to know which system prevailed. Since equity originated as a means of remedying the common law's injustices in individual cases, it is hardly surprising that the old maxim continued to be applied, and equity still prevails over the common law.

Perhaps an even more important aspect of equity's creativity than the invention of additional remedies such as specific performance may be found in its invention of the idea of a TRUST.

When *common law* is contrasted with CIVIL LAW, it means

- the ideas and principles of the English legal system (together with those of the former colonies and Dominions whose legal systems still have at least some foundation in English law); and
- the ideas and principles of the legal systems of the countries of continental Europe (which are based on Roman law).

It is often said that one of the most important functional distinctions between common law and civil law systems is that the latter have no doctrine of binding precedent. However, the general reasons for following earlier decisions (as outlined in the opening paragraph of the entry for binding precedent) apply to all legal systems. Therefore, it is not surprising that the courts of the legal systems of continental Europe routinely follow their own decisions, even though they are not bound to do so. It follows, therefore, that any distinction between legal systems based on whether they embrace a doctrine of binding precedent must be treated with a degree of scepticism.

Finally, it is important to notice that the use of the term *civil law* discussed here has nothing whatsoever to do with the distinction between *civil law* and *criminal* law (see CRIME) within common law systems.

Community law

The law of the EUROPEAN COMMUNITY was often referred to simply as *Community law*. The phrase *union law* (meaning the law of the EUROPEAN UNION) has not gained the same currency (presumably in order to avoid any confusion with that part of industrial relations law which deals with trade unions). The usage *EU law* is, however, very common

Compellable witness

A witness who may be compelled to give evidence (and who, therefore, may be imprisoned for contempt of court if she refuses to do so) is called a

compellable witness. The general – but not universal – principle is that all
COMPETENT WITNESSES are also compellable.

Competent witness

Anyone who is permitted, as a matter of law, to give evidence is a *competent witness.* The general principle is that anyone, whatever her age, is a
competent witness.

Complainant

The person who begins most types of CIVIL LAW proceedings in a MAGISTRATES' COURT is known as the *complainant.* The word is also sometimes
applied to a victim of CRIME.

Complaint

The document which is used to begin most types of CIVIL LAW proceedings
in a MAGISTRATES' COURT is known as a *complaint.*

Compulsory purchase

The phrase *compulsory purchase* relates to the procedure under which a
landowner may be compelled to sell her land to a body (usually a LOCAL
AUTHORITY) to which PARLIAMENT has given the power to buy land by compulsion. (For the purpose of compulsory purchase, these bodies are
known as *acquiring authorities.*)

A wide variety of statutes contain powers of compulsory purchase.
However, whatever the source of the power, there is almost always a
single procedure which involves (a) the making of a compulsory purchase
order, followed by (b) the holding of a public inquiry and, finally (c) confirmation of the compulsory purchase order by a confirming authority (who
is almost always a SECRETARY OF STATE).

An owner whose land is acquired by compulsory purchase will generally receive its market value, together with an amount for *disturbance*
(which includes expenses such as lawyers' and valuers' fees).

Although the phrase *compulsory purchase* is long established in English
law, it is, strictly speaking, inaccurate. An acquiring authority *chooses*
which pieces of land it acquires: it is the owner who is *compelled to sell.*

C

Conciliation

Conciliation is a form of ALTERNATIVE DISPUTE RESOLUTION in which an independent third party tries to help the parties to a dispute to resolve their differences. It is used particularly in employment and family disputes.

Concurrent sentence

Where a defendant is being sentenced for two or more offences, the court may take the view that both sentences should be served at the same time; or, in other words, that they should be *concurrent*. Alternatively, the court may take the view that the sentences should be served sequentially, with one being served, then the next, and so on. Where the court passes sentence on this basis, the sentences are said to be *consecutive*.

Condition

In the context of the law of CONTRACT, the word *condition* is used in two totally distinct senses, one of which relates to circumstances outside the real substance of the contract itself, while the other relates to the classification of the terms of a contract.

1 A *condition* which relates to circumstances outside the real substance of the contract itself, is either a *condition precedent* or a *condition subsequent*. For example, if A agrees to buy B's car, subject to receiving a satisfactory report on it from a qualified motor mechanic, the contract does not become binding unless and until A has received the report. Because the condition must be satisfied *before* the contractual liability is finalised, it is called a condition *precedent*. In other words, if A receives an unsatisfactory report, she can withdraw from the purchase without being in breach of contract. On the other hand, suppose a firm of solicitors agrees with X (who is an outstandingly able Law student) that the firm will pay her £10,000 a year while she is a student, on condition that she passes all her examinations at the first attempt and then joins the firm as a trainee solicitor. Also suppose that, in return, for this promise, X agrees to enter into a training contract with the firm. Finally, suppose that, seduced by the pleasures of student life, X neglects her studies and fails the first year of her degree course. The contractual obligations on both sides will terminate, with neither being in breach of contract. Because the satisfaction of the condition comes *after* the contractual obligations have arisen, the condition in this case is called a condition *subsequent*.

2 The type of contractual term which is classified as a *condition* (as distinct from a *warranty*) is one which is so important that its breach by one party will entitle the other party to treat the contract as being at an end, rather than being limited to a claim in DAMAGES. (Terms which are classified as *warranties* are less important than *conditions*, and breaches of them give rise to claims in damages only.)

Consecutive sentence

See CONCURRENT SENTENCE.

Consideration

Unless a CONTRACT is in the form of a DEED, the promises which it embodies must be supported by *consideration*. The essence of consideration is that there must be a *bargain* in which each party 'buys' the contractual obligation of the other party. For example, if A agrees to sell her car to B, A's promise to transfer ownership of the car is supported by B's promise to pay the price to A. Correspondingly, B's promise to pay the price is supported by A's promise to transfer ownership of the car to B. The classic analysis is that, in respect of each promise, there is a benefit to one party and a detriment to the other. In passing, it must be said that using the word *detriment* in this context may seem odd, since both parties presumably think they are making a bargain which is beneficial to them – otherwise they would not be making the contract. However, when viewed as individual actions, parting with the car and parting with the money are both detrimental to the owners of each. In any event, the use of the word *detriment* is too firmly established to be challenged.

Three consequences flow from the idea that 'buying' the other party's obligation is central to the concept of a contract.

First (and this consequence is really implicit in what has already been said), the person who is seeking a remedy must normally show that she (and nobody else) has 'bought' the promise which she is seeking to enforce. This is often expressed in the phrase *consideration must move from the promisee*. (On this point, see, further, PRIVITY OF CONTRACT.)

Secondly, the idea of *buying* the other party's obligation under the contract suggests that the consideration which is given must have some value. However, this statement needs to be treated with caution, because the doctrine of freedom of contract means that, generally speaking, the parties are free to make whatever bargains they wish. It follows that the court will not inquire whether the consideration which has been given is

C

adequate (in the sense of being fair), provided it can be regarded as having some value (however small this may be). For example, if the manufacturer of chocolate bars wishes to promote the sale of her products by offering something to people who send in a stated number of wrappers from the chocolate bars, the wrappers will be *sufficient* consideration (even though they are practically worthless in monetary terms). Therefore, there will be a contract between the manufacturer and any customer who sends in the correct number of wrappers, and the manufacturer will be in breach of that contract if she fails to send whatever was promised in return for the wrappers. (The classic, if less than transparent, way of expressing this is to say that consideration *must be sufficient but need not be adequate.*)

Thirdly, it follows that something which one of the parties has done *in the past* cannot count as consideration for the purposes of a contract which is being made now. Taking a practical example, if A says to B 'because you gave me £5,000 last year when I was hard up, I will now give you my car', the gift of the money last year is *past consideration* and therefore is not, strictly speaking, consideration at all. Therefore, if A defaults on the promise to give B the car, B will not have a valid claim, because she has not given any consideration for A's promise. However, it is important to notice that although a promise made after the event is normally past consideration, it is not necessarily so. The doctrine (known as *implied assumpsit*) which determines whether such a promise is truly past consideration requires the presence of three factors. First, whatever is claimed to be good consideration must have been done at the request of the party who is now seeking to rely on it. Secondly, there must have been a clear implication that the party who did whatever is claimed to be good consideration would be rewarded for doing it. (In a typical case, this implication will arise from an implied promise, with the result that there will have been an exchange of promises – one express and one implied – each of which will be consideration for the other.) Thirdly, the promise which is made eventually must be one which is enforceable. (Examples of promises which are not enforceable include those made for immoral purposes and, normally, those made to do something which there is already a legal duty to do.)

Finally, and in passing, it is interesting to note that the doctrine of consideration is unique to COMMON LAW legal systems, and therefore has no place in the legal systems of continental Europe – or even the Scottish legal system.

Consolidating Act

A *consolidating Act* of Parliament brings together all the statute law on a given topic, so that it is available in one place. The purpose of a consolidating Act is, therefore, to make the relevant statute law more accessible, and one of the PRESUMPTIONS OF STATUTORY INTERPRETATION is, therefore, that a consolidating Act does not change the law. Indeed, Bills which become consolidating Acts go through a specially streamlined Parliamentary procedure, which is based on the assumption that they do not change the law.

Consolidating Acts may be contrasted with *codifying* Acts. The latter contain all the law (and not just all the statute law) on the topic to which they relate, and will usually be enacted to provide a fresh start for the law on a particular topic. There is, therefore, no presumption that they do not change the law.

Conspiracy

1 The offence (see CRIME) of *conspiracy* exists both at COMMON LAW and under STATUTE (in the form of the Criminal Law Act 1977). At common law, the essence of conspiracy is now limited to agreements to *defraud* or *to corrupt public morals*. The concept of statutory conspiracy is much wider, covering any agreement to a course of conduct which, if carried out, will either amount to, or involve, an offence. A statutory conspiracy will also occur where the agreement is to pursue a course of conduct which would either amount to, or involve, an offence, if it were not for the existence of facts which render the commission of the offence impossible. Thus, for example, an agreement to murder someone who, unknown to the conspirators, is already dead, would be a statutory conspiracy.

2 The TORT of conspiracy takes two forms. One form, which may conveniently be called *conspiracy to injure*, exists where two or more people combine with the intention of injuring someone else. The textbook example is where A and B start up a business in a field in which C is already established, for the purpose of undercutting C's prices and thereby forcing her out of business. If C is to succeed in a claim for conspiracy, she must show that she has suffered financial loss (and not merely, for example, hurt feelings or harm to her reputation), although she need not show that the conduct of A and B was, in its nature, unlawful. (There is, for example, nothing wrong in one trader undercutting another trader's prices.) In practice, it is likely to be extremely difficult for C to show that the purpose of A and B was to

C

harm her, rather than merely to promote their own commercial interests within the context of a free market.

The second form of tortious conspiracy also requires a combination of at least two people, but it differs from conspiracy to injure by requiring conduct which is, in its nature, unlawful. (It may, therefore, conveniently be called *unlawful means conspiracy.*) The unlawful means will typically involve breaches of contract or the commission of torts (or both). For very many years, successive statutes have provided trade unions and their officials with immunity from liability in this tort. However, such provisions may reflect an abundance of caution rather than legal necessity, since it would seldom be difficult to show that the purpose of industrial action is to protect employees' interests rather than harming those of employers.

Constitution

The word *constitution* can mean two things.

The first, and most basic, meaning is *the body of rules and practices which regulate the government of the state.* The most important conceptual point to make at this stage (at least in the context of Western liberal democracy) is that the government does not validate the constitution: the constitution validates the government. Since different states locate governmental power in different people and different institutions, it follows that different constitutions will reflect this basic fact of political life. More particularly, the detailed content of any state's constitution will depend on the *political character* of the state – for example, whether it is an *absolute monarchy*, a *constitutional monarchy*, a *republic*, and so on; and the *political structure* of the state – for example, whether it is *unitary* or *federal*.

The second meaning relates to the physical form in which the constitution is presented, with the traditional distinction being between *written* and *unwritten constitutions*.

In the case of a *written constitution*, there is a single document (or a set of documents) containing a formal statement of the rules (and perhaps some of the practices, although many of these will develop over time as the constitution is made to work effectively and efficiently).

In the case of an *unwritten constitution*, the rules and practices will all be found in a range of sources rather than in a single document (or a set of documents). Strictly speaking, however, the word *unwritten* is misleading since almost all the rules and practices will be written down somewhere, with typical sources being statutes, decisions of the courts, textbooks on political science and constitutional law and practice, and so on. It is more accurate, therefore, to describe the British constitution as being *uncodified* rather than *unwritten*, but the latter usage is so firmly established that it is unlikely to be changed.

Constitutional conventions

Constitutional conventions are principles of constitutional practice which are considered to be binding even though they are not law. They are sometimes described as being a form of *institutionalised political morality*. The following are among the most important constitutional conventions:

- Parliament does not use its unlimited sovereign power of legislation in an oppressive or tyrannical way.
- The Queen does not withhold the Royal Assent from Bills which have been passed by the House of Commons and the House of Lords (or by the House of Commons alone in cases where the approval of the House of Lords is unnecessary under the PARLIAMENT ACTS 1911 AND 1949).
- Where one party has an overall majority in the House of Commons, the Queen must invite its leader to form a government. Similarly, she must grant a Prime Minister's request to dissolve Parliament. Government Ministers accept both collective responsibility for government policy (which means, in practice, that they resign if the government is committed to a policy which they, as individuals, cannot bring themselves to support); and individual responsibility for significant errors perpetrated by their departments.

Constructive notice

See NOTICE.

Constructive trust

Many TRUSTS are created expressly. In these cases the person creating the trust specifies its terms. But in many other cases a situation arises in which EQUITY considers it to be *unconscionable* (or *inequitable* or simply *unfair*) to allow the legal owner of property to be the BENEFICIAL OWNER of it as well. In these cases, equity implies a *constructive trust*, as a result of which the legal owner holds the property on trust for one or more other people. (Where there are two or more BENEFICIARIES, the legal owner may be one of them.)

C

Since the sources of inequity are unlimited, and since constructive trusts are implied when the court thinks they are necessary in order to prevent inequity, it follows that the circumstances in which they can arise are open-ended. However, a typical situation arises where several people have contributed to the purchase price of property but only one of them is named as the legal owner. The legal owner will then hold the legal estate on trust for all those who contributed to the purchase money (unless, of course, a contrary intention can be identified).

Contempt of court

Contempt of court may be either a matter of CIVIL LAW or a CRIME.

Civil contempt occurs where someone disobeys a court order, such as an INJUNCTION. Despite its classification as a civil matter, it is punishable by committal to prison.

Criminal contempt occurs where there is interference with the proceedings of the court, either in the physical sense of disrupting the hearing, or by publishing prejudicial comment on a case before the conclusion of the hearing.

Contempt of Parliament

See PARLIAMENTARY PRIVILEGE.

Contemptuous damages

See DAMAGES.

Contract

A *contract* may be described as an *agreement which is legally enforceable*. It comes into existence through one party making an offer which the other party accepts. An offer to sell something must be distinguished from an *invitation to treat* (or, to use a more old-fashioned phrase, an *offer to chaffer*). An invitation to treat is, strictly speaking, an invitation to *negotiate* terms, although in practice, as everyone knows, the vast majority of sales in shops involve no negotiation, with the customer paying the marked price without question. (However, there are some contexts where negotiation, or to use a more ordinary word, haggling, is expected, with the motor trade being a prime example.)

Curiously, it is firmly established that shops which display goods for sale do not *offer them for sale* for the purposes of the law of contract. The display is merely an invitation to treat, in response to which the customer makes an offer to buy and the shopkeeper then accepts that offer. So a customer in a self-service shop offers to buy goods by presenting them to the cashier at the checkout. Routinely, of course, the cashier accepts that offer either by scanning the goods (with the scanner's display showing the correct price) or by simply taking the customer's money; but it is not until one of these events occurs that the customer's offer is accepted and a contract is formed.

So far it has been assumed that the acceptance of an offer will be communicated by the person to whom the offer is made (who is known as the *offeree*) to the person making the offer (who is known as the *offeror*). While the need for acceptance to be communicated is, indeed, a general principle of contract law, there is an exception where an offer is made to the whole world. In this situation, individual acceptances are not required. Taking the classic example, where the manufacturer of a patent medicine advertises that she will pay £100 to anyone who catches 'flu after taking the medicine, each individual customer who takes the medicine is regarded as having accepted the offer. It follows that every customer who catches 'flu despite taking the medicine is entitled to receive £100. (Cases of this sort are commonly said to involve *unilateral contracts*, although this is a somewhat misleading expression, since there are two parties to each manifestation of the contract, and therefore each contract is, when correctly analysed, bilateral. After all, an agreement to which there is only one party is as surreal as the idea of one hand clapping.)

Silence cannot count as acceptance of an offer, unless either the parties have agreed that it shall, or there is either an established practice within a particular trade or an established course of dealing between the parties, that it shall.

An offer can be revoked at any time before it is accepted.

Where communication by post is reasonable, an acceptance is effective when it is posted even if it never arrives (provided the parties have not agreed to the contrary and the envelope containing the acceptance is correctly stamped and addressed). However, this rule is strictly limited to acceptances and neither offers nor revocations will be effective unless and until they are received.

Subject to specific statutory exceptions (notably, but not exclusively, contracts for the sale of LAND), there is no need for contracts to be in writing. However, even where writing is not required, there is often something to be said for having a written statement of the terms of a contract in order to reduce the scope for subsequent argument as to exactly what was agreed. (This is particularly likely to be the case where the terms of the contract are long and complicated.)

A contract must be either in the form of a DEED or supported by CONSIDERATION.

Contract of service

See VICARIOUS LIABILITY.

Contract for services

See VICARIOUS LIABILITY.

Contributory negligence

Where a CLAIMANT in NEGLIGENCE (or under the rules governing OCCUPIERS' LIABILITY) has been careless as to her own safety, the defendant will be able to argue that her *contributory negligence* should reduce the amount of damages she should be awarded. For example, if A, while a passenger in a car driven by B, fails to wear a seatbelt, and is injured in an accident caused by B's negligent driving, the damages which B will have to pay to A will be reduced in order to take account of the fact that A was (to some extent at least) the author of her own misfortune.

Two important points arise. First, in the context of *contributory negligence*, the word *negligence* has its everyday meaning of *carelessness*, rather than its technical meaning which has developed in the context of establishing liability in the tort of negligence itself.

Secondly, when reading cases arising from fact-situations which occurred before the Law Reform (Contributory Negligence) Act 1945, it must be remembered that, before that Act, both contributory negligence and ASSUMPTION OF RISK were absolute defences (in the way that only assumption of risk now is). One consequence of this was that neither advocates nor judges needed to distinguish the two concepts with any great care, with the result that what should properly have been called *assumption of risk* may have been referred to as *contributory negligence*; and *vice versa*.

Convention rights

See HUMAN RIGHTS ACT 1998.

Conversion

1 The TORT of *conversion* consists of intentionally dealing with goods in a way which is seriously inconsistent with someone else's right to possess those goods. (The word *conversion* comes from an old-fashioned meaning of the word which meant that the defendant had *converted the goods to her own use*.)

2 In the context of equity, the doctrine of conversion is simply an application of the MAXIM OF EQUITY that *equity looks on that as done which ought to be done*. Suppose, for example, that A has entered into a binding contract to sell her freehold (see ESTATES IN LAND) property, Blackacre, to B. Also suppose that A and B have both made wills leaving their REAL PROPERTY to W and X respectively and their PERSONAL PROPERTY to Y and Z respectively. Finally, suppose that both A and B die before the conveyancing formalities have been completed. Since A was under a binding obligation to sell Blackacre, in the eyes of equity Blackacre has already become (or been *converted into*) personal property (in this case, money) in the hands of A. Therefore Y(rather than W) will inherit Blackacre. Similarly, in the eyes of equity, the money with which B was going to pay for Blackacre has already become (or, again, been *converted into*) real property, and therefore X (rather than Z) will inherit it.

Conveyance

1 Although the word *conveyance* is most commonly used to describe a document which transfers legal ownership of REAL PROPERTY from a vendor (or seller) to a purchaser (or buyer), for the purposes of the Law of Property Act 1925 it includes any INSTRUMENT, except a WILL, which transfers an interest in land.

2 A different meaning is plainly relevant in relation to the offence, contained in the Theft Act 1968, of *taking a conveyance without having the owner's consent or other lawful authority*. According to the *Shorter Oxford English Dictionary*, the meaning of the word *conveyance* (which is plainly the relevant one for the purposes of this offence), is a *vehicle or means of transport*. The 1968 Act refines this definition for the purposes of that Act (and, therefore, for the purposes of this offence), to the effect that the word means *any conveyance constructed or adapted for the carriage of people, whether by land, water or air, except that it does not include a conveyance constructed or adapted for use only under the control of a person who is not carried on it*.

Co-ownership

Two or more people who own the same interest in a single piece of land at the same time are called *co-owners*. *Co-ownership* takes two forms, namely *joint tenancy* and *tenancy in common*. However, it is important to notice that co-ownership is possible in relation to both LEASEHOLD and FREEHOLD land, so to this extent the use of the word *tenancy* in relation to co-ownership constitutes an obstacle to intuitive understanding.

The shortest way of expressing the difference is to say that where there is a *joint tenancy*, each co-owner has a *part share in the whole* of the land; but where there is a *tenancy in common*, each co-owner has a *whole share in part* of the land.

Where there is a *tenancy in common*, the underlying idea is that each co-owner owns a specific part of the land, but while the co-ownership continues the land is not divided between them. (This is why tenants in common are sometimes said to hold the land in *undivided shares*, with the word *undivided* indicating that the shares could be, *but have not yet been*, divided between the co-owners.)

Joint tenancy is characterised by the *right of survivorship*, which means that when one joint tenant dies, her share automatically passes to the survivor (or survivors). Where there were more than two joint tenants originally, this process continues on subsequent deaths until there is a sole owner.

There is no right of survivorship between *tenants in common*, who can, therefore, leave their shares by WILL to anyone they choose. A *joint tenancy* can be converted into a *tenancy in common* by a process called *severance*. Conversion to a tenancy in common does, of course, automatically terminate the right of survivorship.

Co-ownership of a *legal estate* (see ESTATES IN LAND) can only take the form of a *joint tenancy* (because the fact that each joint tenant has a share in the whole of the land means that they must all be holding the land under a single title, and this fits in with the simplification of conveyancing which was a major aim of the 1925 property legislation). In *equity* (see COMMON LAW), however, there can be *either* a joint tenancy *or* a tenancy in common (although equity dislikes the potential unfairness of the right of survivorship, and therefore prefers tenancies in common). There is no limit to the number of co-owners in equity.

Coroner

The office of *coroner* originated in the 12th century, and holders of the office had a variety of functions as one of the King's local representatives.

(The word *coroner* derives from *Crowner*.) In modern times, coroners are appointed by LOCAL AUTHORITIES. Coroners' courts exercise two JURISDIC-TIONS, both of which are called *inquests*. A coroner may conduct an inquest on her own, or may sit with a jury. A coroner's jury consists of from 7 to 11 members. Its decision need not be unanimous, provided no more than two jurors dissent.

A coroner's principal jurisdiction is to inquire into deaths which are violent or unnatural; or which are sudden and the cause of which is unknown; or which occur in prison. An inquest is intended to decide how, when and where the death occurred: it is not concerned with allocating criminal responsibility.

A coroner's secondary jurisdiction is to investigate findings of property which may fall within the definition of *treasure*, which is contained in the Treasure Act 1996 and which includes what the COMMON LAW previously knew as *treasure trove*. If an inquest decides that property is treasure, it belongs to the Crown but the finder receives a reward, the amount of which depends on the value of the property.

Because a coroner's procedure involves conducting *inquiries* (as the word inquest itself indicates), it is said to be *inquisitorial*, which contrasts with the ADVERSARIAL PROCEDURE which English courts generally follow.

Coroner's court

See CORONER.

Corporation

A *corporation*, or *body corporate*, is an entity which the law recognises as having both members and its own legal identity, which exists alongside, while being totally distinct from, the identities of those members. Corporations are either *sole* or *aggregate*.

A *corporation sole* (such as the Crown), has only one member at a time (in the case of the Crown, the monarch), while a *corporation aggregate* (such as a company or a local authority) has a number of members at the same time (namely shareholders in the case of companies and councillors in the case of local authorities).

The main practical consequences of saying that a corporation has an independent existence are (a) that its legal rights, duties, entitlements and obligations are separate from those of its members (and, for example, continue in unbroken existence despite changes in its membership); and (b) it is subject to the doctrine of *ULTRA VIRES*.

C

Nothing further needs to be said in relation to the first of these points, but two comments are required in relation to the second.

The first comment is that there is a presumption that a corporation created by ROYAL CHARTER will have the same powers as a NATURAL PERSON; and, therefore, will not be subject to the doctrine of *ultra vires*. In practice, however, this exception is almost always inapplicable, because it does not apply where (as is the case with many LOCAL AUTHORITIES) either a Royal Charter has been granted under a statutory power (rather than under the Royal Prerogative), or a corporation which was originally created by Royal Charter (whether exercised under statutory powers or the Royal Prerogative) has subsequently been re-created by statute. In these cases, the doctrine of *ultra vires* applies in the usual way.

The second comment is that the doctrine of *ultra vires* does not enable the validity of an act done by a company to be called into question on the ground that it is *ultra vires* by reason of anything in the company's memorandum of association. Furthermore, in favour of a person dealing with a company in good faith, the power of the board of directors to bind the company is deemed to be free from any limitation which is contained in the company's constitution. Similarly, a party to a transaction with a company is not bound to inquire as to the contents of the company's memorandum of association or as to the extent of any limitations to which the board of directors may be subject.

Corroboration

Corroboration is evidence which supports the truth of other evidence.

Council of Europe

The *Council of Europe*, which was founded in 1949 and which is based in Strasbourg, consists of 46 countries, including 21 countries from Central and Eastern Europe. (Additionally, the Holy See, the United States of America, Canada, Japan and Mexico have observer status.) It is a totally different organisation from the EUROPEAN UNION, but in practice no country has ever joined the Community or Union without first joining the Council of Europe.

The Council was created to:

- defend human rights, parliamentary democracy and the rule of law;
- develop continent-wide agreements to standardise member countries' social and legal practices;

- promote awareness of a European identity based on shared values and cutting across different cultures.

However, since the collapse of the Communist bloc at the end of the 1980s, the Council has developed a major aim of helping the states of Central and Eastern Europe by

- providing expertise in relation to
  - achieving political, legal and constitutional reform, alongside economic reform; and
  - the promotion and protection of human rights, local democracy, education, culture and the environment.

The Council's principal tasks for the future, as formulated by the third Summit of Heads of State and Government, held in Warsaw in May 2005, are

- promoting the common fundamental values of human rights, the rule of law and democracy;
- strengthening the security of European citizens, in particular by combating terrorism, organised crime and trafficking in human beings; and
- fostering co-operation with other international and European organisations.

The Council's principal decision-making body is

- the Committee of Ministers, which consists of 46 Foreign Ministers (or their deputies who may be either ambassadors or permanent representatives);

but there is also

- the Parliamentary Assembly, which consists of 630 members (namely 315 representatives and 315 substitutes) drawn from the 46 national parliaments; and
- the Congress of Local and Regional Authorities, composed of a Chamber of Local Authorities and a Chamber of Regions.

However, from the perspective of English law on a day-to-day basis, by far the most important of the Council's institutions is the EUROPEAN COURT OF HUMAN RIGHTS, which deals with alleged breaches of the EUROPEAN CONVENTION ON HUMAN RIGHTS.

For more than 40 years, the relationship between the law of the European Convention on Human Rights and the law of the United Kingdom proceeded

C

on the basis of the longstanding presumption that the United Kingdom intends to comply with its international obligations. This presumption manifested itself more particularly in the presumption of statutory interpretation to the effect that any ambiguities in United Kingdom statutes and delegated legislation should be resolved by adopting the meaning that best reflects any relevant international agreement (which may, of course, include the Convention). However, the relationship between the two systems was fundamentally altered by the HUMAN RIGHTS ACT 1998, which created the concept of *Convention rights* and gave them special status.

Council of the European Union

The *Council of the European Union*, which consists of government ministers representing the member states, is the European Communities' main legislative body. Before the TREATY ON EUROPEAN UNION 1992, it was technically known as the *Council of Ministers*, but in practice it is, and always has been, known informally simply as *the Council*. Although the Council is a single body, it does not have a fixed membership. For example, a Council meeting which is dealing with agricultural matters will consist of agriculture ministers; a meeting which is dealing with environmental matters will consist of environment ministers; and so on. A Council meeting consisting of foreign ministers is known as a meeting of the *General Council*.

Unlike members of the Commission, who are required to act in the interests of the Community has a whole, members of the Council represent their own states' national interests.

Council on Tribunals

See ADMINISTRATIVE JUSTICE AND TRIBUNALS COMMITTEE.

Counsel to the court

Counsel to the court is the modern replacement for the Latin phrase *amicus curiae* (which may be pronounced *am-eek-us kew-ree-eye* and is literally translated as a *friend of the court*). Counsel to the court appears at the invitation of the court in order to present whatever arguments are possible in support of an important point of view which would otherwise be unrepresented.

County court

All *county courts* have jurisdiction in relation to claims in CONTRACT and TORT and claims for the recovery of land. Some county courts also have other jurisdictions in relation to a very diverse range of matters, including certain aspects of racial, sexual and disability discrimination; divorce and certain other matrimonial proceedings; insolvency; and patents.

Court of Appeal

Although the *Court of Appeal* is nominally one court, it operates through two *Divisions*, namely the *Criminal Division* and the *Civil Division*. The Criminal Division hears appeals from the Crown Court against either conviction or sentence or both. It also has a limited quasi-appellate jurisdiction, hearing certain types of case which are referred to it by the Attorney-General or the Criminal Cases Review Commission. These cases arise from acquittals by juries, sentences passed by the Crown Court which the prosecution consider to be too lenient, and convictions which are alleged to have been miscarriages of justice.

The Civil Division hears appeals from both the county courts and the High Court. Judges of the Court of Appeal are formally known as *Lord* (or *Lady*) *Justices of Appeal*. They have the style of *Lord* (or *Lady*) *Justice Black*, which is written in either case as *Black LJ*. The correct oral style when speaking about a judge of the Court of Appeal is *Lord* (or *Lady*) *Justice Black*, or *His Lordship* (or *Her Ladyship*); and when speaking *to* such a judge, it is *My Lord* (or *My Lady*) or *Your Lordship* (or *Your Ladyship*), depending on the grammatical requirements of the sentence.

Court of first instance

1 The *court of first instance* is the first court which hears a case.

A court which hears a claim for JUDICIAL REVIEW arising from a case at first instance is called a SUPERVISORY COURT.

A court which hears an APPEAL from a case at first instance is called an *appellate court* (see APPEAL).

2 For the *Court of First Instance* of the EUROPEAN UNION, see EUROPEAN COURT OF JUSTICE.

Court of Justice of the European Union

See EUROPEAN COURT OF JUSTICE.

Court of last resort

A *court of last resort* is a court whose decisions cannot be challenged.

C

Covenant

Strictly speaking, a *covenant* is a promise or an agreement contained in a DEED. In practice, however, it is sometimes used more loosely to mean any legal agreement or promise.

See also RESTRICTIVE COVENANTS RELATING TO FREEHOLD LAND.

CPS

See CROWN PROSECUTION SERVICE.

Crime

The concept of *crime* includes a vast number of individual offences from matters such as MURDER, RAPE and THEFT through to matters such as driving a motor vehicle without reasonable consideration for other road users. As this very brief list indicates, crimes may usefully be thought of as being *public* wrongs, and not merely wrongs against individual victims. The public nature of crimes distinguishes matters within the scope of criminal law from those within the scope of topics such as the law of TORT and the law of CONTRACT, which deal with powers, rights and duties governing relationships between individuals and which are classified as CIVIL LAW. In other words, while both categories involve antisocial conduct, crimes are regarded as harming society as a whole, and not just the victims of the wrongdoing. This conceptual difference is reflected in the fact that the state (usually acting through the police and the CROWN PROSECUTION SERVICE) investigates allegations of criminal conduct and, where it appears to be appropriate to do so, brings a PROSECUTION.

Moreover, assuming the prosecution ends in a conviction and sentence, the state automatically enforces the sentence (for example, by imprisoning the defendant or making her pay whatever fine the court has imposed). In the case of civil wrongs, however, it is entirely a matter for the victim to decide whether to spend the time, energy and money required to prepare a case and then to put that case before the court. Moreover, assuming the claim succeeds, it is then entirely a matter for the claimant to decide whether to enforce any remedy which the court awards her.

However, despite the distinction outlined above, it is not uncommon for a single piece of conduct – such as an ASSAULT – to constitute both a crime and a tort. In such cases there may be proceedings in respect of both, or only in respect of one, or in respect of neither. It is therefore appropriate to consider the principal distinctions between criminal and civil procedure.

- The standard of proof is higher in criminal cases (where the prosecution must prove guilt *beyond reasonable doubt*) than in civil cases (where the claimant needs to establish liability only on the lower standard of the *balance of probabilities* or, in other words, that it is *more likely than not* that what she alleges to have happened did actually happen).
- The rules of evidence are different between criminal and civil cases, with some evidence being excluded in criminal cases when it would be admitted in civil ones.
- Civil cases are very seldom heard by a JURY.
- The avenues of APPEAL differ between criminal and civil cases.

Criminal law

See CRIME.

Criminal libel

Although *libel* is usually a TORT (see DEFAMATION) and, therefore, part of the CIVIL LAW, it may also fall within the scope of the criminal law (see CRIME). More particularly, there are two offences of *criminal libel*, one at COMMON LAW and one under the Libel Act 1843.

For the purposes of the common law version of criminal libel, the following points of comparison with the tort of libel may usefully be made.

- The test is whether the statement in question would bring the victim into *hatred, ridicule and contempt*, rather than the alternative formulation of whether it would *tend to lower her in the estimation of right-thinking members of society*.

The original policy which gave rise to the creation of the offence was the prevention of BREACHES OF THE PEACE rather than the protection of reputation. This has the important consequence that, generally speaking, communication to the victim is sufficient for the offence, whereas publication to a third party is an essential element of the tort. However, this original policy consideration has been almost entirely replaced by a requirement that the libel must be *serious* (although this is subject to the refinement that, in the absence of publication to a third party, the danger of a breach of the peace remains essential).

C

- It is unclear whether a statement which is defamatory of someone who is dead can constitute a criminal libel.
- A defendant who wishes to rely on the defence of justification must show not only that her statement is true but also that its publication is in the public interest. It is unclear whether the defence of fair comment on a matter of public interest is available.
- The defences of privilege apply to criminal libel in the same way as they apply to the tort.

The statutory offence of criminal libel is governed by the Libel Act 1843, under which the publication of any libel which the defendant knows to be false is an offence. If the prosecution fails to prove that the defendant knew of the falsity of the statement, she may still be convicted of the common law version of the offence.

Criminal offence

See CRIME.

Criteria for direct effect

See DIRECT APPLICABILITY AND DIRECT EFFECT.

Cross-examination

See EXAMINATION (OF WITNESSES).

Crown

Although the *Crown* may occasionally be used to refer to the monarch in her personal capacity, it is much more commonly used in the wider sense of CENTRAL GOVERNMENT *departments and their staff.*

Crown Court

The Crown Court tries criminal cases on INDICTMENT and sentences defendants who have been committed for sentence by the MAGISTRATES' COURTS. It also hears appeals against convictions in the magistrates' courts. (These are appeals on the facts.) Additionally, it still exercises a residual JURISDICTION in a variety of ADMINISTRATIVE LAW contexts (such as the law relating to HIGHWAYS). (This jurisdiction is described as *residual* because it is part of a much larger jurisdiction which was, historically, exercised by the magistrates sitting at QUARTER SESSIONS, and which has, during the last two centuries or so, been almost entirely transferred to democratically elected LOCAL AUTHORITIES.)

Crown Office

See ADMINISTRATIVE COURT.

Crown privilege

See PUBLIC INTEREST IMMUNITY.

Crown proceedings

The phrase *Crown proceedings* is generally used to mean claims in TORT and CONTRACT against the CROWN.

Crown Prosecution Service

The *Crown Prosecution Service* (or *CPS*) undertakes almost all prosecutions. The executive head of the CPS is the *Director of Public Prosecutions* (*DPP*), who is answerable to the Attorney-General (see LAW OFFICERS OF THE CROWN), who, in turn, is answerable to PARLIAMENT.

Cur adv vult

Cur adv vult is an abbreviation of *curia advisari vult*, which may be pronounced *kew-ree-a ad-vee-sahri vult*, means, literally, *the court wishes to be advised*. However, this is misleading if it is taken to mean that the court wishes to obtain external advice, because what it really means is that the court wishes to think about its decision rather than giving an off-the-cuff judgment.

Where it is used, the phrase is found either at, or towards the end of, the headnote to a law report. Now that lawyers use much less Latin than they used to use, law reporters use phrases such as 'the court took time for consideration' and 'the court reserved judgment', rather than *cur adv vult*.

Although all decisions made at any given level in the hierarchy of the courts are equal, some are more equal than others, with one factor which gives added weight to a decision being the fact that it was considered rather than being delivered immediately after the court had heard the arguments.

C

Cy-près

Where the objects of a CHARITY cannot be achieved, the CHARITY COMMISSION or the HIGH COURT may order that the charity's funds should be applied *cy-près* (to use the Norman French phrase which is still current and which is pronounced *see-pray*) or, in English, *as nearly as possible* to the original objects. For example, a donor may give money to fund research into a particular disease, which, in due course, becomes easily curable and does not need any further research. The *cy-près* doctrine could be used to enable the funds to be applied for the benefit of another charity engaged in supporting medical research.

C

Damages

Damages are based on the *compensation principle*. This principle requires that a party who has suffered loss or harm as the result of unlawful conduct should be put back into the position he would have been in if the unlawful conduct had not occurred, so far as money is capable of achieving this end. The interests which are protected by the compensation principle are usually said to fall into two categories, namely the *reliance interest* and the *expectation interest*.

The *reliance interest* is protected by damages in the law of TORT, where an award of damages is intended to put the claimant back to the position he would have been in if the tort had not been committed. One of the most obvious and most common examples of damages falling into this category is compensation for loss of earnings following an injury caused by someone's NEGLIGENCE.

The *expectation interest* is protected by damages in the law of CONTRACT, where an award of damages is intended to put the claimant into the position in which he would have been if the contract had been performed.

For example, suppose a particular model of car is very difficult to find second hand, and that, accordingly, second hand prices are going up. Also suppose that a purchaser does manage to find one, and agrees to buy it, but the seller then fails to perform his part of the contract by delivering the car. The buyer's damages will be calculated by reference to the difference between what he agreed to pay and what he will have to pay for another car of the same type. (If the car is unique, it follows that he will not be able buy another one at any price, in which case damages will be an inadequate remedy and the buyer will be seeking SPECIFIC PERFORMANCE of the contract.)

It will be obvious that the terminology (*reliance* and *expectation*) is not transparent, because whatever area of law may be applicable, anyone is entitled to *expect* other people to obey the law, and to *rely* on them doing so. However, the terminology is firmly established and must, therefore, be understood and used.

One major sub-division within compensatory damages is between *general damages* and *special damages*. General damages are awarded in respect of those losses, such as pain and suffering, which cannot be quantified precisely. Special damages are awarded in respect of those losses which can be quantified precisely, such as loss of earnings, the cost of repairing or replacing damaged property, and so on.

There are three true exceptions to the compensation principle, namely *punitive* (or *exemplary*) damages; *nominal* damages; and *contemptuous* damages; and one quasi-exception, namely *aggravated* damages.

Punitive (or *exemplary*) damages are intended to *punish* (or *make an example of*) the defendant, and are, therefore, not restricted to compensation. They are not available in contract and are strictly limited in tort, where they are available in only three situations, namely (i) where the defendant has calculated to make more from his wrongdoing than the claimant will lose (where the compensation principle alone would result in the defendant making a profit at the expense of the claimant); (ii) where there is oppressive, arbitrary or unconstitutional action by servants of the government (with *servants of the government* being interpreted loosely to include local government employees and police officers); and (iii) where they are authorised by statute. The third situation is really nothing more than an acknowledgment of the legislative supremacy of Parliament, and such statutory provisions are so rare that this ground for awarding punitive (or exemplary) damages is of virtually no practical importance.

Nominal damages are the court's way of acknowledging that the claimant has acted properly in bringing the case in order to protect his rights or interests, even though he has suffered no actual harm or loss, without which the idea of compensation is simply irrelevant. Nominal damages were traditionally £2, but other relatively small sums are also common. Nominal damages are available both in contract and in respect of those torts which are actionable *per se* (or, in other words, where the cause of action is complete without proof of actual damage).

Contemptuous damages are the court's way of indicating that the case should never have been brought, even though the claimant has established some technical illegality. They are available both in contract and in respect of torts which are actionable *per se*. They are traditionally the smallest coin of the realm.

Although the financial difference between nominal and contemptuous damages is small, the financial consequences of the difference are substantial. An award of nominal damages will normally be accompanied by an order that the defendant shall pay the claimant's costs. An award of contemptuous damages, on the other hand, will normally be accompanied by an order that the claimant (even though he has been technically successful) shall pay the defendant's costs.

D

The quasi-exception to the compensation principle is *aggravated* damages. These damages are available in tort, but only where the tort was committed in a way which injured the claimant's pride or dignity, or caused particular harm by way of humiliation or insult. For example, aggravated damages may be awarded in a libel action where the defendant repeats, or fails to apologise for, and withdraw, the defamatory allegation. However, these damages are not a true exception to the compensation principle because they are intended to compensate for the additional harm that has been unnecessarily caused.

Finally, it must be noted that the phrase *substantial damages* simply means damages which are neither nominal or contemptuous. It does not necessarily mean that they are a large amount of money.

De bene esse

The Latin phrase *de bene esse* (which may be pronounced *day ben-eh esseh*), which is more or less untranslatable, means allowing or accepting something for the time being, but determining its worth at a later stage if this becomes necessary. The classic context within which the phrase is used arises where the court agrees to hear evidence which may (or may not) become relevant at a later stage in the proceedings, but where it is already known that, by the time the relevance or otherwise of the evidence is established, it will be inconvenient or impossible for the witness to appear. Under these circumstances, the court may agree to receive the evidence *de bene esse*.

Debenture

A *debenture* is a document in which a company acknowledges that it has borrowed money. It will almost always be used where security for the loan is being taken in the form of a CHARGE over the company's assets, although a debenture may also acknowledge an unsecured debt (in which case it is called a *naked debenture*).

D

Deceit

The TORT of *deceit* is committed by a person who makes a false statement (either knowing, or being reckless as to whether, it is false) with the intention that another person shall act upon it; and that other person does in fact act on it, and suffers loss as a result.

Decisions (European Community and European Union law)

See DIRECT APPLICABILITY AND DIRECT EFFECT OF EUROPEAN COMMUNITY AND EUROPEAN COMMUNITY LAW and SOURCES OF EUROPEAN COMMUNITY AND EUROPEAN UNION LAW.

Declaration

See DECLARATORY ORDER.

Declaration of incompatibility

See HUMAN RIGHTS ACT 1998.

Declaration of Right

See BILL OF RIGHTS 1689.

Declaratory order

A *declaratory order* (which was known as a *declaration* before the intro-duction of the CIVIL PROCEDURE RULES) declares what the law is on a partic-ular matter. It is simply a declaration and, as such, does not order anyone to do anything. It follows that it cannot be enforced and if one party to a case chooses to ignore it, there is nothing the other party can do about it. On the other hand, many people and organisations (and particularly public officials and bodies) will obey the law once they know what it is. In practice, therefore, a declaratory order is often very useful, although sometimes the court does not feel the need even to make the order, because it is confident that its judgment contains a sufficiently clear statement of the relevant law.

Declaratory theory of the common law

The *declaratory theory of the COMMON LAW* states that the common law has its own existence and the role of the courts is merely to declare it. It is practically impossible to defend this theory, because it fails to explain (i) how the common law can exist independently of the decisions of the courts; and (ii) how it can change to meet the changing needs of society and then become identifiable, so that the courts may declare it in its cur-rent form. However, it has the attractions of avoiding (i) having to explain how a law can apply to situations which existed before it came into effect; and (ii) the conclusion that the courts breach the SEPARATION OF POWERS by making law.

Deed

Certain documents (for example, most transfers of title to land), require a high degree of formality. The usual way of achieving this has been to require such transactions to be by *deed*. Before the Law of Property (Miscellaneous Provisions) Act 1989, a deed would be *signed, sealed* and *delivered*.

- *Signature* requires no comment.
- *Sealing* originally involved making an impression on hot wax, but in more modern times it developed into the mere formality of sticking a small, red, paper disc onto the document.
- *Delivery* was either by *acts* or by *words*. Delivery by *acts* meant giving the deed to the other party, while delivery by *words* meant saying 'I deliver this as my act and deed' (although, in practice, this seldom happened).

The 1989 Act was passed in the light of a widespread acceptance that the technical requirements surrounding the execution of deeds were unduly artificial. Accordingly, under the Act, a document is a deed provided

- it is clear on its face that it is a deed;
- it is witnessed; and
- it is delivered.

The first of these points is a simple matter of including the appropriate statement in the document.

The second point requires that

- where the maker of the deed signs the deed personally, one independent witness, who is present when the maker signed it, must also sign it; or
- where the deed is signed by someone else at the direction of the maker of the deed (for example, because the maker himself is too ill to sign it personally), it must also be signed by two independent witnesses, who are present together when the maker directs the signing and the signing takes place.

D

The third point, namely the requirement of delivery, simply continues the old law as it was before the 1989 Act.

Deed poll

A *deed poll* is a DEED to which there is only one party. A deed by which someone changes his name is a classic example. Deeds poll are contrasted with *indentures*, which were deeds made by two (or more) parties.

Originally, indentures were written out two (or more) times on a single piece of paper which was then torn (or cut) jaggedly into separate documents. If a dispute ever arose as to the authenticity of something which purported to be one of those documents, it would be a simple matter to hold the disputed document against the one which it had originally adjoined. If, but only if, the ragged edges matched each other, the disputed document was genuine.

De facto

The Latin phrase *de facto* (which may be pronounced *day fac-toh*) means *as a matter of fact* and is contrasted with *de jure* (pronounced *day jew-ray*) which means *as a matter of right* (or *as a matter of law*). So, for example, if someone is occupying a piece of land without having any right to do so, his occupation is *de facto* but not *de jure*.

Defamation

Defamation is an umbrella term for two TORTS, namely *libel* and *slander*. The purpose of both torts is to protect interests in reputation, so the most useful short definition of them is the *publication of a false statement about someone to his discredit*.

The requirement of *publication* simply means *communication to a third party*, while the word *statement* includes anything (such as a gesture) which is capable of conveying meaning.

The requirement that the statement must be *false* prevents a CLAIMANT from using the law to protect a good reputation which he would not have if the truth were known. Whether something is to the claimant's *discredit* (or, in other words, whether it is *defamatory*), depends on whether it would *lower the claimant in the estimation of right thinking members of society*.

The means of communication goes to the heart of the formal distinction between libel and slander. At common law, this distinction is that libel is contained in a permanent form while slander is contained in a transient form. In practice, this usually means that libel is written while slander is spoken, but other permanent forms of expression, such as waxworks, may be libellous, while other transient forms of expression, such as gestures, may be slanderous. However, statute has clarified some situations which could be borderline at common law, by providing that spoken statements made in radio and television broadcasts, or in theatrical performances, are libels.

D

The functional distinction between libel and slander is that libel is always actionable *per se* (or, in other words, an action will succeed even if the claimant cannot prove that he was actually harmed by the libel), while slander is, generally, actionable only on proof of *special damage* (or in other words, the claimant must prove that the statement caused him harm which can be quantified in terms of money). However, there are four exceptional situations in which slander is actionable *per se*, namely

- imputations of criminal conduct punishable by imprisonment;
- imputations that the claimant is suffering from an infectious or contagious disease;
- imputations of unchastity (including lesbianism) in a woman; and
- imputations calculated to disparage the claimant in his office, profession, calling, trade or business.

The main defences available to a claim in defamation are

- justification – which means that the statement is true in substance and in fact;
- fair comment on a matter of public interest – which means that the statement consists of honest (and not, for example, malicious) comment on a matter which is of legitimate public interest (as distinct from something which a lot of people simply happen to find interesting);
- absolute privilege – which means that the statement was made in parliamentary or judicial proceedings, or by one high-ranking officer of state to another; or in a context which statute provides to be absolutely privileged; and
- qualified privilege – which means that the statement was made in circumstances where both the maker and the receiver of the statement had a common duty or interest (which could be either legal, moral or social) in relation to making or receiving the statement.

The defences of *fair comment* and *qualified privilege* may both be defeated by *malice*, which means either dishonesty (in the sense of knowing the statement to be untrue, or being reckless as to whether or not it was true) or acting on an improper motive (such as personal spite or ill will).

There is also a statutory procedure under which a potential defendant can publish a suitable apology and agree to pay legal costs and compensation. A potential claimant who accepts such an offer cannot subsequently pursue a claim through the courts. (In other words, this procedure amounts to settling the claim rather than defending it.)

D

Specific defences are available to people who prepare or distribute various kinds of reports (such as reports of parliamentary or judicial proceedings) or whose trade it is to distribute publications such as books and periodicals.

Defendant

The person against whom CIVIL LAW proceedings are brought is usually known as the *defendant*. However, where proceedings are begun by way of *petition* (for example, divorce proceedings) or COMPLAINT (for example, civil law proceedings in MAGISTRATES' COURTS) the word *respondent* is standard usage.

The person against whom CRIMINAL LAW proceedings are brought may also be called the *defendant*, although the word *accused* may be used. (Historically, the word *prisoner* was also used, but this is no longer the case.)

Degrading treatment or punishment

See TORTURE.

De jure

See DE FACTO.

Delegated legislation

Delegated legislation can take many forms, of which the most common are STATUTORY INSTRUMENTS (which are usually given names which include the words *Regulations*, *Rules* or *Orders*), BYELAWS and COMPULSORY PURCHASE orders.

The one feature which all delegated legislation has in common is that it is made not by Parliament itself but by someone (who could be anybody, but is most commonly a SECRETARY OF STATE or a LOCAL AUTHORITY) to whom Parliament has *delegated* the power to legislate.

Because they result from the exercise of *delegated powers*, all forms of delegated legislation can be quashed (by the HIGH COURT, in proceedings by way of JUDICIAL REVIEW) if the person to whom the power is delegated has purported to do something which is ULTRA VIRES (or *beyond the powers*) which Parliament has delegated. There is a great deal of case law on when delegated legislation will be held to be *ultra vires*, but the common thread running through it all is that the court will not intervene unless it is satisfied that there has been an *abuse of the power which has been delegated*.

Delegatus non potest delegare

The literal meaning of the Latin maxim *delegatus non potest delegare* (which may be pronounced *deh-leg-ah-tus noan pot-est deh-leg-ah-ree*) is that a person to whom some function has been delegated cannot further delegate the performance of that function to anyone else. This maxim originated in the law of agency where it prohibits someone who has been appointed as an AGENT in a particular matter from appointing someone else to act as his agent in that matter.

In practice, the maxim is also, misleadingly, applied to the situation where a person, having been authorised by statute to perform a particular function, arranges for someone else to perform that function on his behalf. In this situation, there is no original act of delegation and therefore the *delegatus* maxim has, strictly speaking, no legitimate application. The law which applies to this situation is better explained on the basis that where Parliament has authorised someone to do something, it wants that person – and nobody else – to do it.

De minimis non curat lex

The Latin maxim *de minimis non curat lex* (which may be pronounced *day minimeese noan cue-rat lex*) means *the law does not concern itself with trifles*.

For example, when a newsagent has a rack of newspapers hanging on the external wall of his shop so that they protrude into the airspace above the HIGHWAY, he will not be guilty of the offence of obstruction of the highway.

Demurrage

A charterer of a ship who retains the vessel beyond the date specified in the CHARTERPARTY may be liable to pay a sum of money, called *demurrage*, to the owner of the ship.

D

Derogation

Article 15 of the EUROPEAN CONVENTION ON HUMAN RIGHTS permits parties to the Convention to derogate from their obligations under the Convention by restricting the exercise of many of the rights and freedoms guaranteed by the Convention without breaching their obligations under the Convention. However, no *derogation* is permitted in respect of

- the right to life (except in respect of deaths resulting from lawful acts of war);
- freedom from torture or inhuman or degrading treatment or punishment;
- freedom from slavery or servitude; or
- retrospective criminal law.

Devise

As a noun, *devise* is a gift of REAL PROPERTY in a WILL. As a verb, it is the act of leaving a gift of real property in a will (as in 'I devise Blackacre to my son John').

Devolution

1 In property law (see REAL PROPERTY), the word *devolution* originally referred only to the passing of title by operation of law (as, for example, where title to a bankrupt's property vests in his trustee in bankruptcy). Its use is still often confined to such situations, but it is now sometimes also used more loosely to refer to any transfer of title, including sales and purchases.

2 In PUBLIC LAW, the word *devolution* refers to the transfer of governmental power to specific areas. Thus the SCOTTISH PARLIAMENT, the NATIONAL ASSEMBLY OF WALES and the NORTHERN IRELAND ASSEMBLY all exercise devolved powers under the Scotland Act 1998, the Government of Wales Act 1998 and the Northern Ireland Act 1998 respectively.

D

Dictum

The phrase *obiter dictum* is often shortened to *dictum*.
See BINDING PRECEDENT.

Dilapidations

Where, as is almost always the case, a tenant has agreed to give up the property in a good state of repair at the end of the tenancy, any lack of repair is usually described as *dilapidations*. The outgoing tenant who has left the premises in disrepair will be liable for the cost of making it good.

Diminished responsibility

Diminished responsibility is available as a defence to MURDER and to no other charge. Where the plea succeeds, it has the effect of reducing the charge to MANSLAUGHTER, to which it is then a guilty plea. The point of the plea is that the only sentence which can be imposed for murder is life imprisonment, while the sentence for manslaughter can be as lenient as the judge thinks appropriate in all the circumstances of the case. In order to establish diminished responsibility, the defendant must show, on the balance of probabilities, that his mental responsibility was (at the time of the killing) substantially impaired by an abnormality of mind. The abnormality of mind may be either inherent or induced by disease or injury.

Direct applicability and direct effect of European Community and European Union law

A provision of either EUROPEAN COMMUNITY or EUROPEAN UNION LAW is *directly applicable* if it *becomes part of the law of member states automatically* (or, in other words, without any action on the part of member states).

Direct applicability must be carefully distinguished from *direct effect*. A provision of European Community or European Union law is *capable of* having direct effect if it

- creates rights which are enforceable in the courts of a member state by people who are aggrieved by breaches of the provision;

but it *actually* has direct effect if, and only if, it also

- satisfies the *criteria for direct effect*.

Reduced to their most basic formulation, the criteria for direct effect are that the provision in question must be

- clear and precise in its expression (so that the court can know what it is being asked to enforce); and
- self-contained (in the sense that its implementation must not depend on the exercise of discretion by the public authorities of member states).

Although many provisions which are directly applicable are also capable of having direct effect, some legal provisions confer *powers* – which may be called by other names, such as *capacities* or *discretions* – which enable one person to do something without giving anyone else the right to insist that it is done. For example, you have the legal power to change your name; but you do not infringe anybody's rights if you choose not to do so. In summary, both treaty articles and regulations share the quality of being both *directly applicable* and (provided they satisfy the criteria for direct effect) *directly effective.*

On the face of it, directives cannot be either directly applicable or capable of having direct effect; but one of the consequences of this conclusion seems to be fundamentally unjust. Suppose a member state fails to implement a directive within the time which the directive itself permits, and an individual brings a case in which he claims a right against the state which he would have had if the directive had been implemented. (For example, the directive may have required a minimum annual allowance of paid leave and the individual may be an employee of the state who would have benefited from the introduction of such a measure.)

If the member state defends the case on the basis that the legal right which is being claimed does not exist, what it is really doing is trying to avoid liability by relying on the fact that it is in breach of its obligation to give effect to the directive. Accordingly, in this kind of situation, the ECJ has held that the directive may be enforced against the member state. In other words, a directive may be directly effective even though it is *not* directly applicable.

But the argument which justifies this conclusion does not hold good where an individual brings a case against another individual (since it is only the state, and not individuals, who can change the law). The European terminology which makes this distinction clear, is that claims against the state require the existence of *vertical* direct effect, while those against other individuals require *horizontal* direct effect.

The direct effect of both treaty articles and regulations is capable of being both *vertical* and *horizontal*.

DECISIONS are both *directly applicable* and *capable of having direct effect*; and their direct effect (assuming it exists in a given case) is certainly *vertical*. Decisions are probably also capable of *horizontal* direct effect.

Finally, even where European Community and European Union law lacks direct effect, it may still have an *indirect effect* on the laws of member states, in the sense that a relevant provision may influence the interpretation of existing national laws of member states. This proposition is sometimes known as the *von Colson principle* or the *Marleasing principle* after the leading cases of *von Colson v Land Nordrhein Westfalen* [1986] 2 CMLR 702 and *Marleasing SA v La Comercial Internacional de Alimentacion SA* [1992] 1 CMLR 305.

Direct effect

See DIRECT APPLICABILITY AND DIRECT EFFECT OF EUROPEAN COMMUNITY AND EUROPEAN UNION LAW.

Directives (European Union law)

See DIRECT APPLICABILITY AND DIRECT EFFECT OF EUROPEAN COMMUNITY AND EUROPEAN UNION LAW and SOURCES OF EUROPEAN COMMUNITY AND EUROPEAN UNION LAW.

Director of Public Prosecutions

See CROWN PROSECUTION SERVICE.

Discharge

1 A DEFENDANT whose PROSECUTION ends in an ACQUITTAL will be *discharged*.

2 Where a prosecution ends in a conviction but the court thinks that no punishment is appropriate, it may impose either an *absolute discharge* or a *conditional discharge*. An absolute discharge is a discharge pure and simple. A conditional discharge is a discharge subject to a condition that the defendant does not re-offend within the period (not exceeding three years) which the court specifies. A defendant who does re-offend will be liable to be sentenced for both the original offence and the subsequent one.

3 When contractual obligations are fully performed, the CONTRACT is *discharged*.

Dishonestly handling property knowing or believing it to be stolen

A person commits an offence (see CRIME) if he *DISHONESTLY handles property (except while stealing it), knowing or believing it to be stolen*. The handling can take the form of dishonestly receiving the goods, or dishonestly undertaking or assisting in their retention, removal, disposal or realisation by, or for the benefit of, another person; or arranging any of these activities.

Handling property once it has been stolen is (all other things being equal) a more serious offence than theft. Although many people find this counter-intuitive, the policy of the law proceeds on the assumption that relatively few thefts are committed because the thief has a personal use for the property which is stolen. From this, it follows that if thieves were unable to sell their ill-gotten gains, the number of thefts would fall dramatically. (This policy is summed up in the old saying *if there were no*

D

handlers there would be no thieves. While this comment is clearly an over-statement, it equally clearly contains more than a grain of truth.)

Dishonesty

A finding of dishonesty cannot properly be made unless the conduct in question

- was dishonest according to the ordinary standards of reasonable and honest people; and
- the person whose conduct it was must have realised that it was dishonest according to those standards.

Dissentiente

The Latin word *dissentiente* (which may be pronounced *dis-sen-shee-enteh*) means *dissenting* and may be found in older law reports where, say, two judges agreed as to the result and one dissented. The headnote may well say something along the lines of 'Held: Green and Brown LJJ, White LJ *dissentiente*): ...'.

The modern style is simply to use the word *dissenting*.

District judge

District judges are full-time junior judges in COUNTY COURTS, who perform administrative as well as judicial functions. District judges were formerly known as *Registrars*.

District judge (magistrates' courts)

District judges (magistrates' courts) are full-time, legally qualified, judges in MAGISTRATES' COURTS. Historically, they were called *stipendiary magistrates*. They generally sit in large urban areas, while LAY MAGISTRATES still sit in magistrates' courts in smaller urban areas and in rural areas.

Divisional Court

In all three Divisions of the HIGH COURT, *Divisional Courts* hear certain types of APPEAL (and, in the case of the Queen's Bench Division, some claims for JUDICIAL REVIEW). A Divisional Court consists of two or more judges.

Doli capax

The Latin phrase *doli capax* (which may be pronounced *doh-lee cap-ax*) means *capable of committing a crime*, and is the opposite of *doli incapax*.
See CAPACITY.

Dominant tenement

See EASEMENT.

DPP

Director of Public Prosecutions.
See CROWN PROSECUTION SERVICE.

Dualism

National legal systems differ in their approach to Public International Law (see INTERNATIONAL LAW). Some take the view that it is separate and distinct from the national legal system; and therefore it becomes part of national law only on those occasions when the national legal system says so. Others take the view that the two systems are, in effect, one. The first approach is called *dualism*, while the second is called *monism* (from *mono* meaning *one*). The English legal system is dualist, which has the important consequence that the provisions of treaties and other international agreements do not become part of English law unless and until Parliament passes an Act saying that they do.

Dubitante

The Latin word *dubitante* (which may be pronounced *dew-bit ant-eh*) is sometimes found in the *headnote* to a LAW REPORT, which might say, for example: 'Held: Green and Brown LJJ, White LJ *dubitante*): ...'. This means that the first two judges were confidently agreed as to the decision, but the third one, while not wishing actually to dissent from the opinion of the majority, was nevertheless *doubtful* as to its correctness.

D

Duress

Duress exists where a person acts in an unlawful way as a result of threats (or, sometimes, circumstances). Although it is sometimes said that the effect of duress is that its victim is not acting voluntarily, it is more accurate to say that the action is voluntary but is the result of the realisation that there is no practical alternative. Duress is a defence to all crimes except MURDER (including attempted murder) and TREASON, while contracts entered into under duress are voidable, unless they have been adopted after the duress has ceased to be effective.

Duty of care

The existence of a *duty of care* is an essential element in the TORT of NEGLIGENCE.

D

Easement

An *easement* is a right which benefits one piece of land and burdens another. Common examples include rights of way and rights of light. These examples are particularly useful because they illustrate the fact that easements may be either positive or negative. A right of way is positive because it entitles the holder of one piece of land to do something (i.e. cross over) the other land. A right of light, on the other hand, is negative because it restricts what the owner of the land which is burdened by the easement can do, by preventing anything that would block the light that would otherwise fall on the land that has the benefit of the easement.

The land which has the benefit is called the *dominant tenement* and the land which has the burden is called the *servient tenement*. Easements may exist as either legal interests or equitable interests (see INTERESTS IN LAND for both of these terms).

Easements are in some ways similar to PROFITS À PRENDRE, such as grazing rights, fishing rights and rights to take timber.

Ecclesiastical law

Ecclesiastical law is the body of law relating to the internal affairs of the Church of England.

ECHR

See EUROPEAN CONVENTION ON HUMAN RIGHTS.

ECJ

See EUROPEAN COURT OF JUSTICE.

ECtHR

See EUROPEAN COURT OF HUMAN RIGHTS.

EC Treaty

See TREATY OF ROME 1957.

Effective remedy

Article 13 of the EUROPEAN CONVENTION ON HUMAN RIGHTS requires that everyone whose rights under the Convention are infringed shall have an *effective remedy* in their own state. This article is not included in the list of articles which give rise to *Convention rights* in English law under the HUMAN RIGHTS ACT 1998, because the government of the day took the view that the scheme of the Act, when taken as a whole, is sufficient to guarantee those rights which are not formally accorded the status of Convention rights.

Effet utile

The French phrase *effet utile* (pronounced *eff-ay yew-teel*) means *full effectiveness* and is sometimes rendered in English as the *effectiveness principle*.

Article 10 of the EC Treaty requires member states to take all appropriate measures to ensure compliance with Community law and to facilitate the achievement of the Community's tasks.

Eggshell skull

The so-called *eggshell skull* principle applies in both TORT and CRIME.

In the context of *tort*, this principle states that defendants must take their victims as they find them. Suppose, for example, that D assaults V in a minor way, but V happens to have a physical abnormality such as a very thin skull. Also suppose that, as a result of this physical abnormality, V suffers serious brain damage, although a person with a normal skull would suffer no more than concussion. D is liable to V for the actual harm V suffers, even though D had no way of knowing that V is particularly vulnerable.

For many years this principle was limited to physical abnormalities (although not, of course, only to eggshell skulls) with the result that victims of tort who were short of money, and who suffered greater loss as a result, were not compensated for any additional loss due to their lack of resources. Suppose, for example, that D negligently damages V's car, as a result of which it is off the road for several weeks awaiting repairs. Also suppose that V needs a car in order to get to work and, therefore, has to hire another car until her own car is repaired. V would not have been able to recover the cost of car hire by way of damages because this loss was caused by the fact that she did not already own, and was not sufficiently wealthy to be able to afford to buy, another car. This result was widely believed to be unjust, and the House of Lords has developed the law so that defendants must take their victims as they find them in terms of their lack of financial resources as well as their physical abnormalities.

In the context of *crime*, the application of the eggshell skull principle can be a little more complicated. As far as the ACTUS REUS is concerned, the principle applies in the same way as it does in tort. However, assuming MENS REA is also an element in a particular offence (as it always is at COMMON LAW and often is under STATUTE), it is also necessary to consider the requisite *mens rea*.

For example, as a matter of criminal law the *mens rea* element of the offence of assault occasioning grievous (or, in other words, really serious) bodily harm is satisfied if V suffers really serious bodily harm even though D intends to inflict only actual (but not really seriously) bodily harm. So if D assaults V with the intention of inflicting actual (but not really serious) bodily harm but V suffers really serious bodily harm because she has an eggshell skull, there is sufficient *mens rea* for D to be guilty of assault occasioning grievous bodily harm. (The *actus reus* is, of course, also present.)

Similarly, as a matter of criminal law, if D assaults V intending to cause V really serious bodily harm (but not to kill her) and V actually dies because she has an eggshell skull, D can be convicted of murder (because the *actus reus* is plainly present and the intention to cause really serious bodily harm is sufficient *mens rea* for murder). But if D's intention had been to inflict only some relatively trivial (but nevertheless actual) bodily harm and V's eggshell skull had led to her dying, D would not be guilty of murder because an intention to cause only actual bodily harm is not enough to support a conviction for murder.

E

Ejusdem generis

The Latin phrase *ejusdem generis* (which may be pronounced *ay-us-dem jen-er-is*) means *of the same class* and the *ejusdem generis* principle of interpretation is a specific example of the EXPRESSIO UNIUS principle of interpretation. The *ejusdem generis* principle states that where general words follow particular words, the general words are restricted to things *of the same class* as the particular ones. For example, where a statutory provision refers to 'cathedral, collegiate, chapter or other schools' there is a presumption that the closing words do not mean 'or any other schools' (because if they did, the preceding words would be redundant). The court will, therefore, seek to identify the common characteristic which is shared by cathedral, collegiate and chapter schools, and it will then limit the scope of the provision to those schools and other schools *of the same class*. (In this example, the court concluded that the class was schools connected to the Church of England.)

Embezzlement

The offence of *embezzlement*, which was, in effect, THEFT of an employer's property by an employee, was abolished by the Theft Act 1968. Conduct of this type would now be simply theft, although in some cases it might well be accompanied by FALSE ACCOUNTING.

Employment Appeal Tribunal

The main function of the *Employment Appeal Tribunal* is to hear appeals on points of law from EMPLOYMENT TRIBUNALS.

Employment tribunals

Employment tribunals, which consist of a legally qualified chair and two 'wing' members (one representing employers' organisations, the other representing trade unions) have a wide-ranging jurisdiction, including claims of unfair dismissal, various types of discrimination in relation to employment and disputes arising from contracts of employment.

Encouragement and assistance to commit an offence

The Serious Crime Act 2007 abolished the COMMON LAW offence (see CRIME) of INCITEMENT and replaced it with three new offences as follows:

- A commits an offence if, intending to encourage B to commit an offence, she does an act which is *capable* of *encouraging* or *assisting* B to do so;
- A commits an offence if she does an act which is *capable* of *encouraging* or *assisting* B, to commit an offence, believing (i) that B will commit the offence; and (ii) that her act will encourage or assist B to do so;
- A commits an offence if she does an act which is *capable* of *encouraging* or *assisting* B to commit one or more offences, believing (i) that B will commit one or more of those offences (but without having any

E

belief as to which one or more of the offences B will commit); and (ii) that her act will encourage or assist B to do so.

The Act also defines what amounts to *relevant* conduct on the part of A and subdivides the elements of the offences to be committed by B into *conduct, circumstances* and *consequences.*

Encumbrance

An *encumbrance* is a right or interest in land which is owned by someone other than the owner of the land. Examples include MORTGAGES, LEASES and RESTRICTIVE COVENANTS RELATING TO FREEHOLD LAND.

Endorsement

Strictly speaking, *endorsement* means any kind of writing *added to the back* of a document after the document has been completed. (The origin of the word is the same as the origin of the word *dorsal*, as in a *dorsal* fin *on the back* of a shark or other fish.) In practice, however, the word is sometimes applied to any kind of addition, irrespective of its location on a document. For example, endorsements relating to penalty points appear on the front of counterpart driving licences.

Engrossment

An *engrossment* is the final version (as distinct from a draft) of a document. The term is usually applied to DEEDS, but may also be applied to any formal document.

Entail

Entail means the same as *fee tail.*
See ESTATES IN LAND.

E

Epitome of title

See ABSTRACT OF TITLE.

Equitable

See COMMON LAW.

Equitable interest

See INTERESTS IN LAND.

Equitable maxims

See MAXIMS OF EQUITY.

Equity

See COMMON LAW.

Equity of redemption

See MORTGAGE.

Equity's darling

A *bona fide* PURCHASER *for value of a legal estate without notice of an equitable interest* takes the legal estate without being bound by the equitable interest. The historical importance of this principle has been greatly reduced by the impact of registration on the doctrine of NOTICE.

The phrase *Equity's darling* is seldom if ever used in modern times but it may still be encountered in reports of some old cases to reflect the markedly preferential treatment accorded to *bona fide* purchasers without notice.

On mature reflection, the phrase is somewhat counter-intuitive, because it indicates that equity (see COMMON LAW) is enamoured of someone who is not bound by interests which exist only in equity. But the phrase is too firmly established to be vulnerable to such straightforwardly logical attack.

E

Estate

All the property, of whatever kind, which belongs to a person at the time of her death is called her *estate*. This property will be administered by her PERSONAL REPRESENTATIVES, according to the terms of her WILL or the rules of INTESTACY (or, where some of her property is included in her will while some is not, partly according to the terms of her will and partly according to the rules of intestacy).

See also ESTATES IN LAND.

Estate contract

An *estate contract* is a contract to convey or create a legal estate or interest in land, including an option to purchase, a right of pre-emption and any other similar rights. It is registrable as a LAND CHARGE.

Estates in land

It is the most basic proposition of English land law that only the Crown can actually own land and that the most that anyone else can own is an *estate in land*.

There are only *four* estates in land, namely *fee simple*, *fee tail* (or *entail*), *life estate* and *term of years*. Furthermore, under the Law of Property Act 1925, only the first and the last are capable of existing at COMMON LAW (and, therefore, being *legal estates*) rather than only in equity. The fact that these two estates are capable of existing at common law does not mean that they will always do so. More particularly, a fee simple will be a legal estate if, and only if, it is *absolute* and in *possession*, while a term of years will be a legal estate only if it is *absolute*.

The word *fee* means an *estate which is capable of passing on inheritance*; and a *fee simple* is simply that. In other words, it is an inheritable estate which is not limited as to who can inherit it, and which, in practice, is practically indistinguishable from ownership of the land itself.

The requirement that it must be *absolute* excludes a fee simple which is *conditional* (for example, if A transfers a fee simple 'to B, unless she shall be convicted of a criminal offence', B holds the fee simple subject to the stated condition and not absolutely).

The requirement that it must be *in possession* means that, for example, a gift of land 'to B for life and then to C in fee simple' does not give C an immediate legal estate (because, while B is alive, C's estate is only *in remainder*). Of course, it will become an estate *in possession* – and, therefore, a legal estate – when B dies.

Unlike a fee simple, a *fee tail* is restricted (or cut down, since the word *tail* comes from the Law French *tailler* – pronounced *tye-ay* and meaning *to cut* – which, incidentally, gives the English word *tailor*, who, of course, cuts cloth. (*Entail* is another way of saying the same thing as *fee tail*.)

The essential characteristic of a fee tail is that it descends through a bloodline, but the details may be fine-tuned to fit the circumstances. The following kinds of fee tail are possible:

- a straightforward *fee tail*, which will descend to the estate owner's oldest child (or remoter issue claiming through him or her);

E

- a *fee tail male*, which will descend to the estate owner's oldest *male* child and remoter issue claiming through him;
- a *fee tail female*, which will descend to the oldest *female* child and remoter issue claiming through her;
- a *fee tail special*, in which case it will descend only to the oldest child (and remoter issue) of a specified person and one wife. (This is not an implicit recognition of bigamy but of the much more common occurrence of a man remarrying on the death of his wife. When these categories were developed, divorce was so rare as to be negligible.)

The second or third of these possibilities may be combined with the fourth, to produce either

- a *fee tail male special*; or
- a *fee tail female special.*

Under the Trusts of Land and Appointment of Trustees Act 1996, no new fees tail can be created, but existing ones continue until they either expire for want of anyone to inherit them (in which case they revert to the Crown as BONA VACANTIA) or they are converted into fees simple by a process called *barring the entails*.

A *life estate* is created where, for example, A gives property to B for her lifetime, after which the property goes to C.

A *term of years* is simply another expression meaning a *lease*. The expression *term of years* is a little confusing, since a lease can be for any period of time and does not have to last for even a single year, let alone a number of years. The meaning of *absolute* is the same as for a fee simple (as explained above), but it is worth noting that there is no requirement that a term of years must be *in possession* before it can be a legal estate.

Since only a *fee simple absolute in possession* and a *term of years absolute* are capable of existing *at law* (or, in other words as *legal estates*), it follows that *life estates* and *fees tail* can exist only *in equity*.

In brief, therefore, the concept of *estates* deals with ownership, and the right to deal with land. Other, lesser, rights in respect of land (such as EASEMENTS and RENTCHARGES) are known as INTERESTS IN LAND (and, going one stage further down the hierarchy, there are also MERE EQUITIES, which are, by definition, not rights in land at all).

Estoppel

Estoppel may arise in a variety of ways, but all estoppels operate to prevent a person from denying that something is true.

Suppose, for example, that, either by conduct or express representation, A allows B to hold herself out as being A's agent. As against anybody who relies, to their detriment, on B actually being A's agent, A is estopped from denying that this in fact the case. (Expressing the same thing in different words, B's *apparent authority* to act as A's agent creates *authority by estoppel*.)

An estoppel at COMMON LAW can arise only in relation to conduct or express representations as to *existing facts* (as, for example, in the situation outlined in the previous paragraph), but in EQUITY an estoppel can arise in relation to *future conduct*. Suppose, for example, that X is Y's tenant and that Y, knowing that X is experiencing short-term financial difficulties, agrees to accept only half the rent that X owes for the coming year. Y will be estopped from denying that the reduced amount is all that she requires by way of rent for that year (assuming that it would be unconscionable to allow her to so – because, for example, X has arranged her financial affairs on the basis of her reduced liability to Y). (*Equitable estoppel* is also known as *promissory estoppel*.)

Equitable estoppel can be used only as a defence. In other words, it cannot give rise to a CAUSE OF ACTION. (This is often expressed in the classic phrase that *estoppel can be used as a shield but not as a sword*.)

By way of contrast, however, a *proprietary estoppel* can give rise to a cause of action. A proprietary estoppel arises where a person who owns land allows someone else to act to their detriment as if they had an interest in the land. For example, a man who owns a house in which he lives with his girlfriend may leave her for someone else but may also tell her that she can have the house in which they have been living. If she then spends money on maintaining the house, the owner of the house will be estopped from denying that he has given it to her. Crucially, this estoppel allows the girlfriend to apply to the court for an order compelling the owner to transfer ownership of the house to her.

Issue estoppel arises once a court has decided an issue of fact, and there is no possibility of an appeal or a further appeal. The parties are then estopped from disputing the facts as the court has found them to be; and (subject to a few express statutory exceptions) are also barred from reopening the issue by bringing further legal proceedings.

E

Euratom

See EUROPEAN ATOMIC ENERGY COMMUNITY.

European Atomic Energy Community

The *European Atomic Energy Community* (which is often known as *Euratom*) was created by the Treaty of Rome 1957. Its objectives were to develop the creation of nuclear energy, to distribute it throughout the EUROPEAN ECONOMIC COMMUNITY (as it then was) and to sell the surplus to the outside world.

Euratom was created by a Treaty of Rome 1957. However it is important to notice that this treaty is distinct from another Treaty of Rome 1957 which created the *European Economic Community* (which became the *European Community*). In practice, the context usually leaves no doubt as to which Treaty of Rome 1957 is being referred to, but for the avoidance of any possibility of doubt the one dealing with the *European Community* was commonly referred to as the *EC Treaty*. Euratom ceased to have an indepedent existence when it was merged with the new EUROPEAN UNION by the TREATY OF LISBON 2007

European Coal and Steel Community

The *European Coal and Steel Community* (ECSC), which was created by the Treaty of Paris 1951, and which came into operation in 1953 with a fixed life of 50 years, existed in order to create a common market in coal, steel, iron ore and scrap between the member states.

When the ECSC was dissolved in 2003, its functions were absorbed into those of the EUROPEAN COMMUNITY.

European Community and European Union

The *European Economic Community* (EEC) was created by the Treaty of Rome 1957. The purpose of the treaty, and thus the purpose of the EEC, was, in the words of the preamble to the Treaty, to 'lay the foundations of an ever closer union among the peoples of Europe'. Over a substantial number of years, the European Economic Community came to be very often referred to as the *European Community* (EC), even though its name had not been formally changed in any way.

The TREATY ON EUROPEAN UNION 1992 (TEU), which is also known as the *Maastricht Treaty*, not only created the *European Union* (EU) but also formalised the common usage by renaming the *European Economic Community* as the *European Community*. Crucially, that treaty created the EU in the form of a organisation consisting of three pillars, namely

- the *three communities* (the EC, EURATOM and the EUROPEAN COAL AND STEEL COMMUNITY);
- the *common foreign and security policy* (or CFSP); and
- *police and judicial co-operation in criminal matters* (or PJCCM).

However, only the three communities were legal entities, with CFSP, PJCCM and, indeed, the EU itself, functioning only at the political level of inter-governmental co-operation. Unfortunately, these realities rapidly came to be obscured by the fact that many commentators spoke as if the EC had become the EU (even though this was demonstrably not the case) and consequently began to speak of *EU law*.

The structure created by the TEU continued in being (apart from the absorption of the ECSC into the EC in 2003) until the TREATY OF LISBON 2007 merged all three pillars into one entity, which not only carries forward the name of *European Union* but also acquires – for the first time – a legal, as distinct from a merely political, existence. One consequence of this change was that the *Court of Justice of the European Communities* was re-named the *Court of Justice of the European Union*, and acquired jurisdiction over certain aspects of PJCCM.

Now that the Treaty of Lisbon has extinguished the EC and Euratom as distinct entities, and has converted the European Union into a legal entity, many Law students may be tempted to consign the explanation contained in the previous paragraphs to the dustbin of history, even if their political science counterparts pursuing courses such as European Studies cannot afford to do so. However, the case-law of the European Court of Justice inevitably refers to the realities as they were at the relevant time, as do many scholarly articles to which Law students may be referred. Unfortunately, therefore, it follows that any student who wishes to have a fully informed – and technically accurate – understanding of everything that she reads across the whole field of EC/EU law should at least be aware of the issues discussed in this entry as a whole.

See also TREATY OF LISBON.

European Convention on Human Rights

The *European Convention on Human Rights* (as the *European Convention for the Protection of Human Rights and Fundamental Freedoms* is commonly known) came into force on 3 September 1953 (the fourteenth anniversary of the outbreak of the Second World War) and was largely prompted by the European experience of totalitarianism during the second quarter of the 20th century. Strictly speaking, its provisions are not part of English law, but the HUMAN RIGHTS ACT 1998 does designate as *Convention rights* almost all the rights which the Convention seeks to protect, and also gives those rights special status in English law.

E

European Convention for the Protection of Human Rights and Fundamental Freedoms

See EUROPEAN CONVENTION ON HUMAN RIGHTS.

European Court of Human Rights

The *European Court of Human Rights* (which is often abbreviated to *ECtHR* to avoid confusion with *ECHR*, which is the standard abbreviation for the EUROPEAN CONVENTION ON HUMAN RIGHTS) sits at Strasbourg. It hears complaints alleging infringements of the European Convention on Human Rights. A party who is dissatisfied with a decision of an English court may complain to the European Court of Human Rights, but this will involve entirely new proceedings and is not an appeal against the English decision.

The principal remedy available in the European Court of Human Rights is merely a declaratory judgment that a breach of the Convention has occurred. It may also award compensation but there is no mechanism through which the payment of compensation can be enforced.

European Court of Justice

The European Court of Justice of the EUROPEAN COAL AND STEEL COMMUNITY was established in 1954. Following the creation of the EUROPEAN ECONOMIC COMMUNITY and the EUROPEAN ATOMIC ENERGY COMMUNITY by the two Treaties of Rome 1957, it acquired jurisdiction in respect of all three communities and was accordingly renamed as the *Court of Justice of the European Communities*. (The court is commonly known as the *European Court of Justice* or, more simply, the *ECJ*.)

The TREATY OF LISBON 2007 re-designated the Court of Justice of the European *Communities* as the Court of Justice of the European *Union* (although the familiar abbreviation of *ECJ* is obviously unchanged).

From 1989, there was also a *Court of First Instance* (CFI) until the Treaty of Lisbon 2007 re-named it as the *General Court*. However, the original title is somewhat misleading if it is understood to suggest that all cases begin there, with the subsequent possibility of an appeal. While it is true that an appeal may lie to the ECJ, it is also true that many cases begin in the latter court. The identity of the court in which cases begin is subject to detailed rules, but the essence of the scheme lies in distinguishing between cases according to their significance and complexity.

Most of the cases coming before the two courts fall into one of two categories.

The first category involves complaints made by either one of the EU's institutions or a member state alleging that either one of the other institutions or a member state is in breach of EU law.

The second category involves cases where a court of a member state requires an authoritative ruling on a point of EU law which has arisen in a case with which it is dealing. When this happens, the court of the member state may (and sometimes must) seek the opinion of one of the EU's courts, in order to enable it to give its own judgment. This is known as the *preliminary reference procedure*.

It is important to appreciate that the preliminary reference procedure is not, in any way, an appeal.

First, and perhaps most basically, a preliminary reference (as its name suggests) is made before the court of the member state has made its decision (and, therefore, before there is anything to appeal against).

Secondly, any party to the proceedings before the court of the member state may ask that court to refer a question of EU law to one of the EU's courts; but the decision on whether to make the reference is always a matter for the national court itself.

Thirdly, once a reference has been made, and the case has been considered by one of the EU's courts, the matter will return to the court which made the reference, which will then give its judgment in the light of the reply to the reference.

European Economic Area

The *European Economic Area* (EEA) was created by an agreement between the member states of both the EUROPEAN ECONOMIC COMMUNITY (as it then was) and the EUROPEAN FREE TRADE ASSOCIATION (EFTA) (with the exception of Switzerland). Broadly, the EFTA states accepted the benefits and the burdens of EUROPEAN COMMUNITY (now EUROPEAN UNION) law in respect of both

- the FOUR FREEDOMS (except for the provisions relating to agriculture and fisheries, which were and are accepted only on a very limited basis); and
- related areas of social policy, consumer protection, the environment, company law and statistics.

The EFTA states are consulted on relevant proposed changes in EU law but do not participate in the legislative process as such.

E

European Economic Community

Before the Treaty of Maastricht (also known as the Treaty on European Union or the TEU) the EUROPEAN COMMUNITY (or EC) was called the *European Economic Community* (or *EEC*). It ceased to have an independent existence when it was merged into the new European Union by the TREATY OF LISBON 2007.

European Free Trade Association

The *European Free Trade Association* (*EFTA*) was created by the Stockholm Convention 1960 to provide an economically based alternative to the EUROPEAN ECONOMIC COMMUNITY (as it now is), which EFTA members saw as being driven more by political than by economic considerations. The founding states were Austria, Denmark, Norway, Portugal, Sweden, Switzerland and the United Kingdom, with Finland, Iceland and Liechtenstein joining at various later dates. Subsequently, however, Austria, Denmark, Finland, Portugal, Sweden and the United Kingdom all left EFTA at various dates in order to join the EC, with the result that only Iceland, Liechtenstein, Norway and Switzerland remain as members of EFTA.

Apart from providing for free trade within its own area under the Stockholm Convention, EFTA manages the EUROPEAN ECONOMIC AREA Agreement (which covers relations between EFTA and the European Union) and a number of EFTA Free Trade Agreements with other countries. The Convention, and the free trade agreements, are managed from Geneva, while the EEA Agreement is managed from Brussels.

European Parliament

By way of contrast with national parliaments, and despite the fact that it is directly elected by the electorates of the member states, the *European Parliament* cannot be accurately described as a *legislature*. It is, however, involved in policy-making and in drafting legislation.

European Union

See EUROPEAN COMMUNITY AND EUROPEAN UNION.

Evidence

Evidence is anything (apart from mere argument) which tends to prove (or disprove) any fact which is in issue in any legal proceedings. However, the court will not necessarily be willing to receive all the evidence which the advocates wish to present, but only that which is *admissible*.

The essential test of admissibility is *relevance*: is the evidence in question relevant either to a disputed fact or to the credibility of the witness? If it is relevant, it is admissible unless it falls within the scope of a relevant exclusionary rule (such as the rule against HEARSAY), unless – going one stage further – it falls within one of the exceptions to the exclusionary rule in question.

The court has a general discretion to exclude any evidence whose prejudicial value is greater than its probative value.

Examination (of witnesses)

The usual procedure where witnesses give evidence is for the advocate who is calling the witness to ask the witness questions in such a way that the answers will constitute the witness's evidence. (This process is called *examination-in-chief*.)

The advocate for the other side will then have the opportunity to *cross-examine* the witness by asking questions which test the accuracy or reliability (or both) of the witness's evidence.

The advocate who called the witness may wish to clarify points raised by the cross-examination, in which case she then *re-examines* the witness, after which her opponent may *re-cross-examine* the witness. Advocates who are examining their own witnesses are not allowed to ask *leading questions* (except in relation to issues which are not in dispute), but advocates who are cross-examining may do so. (Leading questions are questions which suggest the answer. For example, 'What did you see?' is not a leading question. 'Was the defendant holding a smoking gun?' is a leading question.)

Exchange of contracts

Contracts for the sale of land are usually made by a procedure known as *exchange of contracts*. This means that two copies of the contract are prepared and signed by the seller and the buyer respectively and these are then exchanged so that the seller has a copy signed by the buyer and the buyer has a copy signed by the seller. In very straightforward cases involving land of low value, it is not uncommon to dispense with exchange of contracts altogether and move straight to the preparation and execution of a conveyance (in the case of unregistered land) or a transfer (in the case of registered land).

E

Exclusion clause

An *exclusion clause* (also known as an *exemption clause*) is a clause in a contract which tries to exclude or restrict the liability of a party for loss caused by whatever type of breach of the contract the clause specifies. For example, an insurer who issues a health insurance policy (which is, of course, a contract) may exclude liability in respect of medical conditions which the policyholder already has at the time the policy is issued. Although it is possible to view such clauses as simply defining the extent of the contractual liability, in practice the courts view them as attempts to provide a defence if the other party sues.

On this basis, therefore, the court will usually interpret an exclusion clause strictly, against the person who is seeking to rely on it. In other words, where the clause is capable of bearing two meanings, the court will give it the meaning which is least favourable to the person who is seeking to rely on it. (This is sometimes called the *contra proferentem* rule of interpretation, with *contra* being pronounced in the obvious way and *proferentem* being pronounced *proff-er-en-tem*.)

Going one step beyond the *contra proferentem* rule, legislation relating to consumer protection contracts often authorises the court to decide that an exclusion clause which is unfair is simply VOID.

Ex debito justitiae

The Latin phrase *ex debito justitiae* (which may be pronounced *ex deb-it-oh jus-tit-ee-eye*) means, literally, *from the obligation of justice*. So, a remedy granted *ex debito justitiae* is available *as of right* (because the court is *obliged* to grant it), rather than being available *in the discretion of the court*. (COMMON LAW remedies are available as of right. On the other hand, strictly speaking, EQUITABLE REMEDIES are available only as a matter of *discretion*, although it must be added that the court exercises its discretion according to well-established principles – see MAXIMS OF EQUITY.)

Executive

The *executive* is normally used as another word meaning the GOVERNMENT. However, in relation to the doctrine of the SEPARATION OF POWERS, *executive power* has a wider meaning and may include, for example, the powers exercised by LOCAL GOVERNMENT.

Executor

See PERSONAL REPRESENTATIVE.

Exemplary damages

See DAMAGES.

Exemption clause

See EXCLUSION CLAUSE.

Ex officio

The Latin phrase *ex officio* (which may be pronounced *ex off-ish-ee-oh*) means, literally, *from office*, although in practice it is usually best translated as the single word *automatically*. For example, High Court judges are, *ex officio*, justices of the peace (SEE MAGISTRATES). In other words, appointment as a High Court judge *automatically* carries with it appointment as a justice of the peace.

Ex parte

The Latin phrase *ex parte* (which is pronounced *ex part-eh*) is no longer used in the era of the CIVIL PROCEDURE RULES (CPR) but will frequently be encountered when reading older cases. It has two meanings.

One meaning is *from one side*. For example, an *ex parte* application to the court was one made by an applicant who had *not given notice* to the other side that the application was being made. (Indeed, under the CPR, they are now known as *without notice applications*.) Although there is obviously the potential for considerable unfairness in such proceedings (because the court will hear only one side's case), they are used only in the preliminary stages of the proceedings taken as a whole. Moreover, and crucially, the makers of such applications have a duty to disclose any weaknesses in their cases. (Applications for *permission* to apply for JUDICIAL REVIEW – which were previously called applications for *leave* to apply for judicial review – are classic examples.)

The other meaning, which is also no longer used, is *on behalf of*. This meaning was used in case names such as *R v Secretary of State for the Home Department ex parte Smith*, where there was a legal fiction that the Crown was bringing the case *on behalf of* the applicant (whom we have called *Smith* in this example). The modern practice retains the fiction but presents it differently, so a similar case would now be called *R (on the application of Smith) v Secretary of State for the Home Department* (which, in practice, is often abbreviated to *R (Smith) v Secretary of State for the Home Department*). This revision of the form in which the case name is presented has one significant practical advantage when looking up the law.

E

Lawyers who specialise in PUBLIC LAW tend to think of the cases in terms of the names of the applicants, because they are much more distinctive than the names of the respondents. Therefore, case names which put the applicants' names towards the front are much easier to find in alphabetised lists, such as tables of cases which give case citations in the law reports.

Ex post facto

The Latin phrase *ex post facto* (which is pronounced in the obvious way) means *after the fact*.

Expressio unius

The Latin phrase *expressio unius* (which may be pronounced *express-eeoh oo-nee-us*) refers to a principle of legislative INTERPRETATION, the full version of which is *expressio unius, exclusio alterius* (in which the second two words may be pronounced *ex-clu-si-oh al-tair-ee-us*). (The principle sometimes appears as *inclusio unius, exclusio alterius*, in which the first word may be pronounced *in-clu-si-oh*.) The Latin may be translated as *to express* (or *to include*) *one thing is to exclude another*, so that if one thing is expressly included, it follows that all other things are excluded by implication. For example, suppose an Act of Parliament provides that a court which 'convicts a person of an offence under this Act' has the power to order the defendant to forfeit certain property. Also suppose that a court convicts a defendant of *conspiracy to commit an offence under the Act*. Unless the Act expressly says so, the court will have no power to make an order for forfeiture, because although conspiracy is undoubtedly an offence, it is not an offence *under* – or in other words, *created by* – the Act in question.

Express repeal

See LEGISLATIVE SUPREMACY OF PARLIAMENT.

Express term

See IMPLIED TERM.

Express trust

An *express trust* is a TRUST which is deliberately created and which the trustee (or trustees) deliberately accept. A trust created in this way is to be contrasted with an IMPLIED TRUST.

Extradition

Extradition is the process by which one state surrenders to another state someone who is alleged to have committed a criminal offence in that state. The availability of extradition is governed by individual treaties between states. It is commonplace for these treaties to exclude people who are suspected of political crimes.

Ex turpi causa actio non oritur

The Latin phrase *ex turpi causa actio non oritur* (which may be pronounced *ex tur-pie cow-za act-ee-oh nohn ori-tour*), which is commonly shortened to *ex turpi causa*, means that a legal action cannot arise from a morally flawed basis. So, for example, contracts for immoral purposes are void. Similarly, the court refused to allow a claim for damages made by a drunken pillion passenger on a motor cycle which crashed after he had encouraged the (also drunken) driver to drive dangerously in order to frighten other road users.

E

Fact

Matters which courts have to decide fall into two categories: *fact* and *law*. Matters of *fact* are decided by reference to

- what the parties agree;
- the doctrine of JUDICIAL NOTICE; and
- EVIDENCE.

Matters of *law* are decided by reference to legal argument.

Apart from knowing how matters are to be decided, there may be three further reasons for distinguishing between matters of fact and matters of law.

First, only matters of law are subject to the doctrine of BINDING PRECEDENT. Secondly, the available avenues of APPEAL (if any) will, in many cases, depend on whether the finding which is being challenged is a matter of fact or a matter of law. Thirdly, where there is a jury, matters of fact are decided by the jury while matters of law are decided by the judge.

Fair comment

See DEFAMATION.

False accounting

The offence (see CRIME) of *false accounting* is committed by DISHONESTLY (and for the purposes of causing loss or gain) falsifying, destroying or hiding an account or document used in accounting; or using an account or document which is used in accounting, knowing or suspecting it to be false.

False imprisonment

The TORT of *false imprisonment* consists of directly and intentionally (or, perhaps, negligently, although this is open to debate) placing a total restraint on a person's freedom of movement, without lawful justification. It may be committed by an initial detention, or by continuing an existing detention, or by unlawfully continuing what was a lawful detention after its lawfulness has terminated (for example, continuing to detain a prisoner after his lawful date of release).

False pretences

See FRAUD.

Family Division

See HIGH COURT.

Family Proceedings Court

See MAGISTRATES' COURT.

Fatal Accidents Acts 1846 and 1976

Where the commission of a TORT causes death, there will typically be two types of loss.

First, the victim's dependants will lose the benefits that they would have enjoyed if he had continued to live (for example, that part of his income which the victim would have spent on them). This type of claim is known as the *dependency claim*. The first statute dealing with dependency claims was the *Fatal Accidents Act 1846*, the modern successor of which is the *Fatal Accidents Act 1976*.

Secondly, the victim himself may well have acquired the right to recover damages in respect of losses arising from the accident, but have died as a result of his injuries before he could pursue this claim. (For example, he may have suffered pain and suffering before he died.) Damages based on this type of loss are recoverable, by the victim's estate, under the Law Reform (Miscellaneous Provisions) Act 1934.

F

Fee

See ESTATES IN LAND.

Fee simple

See ESTATES IN LAND.

Fee tail

See ESTATES IN LAND.

Felony

Before the Criminal Law Act 1967, criminal offences (see CRIME) were classified as either *felonies* or *misdemeanours*, with the former comprising what were, generally speaking, the more serious offences and the latter comprising what were, generally speaking, the less serious ones. A number of consequences flowed from the distinction, but these are no longer of any practical importance because the 1967 Act abolished the distinction and provided that the legal consequences which flowed from an offence being classified as a misdemeanour would thereafter be common to all offences. However, no retrospective amendment of existing statutes was attempted, with the result that both terms are still found in pre-1967 statutes.

Fiduciary

1 As a noun, *fiduciary* means someone (A), such as trustee, who stands in a position of trust in relation to someone else (B), in such a way that B is entitled to rely on A acting in his best interests, rather than his own.
2 As an adjective, *fiduciary* means *characterised by a position of trust.* For example, a trustee is in a fiduciary relationship to a beneficiary.

Fine

1 In the context of criminal law, a *fine* is a financial penalty imposed on a defendant who has been convicted of a CRIME.
2 In the context of LEASES, a *fine* is a lump sum paid by a tenant on the grant of a lease.

F

First instance

1 The first court which decides a case (as distinct from one which hears an appeal against a decision of a previous court) is known as a *court of first instance.* The principal courts of first instance in the English legal system are the MAGISTRATES' COURTS, the COUNTY COURTS, the CROWN COURT and the HIGH COURT.
2 The meaning of *first instance* given above must not be confused with the Court of First Instance of the European Union – see EUROPEAN COURT OF JUSTICE.

Fixture

When an object is a *fixture*, it becomes part of the land to which it is fixed. Historically, this principle was embodied in the Latin maxim *quicquid plantatur a solo, solo cedit* (which may be pronounced *quik-quid plan-tahtour a sow-low, sow-low kay-dit*, and may be translated as *that which is attached to the ground belongs to the ground*). This principle is important for a variety of reasons, not least of which is that, in the absence of any contractual provision to the contrary, fixtures will be included in any sale of the land.

There are two tests for deciding whether something has become a fixture. Historically, the test, which is sometimes called the *degree of annexation test*, was *the extent to which the thing was actually fixed to the land*. So, a door which is bought from a builders' merchant is PERSONAL PROPERTY until it is hung on its hinges in a doorframe in a building, at which point it becomes part of the building, and, therefore, part of the land. The more modern approach, sometimes called the *purpose test*, is to ask *why the thing is there*; and, more particularly, whether the thing is *intended to be a permanent feature of the land*.

Applying the purpose test, a substantial chalet which rests on its own weight without any kind of fixing will be a fixture, while a greenhouse will fall on the other side of the line. Objects forming part of the architectural design of a building (such as an Elizabethan tapestry hanging in an Elizabethan house) will be fixtures, even though they are not physically attached to the structure of the building.

Where the court finds difficulty in applying the *purpose* test, it may fall back on the *degree of annexation* test.

Floating charge

A *floating charge* is a charge created by a company by way of a DEBENTURE.

The charge is called *floating* because it hovers over all the assets which the company owns from time to time, but without preventing the company from acquiring and disposing of assets in the ordinary way. However, once the charge becomes enforceable, it crystallises on the particular assets which the company owns at that time, thus restricting the company's ability to dispose of them without the debenture-holder's consent.

Floodgates principle

An advocate may oppose, and a court may reject, an argument on the basis that, although it would produce justice in the instant case, it would

F

also *open the floodgates* to future claims. An American judge formulated the classic statement of this principle by saying that it was based on a fear of creating 'liability in an indeterminable amount, for an indeterminate time, to an indeterminate class' of claimants.

However, there is often a strong view that a court should reject a floodgates argument unless there is some identifiable reason to suppose that, in all the circumstances of the case, the fear as to possible future consequences is valid.

The Latin maxim RUAT COELUM, FIAT JUSTITIA provides another counterargument.

FOB

See CIF.

Force majeure

The French phrase *force majeure* (with the first word pronounced in the obvious way and the second as *ma-zher*), literally means *greater force*. In the context of the law of CONTRACT it is used to mean some overwhelming event which makes it impossible to perform the contract. There are no universally agreed and precise limits to the scope of *force majeure*, and therefore the parties to contracts often agree their own definition. A typical specimen could be in the following terms: 'A party shall not be liable in the event of non-fulfilment of any obligations arising under this contract by reason of Act of God, disease, strikes, lock-outs, fire and any accident or incident of any nature beyond the control of the relevant party'.

Foreclosure

Foreclosure is one of the remedies open to a mortgagee – see MORTGAGE.

Forgery

The criminal offence (see CRIME) of *forgery* is committed by a person who makes a false INSTRUMENT, intending that he (or another person), will use it to induce someone to accept it as being genuine, and, as a result, that person will do (or not do), something to his own (or someone else's) prejudice.

The essence of the forgery is that the instrument must *tell a lie about itself*. For example, A is not guilty of forgery if he submits the manuscript of a law textbook to a publisher, with a covering letter in which he falsely states that B (a very distinguished Professor of Law) believes that the book is an essential addition to the literature of the subject and should be published. On the other hand, A is guilty of forgery if he obtains some headed notepaper from Professor B's university, and uses it to write a letter of recommendation purporting to come from Professor B. In this case, the letter will be telling a lie about itself by appearing to be something which it is not.

Four freedoms

In order to create an *internal market* (which was the original purpose underlying the establishment of the EUROPEAN ECONOMIC COMMUNITY), *goods, persons, services* and *capital* must all be able to move freely between member states. These freedoms of movement are known as the *four freedoms*.

Fraud

The offence (see CRIME) of *fraud* may be committed in three ways, namely by *false representation*, by *failing to disclose information* and by *abuse of position*.

Dealing first with the elements which are common to all three versions of the offence, there must be DISHONESTY, and the defendant must intend to make a gain for himself or someone else, or to cause a loss to someone else or to expose someone else to a risk of loss. Gains and losses may be either temporary or permanent but they must take the form of either PERSONAL PROPERTY (including money) or REAL PROPERTY.

Turning to the different ways in which the offence may be committed, *fraud by false representation* is committed by dishonestly making a false representation, which may be either express or implied and may be as to a matter of either fact or law, including a state of mind. A representation is false if it is untrue or misleading and the person making it knows that this is, or may be, the case. Fraud may be committed against a machine (for example, by putting a foreign coin into a vending machine).

Fraud by failing to disclose information is committed where the failure to disclose is dishonest and there is a legal duty to make the disclosure.

Fraud by abuse of position is committed where the defendant dishonestly abuses a position which he holds and in which he is expected either to safeguard (or, at least, not act against) the financial interests of someone else.

See *also* OBTAINING SERVICES DISHONESTLY.

F

Freedom of assembly and association

Article 11 of the EUROPEAN CONVENTION ON HUMAN RIGHTS protects the right to *freedom of peaceful assembly* and to *freedom of association with others*, including the right to form and join trade unions. The word 'association' means 'a voluntary grouping for a common goal'.

This right is a Convention right under the HUMAN RIGHTS ACT 1998. However, the Convention expressly provides that it may be subject to such restrictions 'as are prescribed by law and are necessary in a democratic society in the interests of national security or public safety, for the prevention of disorder or crime, for the protection of health or morals or for the protection of the rights and freedoms of others'. Any restriction must, of course, comply with the principle of PROPORTIONALITY.

For the full text of art. 11, see Appendix 3.

Freedom of contract

The COMMON LAW doctrine of *freedom of contract* allows the parties to a contract to agree on whatever terms they wish. However, the doctrine is subject to many statutory restrictions, especially in the fields of employment law and consumer law.

Freedom of expression

Article 10 of the EUROPEAN CONVENTION ON HUMAN RIGHTS protects the right to *freedom of expression*, which includes the right to hold opinions and to receive and impart information and ideas.

This right is a Convention right under the HUMAN RIGHTS ACT 1998. However, the Convention expressly provides that this right may be subject to such 'formalities, conditions, restrictions or penalties as are prescribed by law and are necessary in a democratic society in the interests of national security, territorial integrity or public safety, for the prevention of disorder or crime, for the protection of the reputation or rights of others, for preventing the disclosure of information received in confidence, or for maintaining the authority and impartiality of the judiciary'. Any restriction must, of course, comply with the principle of PROPORTIONALITY.

For the full text of art. 10, see Appendix 3.

Freedom of thought, conscience and religion

Article 9 of the EUROPEAN CONVENTION ON HUMAN RIGHTS protects the right to *freedom of thought, conscience and religion*. In reality, this right consists

F

of two more specific rights. The first of the more specific rights is the right to *hold* a belief. The second right is the right to *manifest* a belief. Both rights are *Convention rights* under the HUMAN RIGHTS ACT 1998. However, while the first right is absolute, the Convention expressly provides that the second one may be subject to such restrictions 'as are prescribed by law and are necessary in a democratic society in the interests of public safety, for the protection of public order, health or morals or for the protection of the rights and freedoms of others'. Any restriction must, of course, comply with the principle of PROPORTIONALITY.

For the full text of art. 9, see Appendix 3.

Freehold

See ESTATES IN LAND.

Freezing injunction

Mareva injunctions (named after *Mareva Compania Naviera SA v International Bulkcarriers* [1980] 1 All ER 213, which was one of the earliest cases where this type of injunction was granted) were renamed *freezing injunctions* by the Civil Procedure Rules.

A freezing injunction will be granted in order to prevent a defendant from moving his assets beyond the JURISDICTION of the court, where this would prevent a successful claimant from enforcing a judgment of the court in his favour. A freezing injunction will normally be granted by way of INTERIM RELIEF for the purpose of freezing the defendant's assets before final judgment is given, but it may be granted at the final stage of the proceedings. The essential test at either stage is whether the court is satisfied that the successful claimant would otherwise be likely to be frustrated in enforcing whatever judgment the court either may make in the future, or has already made.

F

Frustration

A CONTRACT will be discharged by *frustration* if

- after the contract has been made, some event occurs, which (through no fault of either party) significantly changes the nature of the contractual rights or duties (or both) from those which the parties could reasonably have contemplated when they made the contract; and

- the contract either makes no provision for the change of circumstances, or (if it does) the provision which it makes is inadequate; so that
- the contract has lost its commercial purpose, or it would be unjust for some other reason, to require that it should still be performed.

For example, a contract for the hire of a building for a pop concert will be frustrated if the building burns down before the concert takes place (assuming that neither of the parties is responsible for the fire and that the contract makes no suitable provision for other accommodation).

Full age

See ADULT.

Fully secret trust

See SECRET TRUST.

F

GBH
See ASSAULT.

Gender recognition certificate

A person suffering from the disorder commonly known as *transsexualism* (but also known as *gender dysphoria* and *gender identity disorder*), may obtain a *gender recognition certificate* on the basis of either having been living in the acquired gender for at least two years, or having changed gender under the law of a country or territory outside the United Kingdom. Apart from issues arising in connection with the inheritance of titles and of property connected with titles, the holder of a gender recognition certificate is to be treated for all legal purposes as belonging to the acquired gender.

General Council of the Bar

The *General Council of the Bar*, which is commonly known as the *Bar Council*, is the governing body of the Bar. It represents the interests of the Bar in all matters relating to the profession, whether by acting as something akin to a trade union, by regulating education and training for the Bar, by providing disciplinary procedures in order to maintain high standards of professional conduct among barristers, by acting as an interest group in relation to matters of substantive law and the administration of justice, or in any other way.

General Court (of the European Union)
See EUROPEAN COURT OF JUSTICE

General damages
See DAMAGES.

General equitable charge

The phrase *general equitable charge* is not defined, but one of the most common examples is an equitable MORTGAGE without deposit of title deeds. A general equitable charge is registrable as a Class C (iii) LAND CHARGE.

General warrant

A *general warrant* is a warrant for arrest which does not identify the person to whom it relates, or a search warrant which does not identify the premises to be searched. Such warrants are unlawful at COMMON LAW.

Good root of title

Where land with unregistered title is being sold, the seller must (unless the contract contains any contrary provision) produce a *good root of title*. This is almost always a CONVEYANCE for value (see PURCHASER), which is at least 15 years old and which deals with the whole legal and equitable title to the land and contains nothing to cast doubt on the seller's ownership.

A legal MORTGAGE may also be accepted as a good root of title – and, indeed, is sometimes said to be even better than a conveyance, and therefore to be the *best* root of title rather than merely a *good* root of title. This is based on the idea that if you are buying a property for your own occupation, you may be particularly attracted to that particular property, and may therefore be tempted to turn a blind eye to relatively minor defects of title. On the other hand, a lender advancing money on mortgage as a purely commercial transaction will not be swayed by any non-commercial considerations, and so will not accept a root of title unless it is perfect.

Goods

In everyday terms, *goods* are physical objects which are capable of being owned. More technically, goods are CHATTELS which are not *chattels real*.

Government

The *government* is the collective name given to all those who hold office as MINISTERS OF THE CROWN, whatever their specific posts may be called.

Government circulars

Government circulars are generally issued to provide advice and guidance on the way in which statutory schemes are administered. Sometimes, however, STATUTE will provide that circulars on specific topics *must* be implemented, thus giving them the force of law.

Grant of representation

See PERSONAL REPRESENTATIVES.

Great Seal

The *Great Seal* is used to authenticate the most important instruments of state, such as international treaties and the LETTERS PATENT which the Queen signs in order to give the Royal Assent to BILLS.

Green paper

A *green paper* is a consultative document, issued by the GOVERNMENT at the stage when policy is still being formulated. It must be distinguished from a *white paper*, which comes at a later stage and is a statement of the policy which the government has decided to adopt.

Ground rent

A landlord who grants a long LEASE will usually require a price which is more or less the same as it would be if the land were freehold (see ESTATES IN LAND). However, in addition to this price, a landlord may require the payment of a further sum by way of *ground rent.*

Ground rent may be a relatively small sum (although there is often provision for periodic increases) and is usually payable annually. It may even be purely nominal, in which case a peppercorn is the traditional way of expressing the amount payable.

Assuming the landlord owns the freehold the reason for insisting on even a nominal payment being expressed is that the person who receives the rents and profits is treated as being in possession of the land, and so receiving a rent means that the freehold continues to be a *fee simple absolute in possession*, which in turn means that it continues to be a *legal estate.*

G

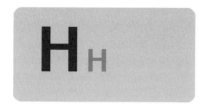

Habeas corpus

The Latin phrase *habeas corpus* (which may be pronounced *hay-bee-us kor-pus*) is the name of the remedy which is used to challenge the legality of detention. It can be sought by the detainee or someone acting on his behalf, and it requires the person who is detaining him to produce the detainee and justify his detention. (*Habeas corpus* means, literally, *you will have the body*.) If the court concludes that the respondent does not have a lawful reason for the detention, it will order the release of the detainee. *Habeas corpus* originated at COMMON LAW but has been governed by statute for over three hundred years. Although it is greatly valued as a protection against any executive detention (or, in other words, detention for no other reason than that the government wishes to take troublemakers out of circulation), in practice *habeas corpus* is now chiefly used as a means of testing the legality of the detention of immigrants. In any event, the doctrine of the LEGISLATIVE SUPREMACY OF PARLIAMENT means that *habeas corpus* can be overridden by express statutory provisions, although the remedy's heritage can create political embarrassment for a government which introduces such legislation into Parliament in any situations other than those where national security is clearly at risk.

Half-secret trust

See SECRET TRUST.

Hansard

Hansard is the official record of proceedings in Parliament. Reports of proceedings from 1988 are available, free of charge, online at http://www.parliament.uk/. *Hansard* takes its title from the name of the 19th century publisher of the reports.

Headnote

See LAW REPORT.

Hearsay

Hearsay is secondhand evidence which arises where a witness giving EVIDENCE in court repeats what someone else has said, in order to establish the truth of what that other person said.

The objection to hearsay is that it is not the best evidence, since the person whose words are being given in evidence was not on oath and cannot be cross-examined, nor can his demeanour be assessed by the court. (Where there is conflicting evidence, the court often forms an impression of who is, or is not, telling the truth from the way in which they give their evidence.)

Hearsay has generally been much more admissible in CIVIL LAW than in criminal law (see CRIME) but the Criminal Justice Act 2003 significantly relaxed the exclusionary tendency in criminal cases by empowering the court to admit hearsay in criminal cases as well where it is satisfied that it is in the interests of justice that the evidence should be admitted.

Heir

An *heir* is the person who, as a matter of law, is entitled to inherit property on an intestacy. An *heir apparent* is someone who will inherit provided he outlives the person whose heir he is. An *heir presumptive* is someone who will inherit provided he outlives the person whose heir he is, and provided that, in the meantime, no one else is born whose kinship to that person would be closer than his own. (For example, if A and B are brothers, A might be B's heir presumptive, but his right to inherit would be defeated if B subsequently had a child.)

Hereditament

Historically, *hereditament* meant any kind of REAL PROPERTY which could be inherited, but is now usually confined to meaning a unit of land which is liable to business rates.

(Business rates survived when domestic rates were replaced by the community charge – commonly called the *poll tax* – which was, in turn, replaced by the council tax.)

H

High Contracting Parties

The parties to a treaty or other international agreement are called the *high contracting parties*.

High Court

Although the *High Court* (or the *High Court of Justice*, to give it its full name) is nominally one court, it functions as three separate units, namely

- the Queen's Bench Division (or, when the monarch is male, the King's Bench Division);
- the Chancery Division; and
- the Family Division.

The High Court's JURISDICTION includes both CIVIL LAW and criminal law (see CRIME), and is exercisable both at FIRST INSTANCE and on APPEAL.

The Queen's Bench Division's jurisdiction at first instance is limited to civil cases and includes not only CONTRACT and TORT, but also a supervisory JURISDICTION (which is simply another way of saying it has jurisdiction by way of JUDICIAL REVIEW).

Its appellate jurisdiction covers both *civil* and *criminal* cases, and takes the form of appeals *by way of case stated* from both magistrates' courts and the Crown Court when that court is exercising its appellate jurisdiction. Appeals by way of case stated can raise points of law only, and must proceed on the basis of the facts as they were agreed by the parties or found by the court of first instance.

In an appeal by way of case stated, the court whose decision is being appealed sends the Queen's Bench Division a written statement containing both the facts of the case (as they were either agreed by the parties or found to be by the court), and the court's understanding of the relevant law. The Queen's Bench Division then says whether the lower court got the law right or wrong. It will then usually send the case back to the court from which it came, telling it either what decision it should make, or leaving it to come to its own decision in the light of the law as it was found to be on the appeal. Sometimes, particularly in minor cases where a substantial period of time has elapsed in waiting for the appeal to be heard, the High Court will content itself by giving judgment on the relevant point of law, without sending the case back.

The Chancery Division has only civil jurisdiction, and deals with cases involving companies, property, wills and associated matters. It is almost entirely at first instance, although it does include a few types of appeal from the county courts.

The essence of the Family Division's jurisdiction is self-evident from its title, and its first instance jurisdiction includes divorce. It has appellate jurisdiction in certain cases originating in magistrates' courts and county courts.

H

Highway

A *highway* is a way over which the public have a right to pass and re-pass, and to do things which are reasonably incidental to the exercise of that right. The owner of property adjoining the highway owns the subsoil which lies beneath it; or, as is much more commonly the case, if opposite sides of the highway are owned by different people, each owns the subsoil as far as the mid-point of the highway.

In practice, some of the most difficult questions arising in relation to highways concern the identification and extent of the rights which are reasonably incidental to the exercise of the right of passage and re-passage. These questions can arise either in actions for trespass brought by the owners of the subsoil, or prosecutions for the statutory offence of wilful obstruction of the highway without lawful authority or excuse.

(Prosecutions for obstruction of the highway are sometimes brought in respect of political activity on the highway.)

Holding over

A tenant who stays in possession of land after his tenancy has expired is said to be *holding over*. Holding over will be a TRESPASS unless the landlord consents to the continued occupation of the land.

Homicide

Homicide is an omnibus term for all the offences which involve the taking of human life. Of those, MURDER and MANSLAUGHTER have the highest profile, but there are also other offences, including causing death by dangerous driving and CHILD DESTRUCTION. English Law does not classify unlawful abortion as homicide.

Honorarium

An *honorarium* is a payment which is made as a matter of honour, rather than as a matter of legal obligation. It follows that no action for non-payment can be pursued in the courts.

Horizontal direct effect

See DIRECT APPLICABILITY AND DIRECT EFFECT.

House of Commons

See PARLIAMENT.

H

House of Lords

The *House of Lords* is the upper chamber of PARLIAMENT. However, until the SUPREME COURT came into existence in October 2009, the phrase *the House of Lords* was also very commonly used as shorthand for the *Appellate Committee of the House of Lords* which, while technically a committee of the upper chamber of parliament, was effectively the highest court of appeal within the English legal system. The Appellate Committee normally sat with five members, but could sit with seven or even nine members in cases which were considered to be particularly important.

The *Appellate* Committee had to be distinguished from the *Appeals* Committee, whose function it was to hear applications (technically known as *petitions*) for permission to appeal to the *Appellate Committee*. The Appeals Committee normally sat with three members.

In practice, towards the end of their lives, both the Appellate Committee and the Appeals Committee consisted entirely of judges who were appointed for the purpose, and who automatically received peerages. (These judges were known formally as *Lords of Appeal in Ordinary* and informally as *Law Lords*.) Although peers who held, or had held, high judicial office were also entitled to sit, so few peers qualified under this heading that it was of no real significance.

With effect from October 2009, the functions of both the Appellate Committee and the Appeals Committee were transferred to a new body called the SUPREME COURT of the United Kingdom.

See also SUPREME COURT.

Human Rights Act 1998

The *Human Rights Act 1998* (the *HRA*) is often said to have incorporated the EUROPEAN CONVENTION ON HUMAN RIGHTS (the ECHR) into English law, despite the fact that it did not do so. What it did do was to create an English law concept of *Convention rights*, and then give those rights special status in English law. However, Convention rights within the meaning of the Human Rights Act do not include all the rights which the ECHR seeks to protect, nor (except in relation to public authorities) does their special status within English law mean that they are binding in English law. The articles and protocols which set out Convention rights within the meaning of the HRA (which are reproduced in full in Appendix 3) may be summarised as:

art. 2   the right to life;
art. 3   prohibition of torture or inhuman or degrading treatment or punishment;

art. 4   prohibition of slavery and forced labour;

art. 5   the right to liberty and security of the person;

art. 6   the right to a fair trial;

art. 7   freedom from the imposition of retrospective criminal liability and punishment;

art. 8   the right to respect for private and family life;

art. 9   freedom of religion;

art. 10   freedom of expression;

art. 11   freedom of assembly and association;

art. 12   the right to marry and found a family;

art. 14   prohibition of discrimination in enjoyment of rights under the Convention.

First Protocol

art. 1   the right to property;

art. 2   the right to education;

art. 3   the right to free elections.

Sixth Protocol

arts 1 & 2   prohibition of the death penalty.

The ECHR contains a system of *derogations* and *reservations*, under which individual states can opt out of those of its provisions which they feel unable to accept.

Apart from the creation of the concept of *Convention rights*, the main points of the HRA may be summarised as follows.

- It is unlawful for public authorities to act in a way which is incompatible with Convention rights.
- Courts and tribunals *must take relevant Convention rights into account.* (While this provision gives no indication as to how much weight should be given to Convention rights, in practice they are likely to be given very substantial weight, because if an English court gives a ruling which contravenes the ECHR, and the losing party takes the case to the EUROPEAN COURT OF HUMAN RIGHTS (ECtHR), that court will almost always follow its own decisions as to the meaning of the ECHR. In other words, the net effect of an English court's failure to follow STRASBOURG JURISPRUDENCE is likely to be simply delay and increased expense in obtaining what the English court could have given in the first place.)
- The courts must, so far as it is possible to do so, read, and give effect to, all domestic PRIMARY LEGISLATION and DELEGATED LEGISLATION (even if made before the HRA was passed) in a way which is compatible

H

with Convention rights. However, a court which finds it impossible to identify a compatible interpretation must apply the domestic legislation over the Convention right.

Beyond this point, it is necessary to tread very carefully. The HRA specifically provides that incompatibility with a Convention right

- does *not* invalidate *primary* legislation (a category which, crucially, includes ACTS OF PARLIAMENT); but it
- *does* invalidate *delegated* legislation (of which STATUTORY INSTRUMENTS are the most common form), *unless* there is a *statute* which specifically provides that the piece of subordinate legislation in question remains valid, notwithstanding its incompatibility with a Convention right (but a specific provision of this sort is very rare in practice); but
- delegated legislation of any type can be quashed only by a court at the level of the High Court or above when dealing with a claim for JUDICIAL REVIEW, and not in the course of other proceedings.

In short, therefore, all courts must always apply both Acts of Parliament and delegated legislation, even if they are incompatible with Convention rights, but practically all *delegated* legislation which is incompatible with Convention rights will subsequently be vulnerable to judicial review.

However, while it is undoubtedly true that Acts of Parliament can no more be quashed for incompatibility with Convention rights than for any other reason, it is important to notice that the HRA does create the possibility of a *declaration of incompatibility* in respect of Acts of Parliament which are incompatible with Conventions rights. These declarations may be made only by a court at the level of the High Court or above and they must specify the statutory provisions to which they relate.

As with any other DECLARATORY ORDER, a declaration of incompatibility is intrinsically unenforceable, but it does create the possibility of the government amending the offending provision by way of delegated legislation in the form of what is known as a remedial order. (The significance of allowing a statute to be amended by delegated legislation is that the process is likely to be much quicker than it would be if Parliamentary time had to be found for an amending BILL to be passed. However, a declaration of incompatibility merely *enables* the government to make a remedial order: it does *not require* it to do so.)

The HRA provides that an application to quash an act of a public authority may be made only in the High Court. On the other hand, however, the Act (together with the Human Rights Act 1998 Rules) provides that reliance may be placed on Convention rights in any proceedings in any court or tribunal.

Implied repeal

See LEGISLATIVE SUPREMACY OF PARLIAMENT.

Implied term

Although many written CONTRACTS consist almost entirely of *express terms*, many will also contain *implied terms*. Perhaps more obviously, in the case of a straightforward oral contract (such as buying a book in a bookshop), practically all the terms (apart from the price and the identity of the book) will be *implied*. Terms may be implied either by STATUTE (with statutes regulating consumer contracts being a particularly fertile source of examples) or at COMMON LAW.

The meaning of a term which is implied by statute is a question of interpretation in the ordinary way. The question of whether the parties can contract out of a term implied by statute also appears to be a question of interpretation. However, in this case it is reasonable to expect the statute itself to make express provision either way, so that the process of interpretation will cause neither delay nor difficulty.

A term will not be implied at common law unless it (i) is reasonable and equitable; (ii) is capable of being expressed precisely; (iii) does not contradict any express term of the contract; (iv) is obvious; and (v) in the context of commercial contracts, is necessary to ensure the business efficacy of the contract.

Something is *obvious* for the present purposes if an *officious bystander* who is present during the parties' negotiations and who suggests the inclusion of an express provision can be told that his suggestion is so obvious that it goes without saying. The content of the requirement of obviousness may be met in various ways. For example, in the context of commercial contracts, a specific term may be implied in order to reflect usage within a particular trade or an established course of dealing between the parties. In the same context, the test of business efficacy requires the court to decide whether the contract would still serve its intended commercial purpose even if the term in question was not implied.

Implied trust

An *implied trust* can come into being either under STATUTE or in equity (see COMMON LAW).

An implied trust will arise under statute, for example, where property is conveyed into the names of two or more people.

An implied trust will arise in equity where it would be inequitable (or *unconscionable*, or simply *unfair*) to allow a legal owner to be the sole BENEFICIAL OWNER as well.

See also CONSTRUCTIVE TRUST and RESULTING TRUST.

Imputed notice

See NOTICE.

Incapacity

See CAPACITY.

Inchoate offences

Attempting to commit offences, or *conspiring* with or *inciting* other people to commit offences, do not, in themselves, cause any harm. Nevertheless, they are all so closely connected with conduct which, if successfully carried out, does cause the type of harm which is prohibited by the criminal law (see CRIME), that they each, in themselves, give rise to criminal liability.

Putting it another way, although ATTEMPT, CONSPIRACY and the provision of ENCOURAGEMENT or ASSISTANCE (together with statutory INCITEMENT) are all offences in their own right, there is a sense in which they are also *incompleted* examples of criminality; and since the word *inchoate* (pronounced *in-koh-ate*) means *incomplete*, they are called *inchoate offences*.

Incitement

Until the Serious Crime Act 2007, incitement was capable of being an offence (see CRIME) either at COMMON LAW or under STATUTE (in which latter context it arises in a variety of statutes). However, while that Act abolished the common law offence (which it replaced with the new offences of ENCOURAGEMENT and ASSISTANCE TO COMMIT AN OFFENCE), it preserved the statutory examples.

A is guilty of *incitement* if she encourages or pressurises B to commit an offence. A is guilty of incitement even if B does not actually commit an offence, but if B does do so, A is also guilty of aiding and abetting B to commit the offence.

Incompletely constituted trust

An *incompletely constituted trust* arises where A declares B to be a trustee of certain property, but B does not in fact have the legal ESTATE in that property (because, for example, A has not yet transferred it to her). When A does transfer the legal estate to B, the trust becomes *completely constituted*.

Incorporated Council of Law Reporting for England and Wales

See LAW REPORTS.

Incorporation

Incorporation has two, distinct meanings, namely

- the process of becoming a CORPORATION; and
- the inclusion in one document of material contained in another, either by merging both into one or merely by one referring to the other. A common form of incorporation by reference occurs where a STATUTE provides that a particular word has the meaning assigned to it by an earlier statute. This practice is convenient for the drafter of the later statute, but inconvenient for the user of that statute, who cannot understand it without also consulting the earlier one.

Incorporeal hereditament

See HEREDITAMENT.

I

Indefeasible

An *indefeasible* interest is one which cannot be made VOID.

Indenture

See DEED POLL.

Independent contractor

See VICARIOUS LIABILITY.

Indictable offence

An offence which is triable only on INDICTMENT (or, in other words, only at the CROWN COURT) is said to be an *indictable offence*. (*Indictment* is pronounced *indite-ment* and *indictable* is pronounced *indite-able*.)

Indictment

An *indictment* (pronounced *indite-ment*) is the formal document containing the charges on which a defendant at the Crown Court is to be tried.

Infant

See MINOR.

Infanticide

A mother commits the offence of *infanticide* if she kills her own child aged less than twelve months, provided she does not have a younger child and, at the time of the killing, the balance of her mind was disturbed by the effect of giving birth to the child, or by reason of lacerations caused by the birth. (The reference to *lacerations* reflects a belief which used to represent orthodox medical opinion as to the cause of post-natal depression.)

As well as being an offence in its own right, infanticide is also available as a plea to a charge of MURDER, which, if successful, reduces the offence to MANSLAUGHTER.

Although the maximum sentence for infanticide is life imprisonment, probation is the usual outcome of a conviction.

Inferior court

When courts are divided into *inferior courts* and *superior courts*, the former category consists of coroners' courts (see CORONER), MAGISTRATES' COURTS and COUNTY COURTS, while the latter consists of the CROWN COURT, the EMPLOYMENT APPEAL TRIBUNAL, the HIGH COURT, the COURT OF APPEAL and the SUPREME COURT. The importance of the distinction between the two categories is that inferior courts are subject to the supervisory jurisdiction of the High Court (or, in other words, to JUDICIAL REVIEW), while superior courts are not. (In the case of the Crown Court, the immunity from judicial review extends only to matters affecting the conduct of trials on INDICTMENT.)

Informed consent

See REAL CONSENT.

Inhuman treatment or punishment

See TORTURE.

Injunction

An *injunction* is an order of the court which either orders the defendant to do something (a *mandatory* injunction) or prohibits the defendant from doing something (a *prohibitory* injunction). Injunctions are equitable remedies and are therefore granted or withheld according to the general principles of equity (see COMMON LAW). (The flavour of those principles is neatly conveyed by the MAXIMS OF EQUITY.)

Injurious falsehood

Injurious falsehood and *malicious falsehood* are alternative names for a single TORT. The tort consists of maliciously making a false statement about a person or his property, with the result that other people are deceived and consequently act in a way which causes loss to that person. The requirement of malice involves either the absence of an honest belief in the truth of the statement, or the presence of a dishonest or other improper motive.

In personam

In the context of rights relating to property, the Latin phrase *in personam* (pronounced *in per-soh-nam*) is contrasted with *in rem* (pronounced in the obvious way). Rights *in personam* are enforceable only against specified people, even when the rights themselves relate to property. On the other hand, rights *in rem* are enforceable against anyone (or, as it is often put, *against the whole world*), and are part of the legal character of the property itself. Equitable rights, and the remedies to enforce those rights operate only *in personam*, while COMMON LAW rights in relation to property are rights in the property itself, and the remedies to enforce those rights operate against the whole world.

Inquest

Proceedings in a CORONER's court are known as an *inquest*.

Inquisitorial procedure

See ADVERSARIAL PROCEDURE.

In re

The Latin phrase *in re* (pronounced *in ree*) means *in the matter of* and is often found in the names of cases involving children, people who are mentally disordered and insolvency. It is sometimes reduced to simply *Re*. Whichever form is used, it is particularly useful where anonymity is required or desired, thus producing case names such as *In re A*. The anonymised case name may also include a few explanatory words, to produce something like *Re X (A Minor)* or *Re Z (A Child: Consent to Abortion)*.

In rem

See IN PERSONAM.

Insanity

See AUTOMATISM.

Instrument

The word *instrument* is commonly used in a very general sense to mean any document having legal consequences.

Intellectual property

Intellectual property means intangible property, such as copyright (or, in other words, the exclusive right to reproduce, or authorise other people to reproduce, artistic works), and patents (or, in other words, the exclusive right to exploit inventions).

Intention

The concept of *intention* occurs in many areas of law. Briefly, however, and purely by way of example, intention is central to most criminal offences (where it is called MENS REA, which may be pronounced *mens raya*); as well as to CONTRACT (where there must be an *intention to create legal relations*); and to some TORTS.

Interests in land

As there are only four possible ESTATES IN LAND (namely *fee simple*, *fee tail*, LIFE INTEREST and TERM OF YEARS), many other property rights are classified as no more than *interests*. For example, if A has a right of way over B's land, this is a property right, which may exist either at COMMON LAW or in equity (or, in other words it may be either *legal* or *equitable*). In order to be *capable* of being *legal*, an interest must be held on a basis which is equivalent to either a fee simple absolute in possession or to a term of years absolute. In order actually to *be* legal, it must *also* comply with any specified formalities as to its creation (which usually means it must be created by DEED). Anything which is classified as an *interest*, but which (for any reason) is not legal, must be equitable.

Interim relief

The need to prepare cases fully, together with pressure on court time, can result in cases taking substantial periods of time to come to trial, to say nothing of subsequent appeals. In some cases, therefore, a claimant will wish the court to grant her *interim relief* (or, in other words, to give her some protection pending the final outcome of the case). For example, if A is claiming that B is infringing her copyright, the court may grant A an interim INJUNCTION to prevent B from continuing the alleged infringement until the case has been heard.

Before the introduction of the CIVIL PROCEDURE RULES, interim relief was called *interlocutory relief*. In either form, it is an omnibus term for all remedies which are granted on a provisional basis until a case has been finally decided.

Interlocutory relief

See INTERIM RELIEF.

Internal market

See FOUR FREEDOMS.

International Court of Justice

The *International Court of Justice* (ICJ), which sits at The Hague in the Netherlands, is the principal judicial organ of the United Nations. Its jurisdiction extends to any disputes referred to it by the member states of the

United Nations, and to types of dispute specifically allocated to it by international agreements.

International Criminal Court

The *International Criminal Court* (ICC) is the first ever permanent, treaty based, international criminal court established to promote the rule of law and ensure that the gravest international crimes do not go unpunished.

The ICC is additional to, rather than a replacement for, the criminal jurisdictions of national courts. The jurisdiction and functioning of the Court are governed by the provisions of the Rome Statute of the International Criminal Court.

The ICC usually sits at The Hague in the Netherlands, but may sit elsewhere as occasion requires. Its jurisdiction covers genocide, crimes against humanity, war crimes and crimes of aggression.

International law

The phrase *international law* can be applied to two distinct subjects. One, known as *public international law* and subtitled *the law of nations*, treats states as being similar to individuals, with a number of other similarities following from this. For example, TREATIES are similar to CONTRACTS, while acts of international aggression are similar to ASSAULT. The other, known as *private international law* and subtitled *conflict of laws*, deals with situations in which domestic legal systems conflict with each other. For example, which legal system's rules would apply to a contract made in England between an Australian and a Brazilian for the sale of goods which are currently in China but which are to be delivered to Denmark? Or to an inheritance scenario where a British national, who has been living in Japan for many years, dies having made a will while on holiday in Thailand, leaving property in Iceland, India and Ghana and Turkey?

Interpretation

Interpretation consists of identifying the meaning of words, phrases, sentences or entire documents. As such, in the context of law it can be applied to any exercise which involves finding meaning. More particularly, interpretation is involved in reading

- cases (in order to distinguish between what is *ratio decidendi* and what is *obiter dictum* (see BINDING PRECEDENT);

- CONTRACTS (in order to identify the terms of the agreement between the parties); and
- ACTS OF PARLIAMENT, DELEGATED LEGISLATION, EUROPEAN UNION legislation and international agreements (such as the EUROPEAN CONVENTION ON HUMAN RIGHTS).

The principles governing the interpretation of Acts of Parliament and delegated legislation are the same in almost all respects, and have traditionally (if less than totally accurately) been called *statutory interpretation*. However, in view of the frequency with which United Kingdom courts are now required to interpret both EUROPEAN UNION LAW and the EUROPEAN CONVENTION ON HUMAN RIGHTS (and, therefore, to come to terms with the somewhat different traditions of interpretation which characterise the legal tradition of mainland Europe), there is something to be said for re-labelling the topic *as legislative interpretation*.

Interpretation Act 1978

Any legal system which contains legislation dealing with legislative INTERPRETATION must choose between three possible models.

- The first model provides general methodological principles (for example, what use, if any, may be made of the long title, or of headings, when interpreting a legislative instrument).
- The second model provides general principles governing
  - the meaning of common words and phrases (for example, *month*); and
  - common situations (for example, the saving of DELEGATED LEGISLATION when the PRIMARY LEGISLATION under which it was made is repealed).
- The third model combines both the other models.

The United Kingdom's *Interpretation Act 1978* (extracts from which are reproduced in Appendix 2) adopts the second of these models, leaving the COMMON LAW to deal with the kind of material which could have been put into the first model.

Intestacy

Intestacy arises where a person dies leaving property which is not disposed of by WILL. The relevant property then passes to members of the dead person's family, in accordance with rules laid down by STATUTE. In the absence of any relevant family members, the property passes to the CROWN as *BONA VACANTIA*.

Where none of a dead person's property is disposed of by will, the intestacy is said to be *total*, but where (as often happens) some property is disposed of by will but some is not, the intestacy is said to be *partial*.

Intra vires

See *ULTRA VIRES*.

Invitation to treat

See CONTRACT.

Invitee

See OCCUPIERS' LIABILITY.

Issue

1 The meaning of *issue* can be restricted to *children* or can be extended to include more remote *descendants* (such as grandchildren, great-grandchildren, and so on – but not, for example, brothers and sisters, nor nieces and nephews, and their descendants). Whether the restricted or extended meaning is appropriate depends on the intention (either express or implied) of the person who uses the word.
2 *Issue* can mean the *disputed facts in the case* (as in 'the issue between the parties was whether the claimant had consented to being touched by the defendant').
3 To *issue proceedings* means to begin legal proceedings.
4 For *issue estoppel*, see ESTOPPEL.

J

The letter J appearing after a judge's name means *Mr* (or *Mrs*) *Justice* and indicates a judge of the HIGH COURT. So, for example, *Black J* means, and is said as, *Mr* (or *Mrs*) *Justice Black*.

Joint and several liability

Where two or more people are *jointly and severally liable*, the person to whom they are liable may sue them collectively in a single action, or may sue any of them individually for the full amount he is claiming. If they are all sued, the court may apportion liability between them. If one of them is sued alone, he may seek to recover a contribution from the other(s).

Joint tenancy

See CO-OWNERSHIP.

Judge

The word *judge* is generally applied to anyone who presides, either alone or with others, in a court. However, by way of exception, lay MAGISTRATES are not called *judges*, nor are CORONERS.

Judicial comity

Judicial comity means the mutual respect which judges have for each other's opinions. Suppose, for example, that two members of the Court of Appeal are clearly of the opinion that a particular appeal should be allowed. If the third member regards the arguments on each side as being very finely balanced, when deciding whether or not to dissent, he will have to decide whether, in the interests of judicial comity, it would be better to concur with the other members.

Judicial Committee of the Privy Council

See PRIVY COUNCIL.

Judicial decision-making

See ADMINISTRATIVE DECISION-MAKING.

Judicial notice

The court may take *judicial notice* of a fact which is so well known that proof would be superfluous. For example, there is no need to prove that Christmas Day falls on 25 December, or that the period surrounding it is traditionally regarded as a season of goodwill. However, the dates (and perhaps the significances) of Jewish and Muslim holy days would need to be established. Unless there was serious controversy between the members of a particular religion as to such matters, the parties would routinely present such matters to the court on the basis that they were agreed. However, if there were any relevant doctrinal differences, the court would no doubt require sufficient evidence to be given to enable it to make an appropriate finding of fact.

Judicial review

Judicial review is the process by which the High Court supervises the way in which a variety of public authorities and officials exercise their powers. The essence of judicial review is that the court is asking itself whether the relevant powers have been exercised in a lawful manner, rather than whether the decision itself is right. In other words, the court recognises that the doctrine of the SEPARATION OF POWERS requires that the quality of public sector decision-making must be left to political mechanisms of control; but, at the same time, the doctrine of the RULE OF LAW requires that questions of legality must be in the hands of the court.

The grounds for claiming judicial review may be summarised as *illegality, irrationality, procedural impropriety*, breach of EUROPEAN UNION law, and breach of a CONVENTION RIGHT under the HUMAN RIGHTS ACT 1998.

Illegality arises where a decision-maker

- purports to exercise a power which, as a matter of law, he simply does not have (or, in other words, he makes a *jurisdictional error*); or
- fails to have regard to the right considerations.

Irrationality (also known as *Wednesbury unreasonableness*, after the case of *Associated Provincial Picture Houses Ltd v Wednesbury Corporation* [1947] 2 All ER 680), arises where a decision is so unreasonable that no sensible person, having applied his mind to the question, could have made it.

Procedural impropriety arises where a decision-maker acts in breach of

- an express procedural requirement (such as an obligation to consult people who are likely to be affected by the decision in question); or
- the COMMON LAW rules of procedural fairness (also known as *natural justice*), under which decisions which affect rights and legitimate expectations must be made by an impartial decision-maker who has
  - considered whatever case has been made by anyone who is likely to be adversely affected by the decision; and
  - stated the reasons for his decisions.

Breach of *European Union law* and breach of a *Convention right* under the HUMAN RIGHTS ACT 1998 are both explained under those headings.

Judiciary

The judges as a whole are known, collectively, as the *judiciary*.

Jurisdiction

The word *jurisdiction* has two meanings, namely

- the power to hear a case (as, for example, in *the jurisdiction of the magistrates' courts includes many motoring offences*); and
- the geographical area which is subject to the court's power (as, for example, in *the jurisdiction of the Court of Appeal does not extend to Scotland*).

Jurist

Strictly speaking, the word *jurist* means a legal theorist, but it is sometimes applied more loosely to any academic lawyer specialising in any field of law. (*Jurist* is not to be confused with JUROR.)

Juror

A *juror* is a member of a JURY.
(*Juror* is not to be confused with JURIST.)

Jury

Criminal trials in the Crown Court are heard by a judge and a *jury* consisting of 12 JURORS.

On the civil side, where there is a jury in the High Court it too consists of 12 jurors, while a jury in a county court consists of eight jurors. (Jury trials in civil cases are very rare, but there is a qualified right to trial by jury in cases involving allegations of fraud and in actions for DEFAMATION, MALICIOUS PROSECUTION and FALSE IMPRISONMENT.

The right is qualified, rather than being absolute, because the judge may refuse to allow trial by jury in cases which require prolonged examination of documents or accounts, or scientific or local investigation, as a result of which the efficient administration of justice will be prejudiced. On the other hand, the judge in a civil case has a discretion to allow trial by jury even in cases falling outside the qualified right if he thinks the interests of justice require it.

A CORONER'S jury consists of no fewer than 7 and no more than 11 jurors.

Apart from a coroner's jury, a jury must make a serious effort to reach a unanimous verdict, although majority verdicts are permissible, provided that at least 10 jurors agree where there is an 11 or 12 member jury, and at least 9 of them agree where there is a 10 member jury. (The numbers may fall below 12 as a result of illness, death or any other circumstance which the judge regards as being sufficient to justify discharging a juror during a trial. If the number falls below 10, the trial cannot continue, and a retrial will usually take place.) Where there is a jury in a county court, at least seven jurors must agree.

A majority verdict of a coroner's jury is acceptable provided no more than two jurors dissent.

Justice of the Peace

See MAGISTRATE.

J

Justiciability

A matter is *justiciable* if it is suitable for determination by a court of law. For example, and putting the matter negatively, the court may refuse to hear a case involving a dispute between members of a religious community where the essence of the dispute is (or depends upon) a matter of theological doctrine. Similarly, the court may decide that some matters (for example, issues of national security) are best suited to being decided by political processes and according to political criteria.

Just satisfaction

Where the EUROPEAN COURT OF HUMAN RIGHTS finds in favour of an applicant it may order the offending state to pay him compensation. However, it will decline to order compensation where it feels that the favourable judgment, in itself, provides *just satisfaction*.

J

KB (or KBD)

KB was originally the abbreviation for the court of *King's Bench*. However, since the Judicature Act 1873, it (or its variant in the form of *KBD*) has been the abbreviation for the King's Bench Division of the HIGH COURT.

KC

See QUEEN'S COUNSEL.

L L

Laches

While the COMMON LAW bars the bringing of legal actions after a prescribed period (with the length of the period depending on the kind of action – see LIMITATION PERIOD), equity takes a more flexible approach. More particularly, the equitable doctrine of *laches* (a Law French word, which may be pronounced *lay-chiz* or *lay-cheez*) bars the bringing of an action to protect an equitable right or interest, or seeking an equitable remedy (such as an order for SPECIFIC PERFORMANCE or an INJUNCTION), where the claimant has been guilty of delay which, in all the circumstances of the case, makes it inappropriate for equity to come to his assistance.

Land

For the purposes of the Law of Property Act 1925, *land* includes not only land itself, in the ordinary meaning of the word, but also buildings which are on the land and rights (such as EASEMENTS) which exist over land.

Land certificate

Until the Land Registration Act 2002, a *land certificate* was the document issued by the LAND REGISTRY to the registered proprietor (which means, in effect, the owner) of the land to which the title was registered. Land certificates are no longer issued.

Land charge

Certain interests in land are capable of being registered as *land charges* by the Land Registry on the application of the person who benefits from them. Although there are six classes of land charge (lettered from A to F) only C, D and F have sufficient practical importance to be worth mentioning here.

- Class C is divided into four sub-classes.

- C(i) relates to *puisne mortgages* (or, in other words, legal mortgages which are not protected by deposit of title deeds. (The word *puisne* is pronounced as if it were the English word *puny*.)
- C(ii) relates to *limited owners' charges*. For example, where a tenant for life under a strict settlement (see SETTLEMENTS OF LAND) pays for something out of his own resources which ought to be paid for by the trustees, he can register the fact that he has a claim for the money against the trustees (and thus against the land).
- C(iii) relates to *general equitable charges*. The scope of the phrase *general equitable charge* may be summarised as including any equitable charge which is either an equitable mortgage not secured by deposit of title deeds or an equitable charge which does not arise from or affect an interest arising under a TRUST OF LAND or a SETTLEMENT OF LAND, but excluding an equitable charge which is either given by way of certain types of indemnity or exoneration, or within the scope of any other class of land charge.
- C(iv) relates to *estate contracts*. A typical estate contract would be the equitable interest acquired by a buyer on entering into a contract to buy a legal estate in land. An estate contract may also be created by an OPTION TO PURCHASE land.
- Class D is divided into three sub-classes.
  - D(i) relates to taxes payable on death. Where an ESTATE includes land, unpaid tax payable on death is a charge upon the land; and Her Majesty's Revenue and Customs may protect itself by registering a land charge.
  - D(ii) relates to RESTRICTIVE COVENANTS relating to FREEHOLD LAND and created after 1925.
  - D(iii) relates to equitable EASEMENTS.
- Class F relates to the statutory right of a spouse (under the Family Law Act 1996, which replaced earlier legislation of 1967, 1970, 1981 and 1983), independently of any proprietary right, to occupy the matrimonial home.

A land charge which is registrable but not registered *may* be void as against a PURCHASER of the land. Whether it actually *is* void will depend on which class of land charge is involved and the kind of consideration which the purchaser gave. The matter may be summarised as follows.

Class of land charge	Void against
C(i)	Purchaser for value
C(ii)	Purchaser for value
C(iii)	Purchaser for value

C(iv)	Purchaser for money or money's worth
D(i)	Purchaser for money or money's worth
D(ii)	Purchaser for money or money's worth
D(iii)	Purchaser for money or money's worth
F	Purchaser for value

A land charge which is not registered is void against a relevant purchaser even if that purchaser actually knows about it, whether or not he searches the register.

Land registration

See REGISTERED LAND.

Land Registry

The *Land Registry* is the government agency which is responsible for the system of registering title to land.

See also REGISTERED LAND.

Lands Tribunal

See TRIBUNALS.

Larceny

The offence of *larceny* was abolished by the Theft Act 1968 and replaced with the offence of THEFT.

Law Lord

See LORD OF APPEAL IN ORDINARY.

Law officers of the Crown

There are two *law officers of the crown*, namely the *Attorney-General* and the *Solicitor-General*.

The *Attorney-General* (which is sometimes spelt without the hyphen and is accordingly abbreviated to either *A-G* or *AG*), is the principal Law Officer of the Crown in England and Wales. He is responsible for, among other things, the prosecution process, although its day-to-day conduct is in the hands of the Director of Public Prosecutions (DPP) and the CROWN PROSECUTION SERVICE (CPS). He is often said to be the Government's principal legal adviser, although in reality much of the advice which he gives (and for which he accepts responsibility) will originate from civil servants. The Attorney-General, who is a MINISTER OF THE CROWN, may be a member of either the House of Commons or the House of Lords.

Although the job title does not reflect the fact, the Solicitor-General (who is also a Minister of the Crown and who may also be a member of either House) is effectively the Attorney-General's deputy. As with the Attorney-General, the hyphen in *Solicitor-General* is sometimes omitted, and the abbreviations are, therefore, either *S-G* or *SG*.

The corresponding officers for Scotland are known as the *Lord Advocate* and the *Solicitor-General for Scotland*.

Law reports

Although an effective system of reporting the decisions of the courts is essential for the proper functioning of the doctrine of binding precedent, there is, strictly speaking, no 'official' series of *law reports*. However, in practice, the reports published by the Incorporated Council of Law Reporting for England and Wales, a non-profit-making body established and run by the legal profession, are sometimes referred to as the 'official' reports.

The Incorporated Council publishes the following series of reports: *Appeal Cases* (AC), *Chancery Division* (Ch), *Family Division* (Fam), and *Queen's Bench Division* (QBD), which are, collectively, often called *the Law Reports* (with upper-case *L* and *R*), as well as the *Weekly Law Reports* (WLR), *Industrial Cases Reports* (ICR), *Business Law Reports* (Bus LR) and *Public and Third Sector Law Reports* (PTSR). The scope of *Business Law Reports* is self-evident, while *Public and Third Sector Law Reports* cover cases involving public sector bodies, charities and voluntary organisations.

Appeal Cases cover the decisions of the HOUSE OF LORDS, the JUDICIAL COMMITTEE OF THE PRIVY COUNCIL, and the SUPREME COURT (and, occasionally, the decisions which gave rise to the appeals). The reports named after the three divisions of the HIGH COURT cover both cases heard in those divisions and appeals arising from them which go to the COURT OF APPEAL. (Criminal appeals from the High Court go straight to the House of Lords and are, therefore, reported in *Appeal Cases*. Anomalously, cases in the Criminal Division of the Court of Appeal appear in the Queen's Bench reports.)

The *Weekly Law Reports* are, as their title indicates, published weekly, but are then bound into three volumes for each year. Those cases which the editor considers to be least important appear in volume 1, while the

L

rest appear in volumes 2 and 3 (with the division between the two depending on the order in which they are reported). In due course, the cases from volumes 2 and 3 appear again in the *Appeal Cases*, *Chancery*, *Family* and *Queen's Bench* series. These versions include outlines of the advocates' arguments.

Industrial Cases Reports contain only cases concerning Employment Law.

In addition to the Incorporated Council's reports, there are many commercially published series of law reports, the most prominent of which is the *All England Law Reports* (All ER), which is a general series published in weekly parts, before being bound as four volumes for each year. (Unlike the *Weekly Law Reports*, no significance attaches to the placing of a case in any particular volume.)

By way of contrast with the *All England Reports*, other commercially published series specialise in particular subject areas and bear corresponding titles, such as *Building Law Reports* (BLR), Family Law Reports (FLR), *Housing Law Reports* (HLR) and *Road Traffic Reports* (RTR).

All the series of law reports noted above reproduce the full transcripts of the courts' judgments, together with at least a *headnote* summarising the case (and perhaps additional apparatus such as cross-references to relevant texts and lists of cases and statutes cited). However, some series, known as *short reports*, consist only of summaries of cases (although some series also include academic commentaries, placing the cases in their contexts and assessing their significance). Most short reports appear in law journals (such as the *Criminal Law Review*), but some are freestanding publications (such as the *Administrative Court Digest*) and the *WLR Daily* section of Incorporated Council's website (http://www.lawreports.co.uk/), which provides brief summaries of the most important cases, on a day-by-day basis and free of charge. Short reports are never as authoritative as their full-transcript counterparts.

No series of law reports is comprehensive: they all contain only those cases which their editors consider to be worth reporting, having regard to their perceptions of the needs of their subscribers.

Appendix 1 lists the citations of most of the law reports which most students will encounter.

Finally, in addition to law reports which have undergone the process of selection and editing including the writing of headnotes, many raw judgments themselves are available online, free of charge. The speeches in House of Lords' cases were generally available online within two hours of being delivered, and the Supreme Court follows the same practice in respect of its own judgments.

A much wider range of raw judgments is available at http://www.bailii.org/.

Lay magistrates

See MAGISTRATES.

LC

LC after a judge's name means *Lord Chancellor.*

Until the Constitutional Reform Act 2005, the Lord Chancellor was Head of the Judiciary and also a MINISTER OF THE CROWN. Since the 2005 Act, he has no longer been Head of the JUDICIARY and, as a matter of practice, he had ceased to sit as a judge more than a decade previously. In fact, the 2005 Act does not even require the Lord Chancellor to be a lawyer.

There has not yet been a Lady Chancellor.

Leapfrog

The fact that, according to the doctrine of BINDING PRECEDENT, the COURT OF APPEAL is generally bound by its own decisions and by those of the HOUSE OF LORDS and the SUPREME COURT, can give rise to inefficiency. More particularly,

- where the HIGH COURT follows a decision of the Court of Appeal because it is bound to do so; and
- the circumstances of the case are such that, if the ordinary avenue of appeal is followed, the Court of Appeal will also treat itself as being bound by either that decision or a relevant decision of the House of Lords or the Supreme Court; but
- there is a general consensus that the point of law involved is one which really ought to be considered by the Supreme Court; it follows that the delay and expense involved in appealing to the Court of Appeal are likely to be simply a wasteful stepping-stone on the way to the final result in the Supreme Court.

The solution lies in the procedure, commonly known as the *leapfrog*, which enables certain appeals from the High Court to go directly to the Supreme Court, thus bypassing the Court of Appeal altogether.

A leapfrog appeal will be available only where the trial judge certifies that

- a point of law of general public importance is involved,

and either

L

- it arises out of a point of statutory interpretation which was dealt with fully at the trial, or
- the point is one on which the trial judge was bound by a decision of the Court of Appeal, the House of Lords or the Supreme Court, and
- the point was dealt with fully in the report of the decision in the Court of Appeal, the House of Lords or the Supreme Court.

The certificate of the trial judge is only a preliminary stage: it is still necessary for either the trial judge or the Supreme Court to decide whether to give permission to appeal.

Since criminal (see CRIME) appeals from the High Court go straight to the Supreme Court anyway, the leapfrog procedure is clearly irrelevant in that context.

Lease

A *lease* is an estate in land which will expire on a fixed date, although it may be (and often is) renewable, thus extending its duration to another fixed date (frequently with the possibility of further renewals).

The person who grants a lease is known variously as the *grantor*, the *lessor* and the *landlord* (or, in accordance with contemporary expectations of gender neutral expression, *landlady*), while the person to whom it is granted is known variously (but correspondingly) as the *grantee*, the *lessee* or the *tenant*. When a lease expires, the property goes back (or *reverts*) to the person who granted it (or to his successor-in-title). The interest which reverts to the grantor is called the *reversion* or the *reversionary interest*.

One problem with the definition of a lease as a *term of years absolute* is that it excludes some interests which the policy of the Law of Property Act 1925 requires to be leases (the policy being that leases are one of the only two possible legal estates – see ESTATES IN LAND). Accordingly, the Act makes special provision for certain forms of words to be interpreted as creating terms of years absolute, even though they expressly do something else. More particularly, provided in each case that the grant is made in return for a RENT or a FINE or both

- the following forms of words each create a 90 year lease:
  - to T 'for life',
  - to T 'for [say] 10 years or his death if this occurs earlier',
  - to T 'for [say] 70 years, provided he remains unmarried'; and
- a perpetually renewable lease creates a lease for 2000 years.

Two points arise. First, in relation to the first three cases, once the relevant death or marriage has occurred, the landlord can give one month's notice to terminate the lease. Secondly, perpetually renewable leases are easily created by accident, as happens where a lease gives the tenant the right to renew the lease on the expiry of the original one, with the renewal to be on the same terms as the original one – which means, of course, that the renewed lease may be further renewed on the same terms, and so on and on indefinitely.

Where the length of the original term is intrinsically uncertain, the court may be willing to interpret the wording as creating a periodic tenancy. For example, in a case where a local authority granted a lease until such time as the land was needed for road widening, the court held that this created a tenancy from year to year which could, therefore, be terminated by giving six months' notice (which, curiously, is the usual period of notice for yearly tenancies).

It may be thought that the human life span being what it is, a lease for more than a hundred years or so is as good as a fee simple (see ESTATES IN LAND). However, this would be a significant overstatement for various reasons, including the following:

- rent will usually be payable under a lease;
- a lease will often contain covenants:
  - restricting the use to which the tenant can put the property, with the consequences of a breach being that the lease may be forfeited (or, in other words, the landlord may reclaim the property); and
  - restricting the right of the lessee to assign his lease to anyone else or to create sub-leases to other people; and
- if the lessor sells his reversion to someone else, the lessee will then be in a legal relationship with the new owner, who may be someone with whom he would not choose to be in such a relationship.

Leasehold

See LEASE.

Leasehold covenants

Leasehold covenants are terms in leases which set out the obligations under the lease of both the landlord and the tenant. Some covenants are express, that is they are contained in the lease, and some are implied by law, for example the covenant of quiet enjoyment in a residential lease.

L

These covenants are binding on the landlord and tenant and their successors in title, whether they are positive or negative – see RESTRICTIVE COVENANTS RELATING TO FREEHOLD LAND for a comparison. This is because the original landlord and tenant are bound by PRIVITY OF CONTRACT and successors in title to both are bound by privity of estate, that is the tenant's lease is part of the landlord's fee simple. As a result the holder of the fee simple can enforce against the current tenant, and *vice versa*, without having to go through the chain of vendors and assignors.

For new leases granted after 1 January 1996, a tenant who assigns the lease is not liable on any covenants after the date of assignment and a landlord is not liable on any covenants after the date on which he sells to a purchaser, provided the tenant has agreed.

The breach of a covenant by the tenant does not automatically entitle the landlord to avoid the lease but in most leases there is a provision allowing the landlord to forfeit and re-enter for any breach of covenant. This is a drastic remedy, so a landlord must issue the appropriate notice and the tenant may then apply for relief from forfeiture.

If anyone is residing on the premises, a landlord cannot forfeit a residential lease otherwise than by action in the courts.

Legacy
See BEQUEST.

Legal estate
See ESTATES IN LAND.

Legal interest
See INTERESTS IN LAND.

Legal owner
See BENEFICIAL OWNER.

Legal personality

Offices and bodies which the law recognises as having *legal personality* have their own existence as well as having members who are natural persons. For example, the *office* of LORD CHIEF JUSTICE is said to have certain powers and duties as head of the JUDICIARY but, in reality, it is the *holder* of that office who exercises those functions. As there can be only one Lord Chief Justice at any given time, the office is said to be a *corporation sole*.

On the other hand, a local authority (for example), which also has legal personality, has many members (in the form of *councillors*) at any given time, and so is said to be a *corporation aggregate*. Similarly, almost all companies have members in the form of shareholders.

There are two essential points about legal personality. First, the existence of a legal person continues despite, and is unbroken by, changes in membership. Secondly, a legal person (other than a company) acts unlawfully if it acts beyond the powers which the law gives it.

See also CORPORATION; LIMITED LIABILITY and *ULTRA VIRES*.

Legislation

See ACT OF PARLIAMENT, DELEGATED LEGISLATION and PRIMARY LEGISLATION.

Legislative interpretation

See INTERPRETATION.

Legislative Supremacy of Parliament

The doctrine of the *legislative supremacy of Parliament* (which is sometimes called the *sovereignty of Parliament*), states that

- Parliament can pass any legislation it wishes to pass; and
- only Parliament can repeal legislation which Parliament has passed.

Three matters require further comment.

First, *Parliament* is *not* the same thing as the *House of Commons*. For something to be an *Act of Parliament*, it must normally have been passed by both the House of Commons and the House of Lords and must always have received the Royal Assent. The only exception to the need for approval by both Houses of Parliament arises where the procedure under the PARLIAMENT ACTS 1911 and 1949 is invoked. Under this procedure, the House of Lords may delay legislation for one year, but cannot veto it. The only exceptions to this exception are

- Bills which the Speaker of the House of Commons certifies as being *Money Bills* (which are exempt even from the one year delaying power); and
- Bills to prolong the life of Parliament, which are exempt from the provisions of the Parliament Acts altogether (and are, therefore, still subject to the House of Lords' power of absolute veto).

L

(For many years there was an academic debate about the status of legislation passed under the Parliament Acts procedure, but it is now clear that such statutes enjoy equal status with statutes passed in the normal way.)

Although the tri-partite analysis of the nature of Parliament is accurate as a matter of law, at a purely practical level it is important to bear in mind two relevant CONSTITUTIONAL CONVENTIONS, namely that *the House of Lords usually defers to the House of Commons*, and that *the monarch does not withhold the Royal Assent*. The combined effect of these conventions is that, in purely practical terms, the political party that dominates the House of Commons will also very largely dominate the whole of the legislative process, unless the party leadership loses the loyalty of its MPs.

Secondly, although it is often said that Parliament cannot legislate contrary to EUROPEAN UNION law, this is not strictly true. As a matter of law, the position is that nobody can prevent Parliament from legislating in any way it chooses; but if it does choose to legislate contrary to Community law, the United Kingdom courts will refuse to apply the statute and apply the Community law instead. (When the courts refuse to apply a statute, they are said to *disapply* it.)

Finally, it is usually said that one consequence of the absolute version of the legislative supremacy of Parliament outlined above is that one Parliament cannot bind its successors (because if it could do so, the successors would no longer be legislatively supreme). Nevertheless, some people argue that the inability of one Parliament to bind its successors is limited to an inability to restrict the *substance* of future legislation, and does not extend to restrictions which are limited to the *manner and form* in which future legislation is passed. For a typical manner and form restriction, see, for example, s. 19 of the HUMAN RIGHTS ACT 1998, which requires Ministers who are in charge of Bills in either House to state that, in their view, either

- the Bill is compatible with Convention rights under the 1998 Act, or
- they wish the Bill to proceed in the absence of such a statement.

There is no English judicial authority to support the view that the courts will recognise *manner and form restrictions* as binding on later Parliaments, so the courts will be likely to apply a later statute even if it has been passed in breach of a *manner and form* requirement. (There is, however, colonial authority that such requirements may be binding, but these authorities deal with non-sovereign legislatures and are, therefore, not directly relevant in the present context.)

Where a later Parliament wishes to repeal an earlier statute it may do so expressly (by enacting a provision to the effect that 'the Whatever Act of Such and Such a Date is hereby repealed') or impliedly by enacting a provision which is incompatible with something (or even everything) contained in an earlier statute. (For obvious reasons, these possibilities are known, respectively, as *express repeal* and *implied repeal*.)

Legislature

Strictly speaking, the word *legislature* simply means a law-making body. As such, it could apply to makers of DELEGATED LEGISLATION, but in the English legal system it is almost always used to mean PARLIAMENT (and this meaning should, therefore, be assumed unless there are clear reasons for assuming that some other meaning is intended).

Letters of administration

See ADMINISTRATOR.

Letters of administration with the will annexed

See ADMINISTRATOR.

Letters patent

Letters patent are documents issued by the Queen (or King, as the case may be) and authenticated by the GREAT SEAL (which is kept in the custody of the Lord Chancellor and is used to authenticate various documents of state). The word *patent* indicates that the documents are open and can therefore be read by anyone.

Libel

See DEFAMATION.

L

Liberty and freedom from arbitrary detention

The right to *liberty and freedom from arbitrary detention* is protected by the COMMON LAW (through the rejection of the idea of a GENERAL WARRANT and the remedy of *HABEAS CORPUS*) and by art. 5 of the EUROPEAN CONVENTION ON HUMAN RIGHTS (which is a CONVENTION RIGHT under the HUMAN RIGHTS ACT 1998).

For the full text of art. 5, see Appendix 3.

Licence

1 A *licence* is a document entitling the holder to engage in some activity which is regulated by law where statute lays down that the regulation shall be undertaken by a scheme of licensing. A driving licence is perhaps the most common example. Some activities which are regulated by law take place under statutory schemes which use other terminology. For example, PLANNING PERMISSION is, broadly speaking, required in order to undertake development in, on, over or under land. Clearly, the legislative drafter could, with equal accuracy, have used the word *licence* rather than *permission*.

2 The concept of a *licence* in relation to land must be distinguished from the concept of a LEASE. Essentially, the difference is that a lease is a property interest in the land itself, while a licence is an arrangement between the occupier of the land (the *licensor*) and somebody else (the *licensee*). However, drawing the line between the application of the two concepts can be difficult in practice. Generally speaking, the main test is whether the person whose status is in question can be said to have *exclusive possession* of the relevant premises. The presence of exclusive possession usually indicates a tenancy, while its absence usually indicates a licence. (For example, a lodger does not have exclusive possession, and is therefore a licensee rather than a tenant.) However, there is a significant exception in the case of people who are required to live on certain premises in order to do their jobs. (For example, a caretaker whose contract of employment requires him to occupy a flat within the building for which he is responsible will have only a licence, even though he will have exclusive possession of the flat.)

In some circumstances there is a hybrid (and unnamed) concept, namely an arrangement which functions as a lease as between the parties (so that, for example, there is an implied covenant that the grantor will keep the premises in repair) but is a licence when viewed from the outside (so that, for example, the 'licensee' cannot assign his 'licence' to a third party).

Lien

See BAILMENT.

Life interest

A person who holds a *life interest* in property may do so either for the duration of his own life or for the duration of the life of someone else. The latter is called an *estate PUR AUTRE VIE*.

Limitation period

For various reasons, including the availability and reliability of evidence, injustice is likely to be caused if legal actions are brought a long time after the occurrence of the events to which they relate. For this reason, any legal system is likely to have rules governing *limitation periods* – or, in other words, specifying periods of time after which actions cannot be brought.

The principal limitation period in the English legal system is six years, which applies to claims in

- TORT (except for claims in DEFAMATION where the period is one year and claims for personal injuries where the period is three years); and
- CONTRACT (except where the contract was made by DEED, in which case the limitation period is twelve years.

There are also various other limitation periods in specialised situations, such as a normal maximum of three months in respect of claims for JUDICIAL REVIEW.

Limited company

When a company is formed, its initial investors put up the capital that the company needs to be able to start trading. In return for this investment, they receive shares in the company. They may, at the outset, put in all the money that they are willing to invest; or they may put in only part of that money, while accepting an obligation to put in the rest when called upon to do so. If they put in all the money at the outset, their shares will immediately be *fully paid up*. If they put in only some of the money at the outset, their shares will, initially, be only *partly paid up*, and will not become fully paid up unless and until the company calls for balance of the money to be paid and it is actually paid.

Provided the company is formed with *limited liability* (or, in other words, it is a *limited company*) the most that the original investors can lose will be the amount of their investment (including the balance which is still outstanding in respect of any partly paid up shares). In other words, where there is a limited company, it is each shareholder's personal liability (rather than the company's liability) which is limited.

In reality, of course, over a period of time, the shares will usually change hands. When this happens, their new owners may well pay substantially more than the amount of money which the original shareholders invested, because they will be effectively buying a share of the company's assets and likely profits at the time when they buy the shares.

L

If the company becomes insolvent, these shareholders will stand to lose the whole of their investment (in the sense of the amount of money which they have paid for the shares), but this bears no practical relationship to the original shareholders' investment.

An alternative form of limited company exists where a company is *limited by guarantee*. Such companies do not issue shares and, therefore, do not have shareholders. Instead, they have *guarantors* who *guarantee* the liabilities of the company up to a stated limit.

Limited liability

See LIMITED COMPANY and PARTNERSHIP.

Limited liability partnership

See PARTNERSHIP.

Liquidated damages

The policy of the COMMON LAW is to encourage people to settle their own differences without going to court. It is not surprising, therefore, that the courts see nothing wrong in principle with the parties to a contract agreeing what their liabilities shall be to each other in the event that either of them shall be in breach of their contractual obligations.

However, since the purpose of the CIVIL LAW (which includes the law of CONTRACT) is concerned with compensating and protecting victims, rather than punishing wrongdoers, the courts require such terms to be genuine pre-estimates of the losses which will flow from breaches which are envisaged. The sums specified in these clauses are known as *liquidated damages*. The problem that arises in practice is that it can be difficult to distinguish between a liquidated damages clause and another type of clause known as a *penalty clause*. The practical essence of the distinction is that *liquidated damages* are intended to *compensate* victims, while *penalty clauses* are intended to *punish* those who are in breach. The key consequence of the distinction is that liquidated damages are lawful but penalties are unlawful.

The courts decide for themselves, in all the circumstances of each case, which category a particular clause falls into, but two things are clear:

- the way the clause is labelled in the contract will not be decisive;
- the payment will be presumed to be a penalty (and therefore unlawful) where a single sum is specified as being payable in respect of any one of a number of events, some of which would cause only trivial

loss to the other party, while others would cause serious loss (because in this kind of situation, it is difficult to see how the sum can be a *genuine pre-estimate* of the loss).

LJ

The letters LJ appearing after a judge's name mean *Lord* (or *Lady*) *Justice* and indicate a judge of the COURT OF APPEAL. So, for example, *Black LJ* means *Lord* (or *Lady*) *Justice Black*, and is said accordingly.

The technical title of a judge designated in this way is a *Lord* (or *Lady*) *Justice of Appeal*.

See also COURT OF APPEAL.

Local authority

Different statutes contain different definitions of *local authority*, depending on the scope of the statutes in question. However, the modern local authorities which are most frequently encountered in case-law are *county* and *district* (or *borough* or *city*) councils. Older cases may involve *urban district*, *rural district* and *county borough* councils.

Local government

The phrase *local government* is used to refer to LOCAL AUTHORITIES generally, and is often contrasted with CENTRAL GOVERNMENT (where the latter means the GOVERNMENT and the CIVIL SERVICE departments.

Local land charge

Local land charges relate to a variety of environmental, highways and planning matters. They are registered in local land charges registers, which are maintained by district councils (see LOCAL AUTHORITIES) and are open to public inspection. Potential purchasers can, therefore, discover whether land which they are proposing to buy is subject to matters such as highway improvement schemes or tree preservation orders.

Locus standi

See STANDING.

Lord Advocate

See LAW OFFICERS OF THE CROWN.

Lord of Appeal in Ordinary

Lord of Appeal in Ordinary was the formal description of a member of the Appellate Committee of the HOUSE OF LORDS, and was (and, of course, still will be while House of Lords' cases continue to be cited) referred to as, for example, Lord Grey. The phrase *Lady of Appeal in Ordinary* was never adopted in relation to Baroness Hale (the only female ever to be appointed as a *Lord of Appeal in Ordinary*). The phrase *Law Lord* was (and will no doubt continue to be) widely used as a convenient shorthand version of *Lord of Appeal in Ordinary*.

With the creation of the SUPREME COURT in October 2009, the office of Lord of Appeal in Ordinary became redundant and the existing holders of that office became *Justices of the Supreme Court*. Although they retained their peerages, they are referred to as, for example, *Justice Grey*.

Lord Chief Justice

The *Lord Chief Justice* is President of the Courts of England and Wales (or, in other words, Head of the JUDICIARY) and is also the President of the Criminal Division of the COURT OF APPEAL. He is referred to in writing as, for example, *Lord* (or *Lady*) *Green CJ* (or, at the expense of a slight tautology, as *Lord* (or *Lady*) *Green LCJ*.)

There has not yet been a Lady Chief Justice.

Lord (or Lady) Justice of Appeal

A *Lord* (or *Lady*) *Justice of Appeal* is a judge of the Court of Appeal, and is referred to in writing as, for example, *White LJ*.

Loss of amenity

Loss of amenity is one of the heads of damages in personal injury cases. It is additional to damages for pain and suffering and loss of expectation of life, and refers to loss of the ability to enjoy life to the full. For example, a claimant who previously derived enjoyment from participating in sporting activities, but whose injuries prevent him from continuing to do so, will receive a sum, under the heading of loss of amenity, by way of compensation for this loss.

L

Magistrates

Until the 14th century, the monarch appointed *Keepers of the Peace*, or *magistrates*, from among local gentry. These appointments were made on an individual basis, and those who were appointed were what would now be called *magistrates*. The Statute of Westminster 1327 systematised the method of appointment; and, by the end of that century, the term *Justice of the Peace* had become standard usage to describe the *Keepers of the Peace*.

In modern terms, the principal significance of the magistracy is that *lay magistrates* are, by definition, not legally qualified. Nevertheless, they sit in MAGISTRATES' COURTS where they deal with a very large number of cases, which they hear with the assistance of legally qualified advisers.

Magistrates' court

The JURISDICTION of the *magistrates' courts* includes both CIVIL LAW and criminal law (see CRIME) elements. It is almost entirely exercisable only at FIRST INSTANCE, but some very limited elements of *civil* jurisdiction involve hearing APPEALS.

The magistrates' *civil jurisdiction at first instance* does not include either CONTRACT or TORT, but does include a very miscellaneous collection of aspects of ADMINISTRATIVE LAW. These relate especially (but by no means exclusively) to the topics of highways and public health, and are largely left over from the time when the magistrates exercised many of the functions that are now exercised by elected LOCAL AUTHORITIES.

The *appellate jurisdiction* of the magistrates is almost entirely limited to appeals against certain decisions made by local authorities which arise out of those aspects of matters such as public health, highways and licensing in respect of which the magistrates no longer exercise jurisdiction at first instance.

When sitting as *family proceedings* courts, only magistrates who are members of a family panel will sit. They deal with a wide range of matters including applications for care orders, adoption proceedings, and certain orders requiring the financial maintenance of spouses and children, but not including divorce.

The magistrates' *criminal jurisdiction* includes both trials (including guilty pleas) and sending people to the Crown Court for trial. In cases where they have convicted people who, in their view, require heavier sentences than they can impose, the jurisdiction of the magistrates also includes committal to the Crown Court for sentence. When sitting as YOUTH COURTS, the magistrates' criminal jurisdiction involves cases brought against young people under the age of 18.

Although the vast majority of magistrates are lay and sit in court on a strictly part-time basis, some are both legally qualified and employed on a full-time, salaried basis. The latter were known for many years as *stipendiary magistrates*, but are now known as *District Judges (Magistrates' Courts)*. In practice, lay magistrates tend to rely heavily on their legal advisers for guidance on the law, although technically the magistrates themselves decide both the law and the facts. Lay magistrates are unpaid.

Magna Carta

The Latin phrase *Magna Carta* (pronounced in the obvious way) is translated as *the Great Charter*. This charter, granted by King John in 1215 (at Runnymede, beside the Thames), provided some protection against abuse of the ROYAL PREROGATIVE. Its modern significance is symbolic rather than practical and is memorably best summed up in the following passage from Rudyard Kipling's verse *What Say the Reeds at Runnymede?*

> And still, when mob or monarch lays
> Too rude a hand on English ways,
> The whisper wakes, the shudder plays,
> Across the reeds at Runnymede.

Majority verdict

See JURY.

M

Malfeasance

The old words *malfeasance*, *misfeasance* and *non-feasance* are seldom encountered, but they are not wholly obsolete. *Malfeasance* consists of doing something which is unlawful. *Misfeasance* consists of doing something in an improper way, when it would otherwise have been lawful. *Nonfeasance* consists of failing to do something which there is a legal duty to do.

See also MISFEASANCE IN PUBLIC OFFICE.

Malice aforethought

See MURDER.

Malicious falsehood

See INJURIOUS FALSEHOOD.

Malicious prosecution

The TORT of *malicious prosecution* is committed by someone who starts (or continues) legal proceedings, without a genuine belief, based on reasonable grounds, that the proceedings are justified. The proceedings must be unsuccessful. The requirement of *malice* means that the proceedings must have been started from an improper or otherwise wrongful motive. Although the name of the tort suggests that the proceedings in question must arise from CRIMINAL LAW, this is not an absolute requirement since it is clear that maliciously instituted insolvency proceedings will also fall within its scope.

Mandamus

See MANDATORY ORDER.

Mandatory order

A *mandatory order* is available by way of JUDICIAL REVIEW in order to compel the performance of a duty in PUBLIC LAW. Before the introduction of the CIVIL PROCEDURE RULES, a mandatory order was known by the Latin name of *mandamus* (which is pronounced as either *man-dah-mus* or *man-day-mus*, and literally means, *we order*).

Manslaughter

The criminal offence of *manslaughter* can be divided into *voluntary* manslaughter and *involuntary* manslaughter, although neither of the words *voluntary* and *involuntary* has its ordinary meaning.

Voluntary manslaughter arises where the ACTUS REUS and the MENS REA of MURDER are present, but one of three possible additional elements is also present. The additional elements are PROVOCATION, DIMINISHED RESPONSIBILITY and the killing of one party to a suicide pact by another party who does not, in the event, commit suicide. The presence of any one of these additional elements will reduce to manslaughter what would otherwise be murder.

M

Involuntary manslaughter can be divided into two sub-categories, namely *constructive manslaughter* (which is also known as *unlawful act manslaughter*) and *manslaughter by gross negligence*. (There is an academic debate as to whether there is a third category, namely reckless manslaughter, which would be committed by a defendant who causes death while being aware that there is a substantial risk that death may occur. However, there is no clear authority on the point; and the circumstances which would give rise to this version of the offence can be properly charged as *constructive* manslaughter anyway.)

Constructive manslaughter arises where death results from an act which was both unlawful and dangerous.

Manslaughter *by gross negligence* arises where (a) the defendant owes a duty of care to the victim; (b) the defendant breaches that duty; (c) the defendant's breach of duty causes the victim's death; and (d) the breach of the duty is so gross that it merits being stigmatised as *criminal*.

Mareva injunction

The CIVIL PROCEDURE RULES renamed *Mareva injunctions* as FREEZING INJUNCTIONS.

Margin of appreciation

In the context of the EUROPEAN CONVENTION ON HUMAN RIGHTS, the concept of the *margin of appreciation* provides a bracket within which a range of possible responses will all be legitimate. In other words, it seeks to give the national authorities as much discretion as is consistent with achieving an appropriate level of protection for the rights which the Convention protects.

Marriage

Marriage is traditionally defined as the voluntary union of one man and one woman, for life, to the exclusion of all others. However, a valid marriage may be terminated by divorce and a voidable (see VOID) marriage may be terminated by a decree of nullity. Although a registered CIVIL PARTNERSHIP is popularly referred to as a *gay marriage*, the legal requirement that the parties to a marriage shall be of opposite genders remains. Therefore, at least as far as English law is concerned, *gay marriage* is a contradiction in terms. However, the holder of a GENDER RECOGNITION CERTIFICATE is, as a matter of law, a member of the acquired gender, and can, therefore, marry a member of his or her original gender.

Master of the Rolls

The old title of *Master of the Rolls* is now held alongside the new one of *President of the Civil Division of the* COURT OF APPEAL. The abbreviation MR appears after his name (there has not yet been a female Master of the Rolls): for example, Lord Black MR.

The title originated when the records of the Court of Chancery (which was the precursor of the Chancery Division of the HIGH COURT) were kept on rolls of parchment or vellum, and the Master of the Rolls was their official custodian.

Master and servant

The old-fashioned expression *master and servant* is still used to describe what would more commonly be thought of in terms of *employer and employee*.

There may be several reasons why it is important to know whether a relationship of master and servant exists, but the two most common ones are the applicability (or otherwise) of employment legislation (and, especially, employment protection legislation), and the relevance (or otherwise) of the doctrine of VICARIOUS LIABILITY.

Maxims of equity

The JURISDICTION of equity emerged in an attempt to avoid the strict rules of the COMMON LAW working injustice in individual cases. As might be expected of a jurisdiction which came into being on this basis, equitable relief began by being discretionary. However, although the desire to avoid unfairness arising from the strict application of rules may be admirable in itself, it can very easily lead to inconsistent decisions being made in different cases arising from substantially similar facts. Since this simply substitutes one kind of unfairness for another, it is not surprising that principles of equity were developed, as an aid to consistency. These principles came to be formulated in pithy statements known as the *maxims of equity*. The most commonly encountered maxim may be stated (and very briefly explained) as follows.

Equity will not suffer a wrong to be without a remedy. This is the very essence of the equitable jurisdiction: see COMMON LAW.

Equity follows the law. For example, equity adopted the common law system of estates in land.

Where there is equal equity, the law shall prevail (a specific version of which appears in the form *where the equities are equal, the first in time shall*

M

prevail). This simply means that where two or more people have competing equitable interests, if all other things are equal, the interest which came into existence first will take priority over the other(s).

He who seeks equity must do equity. Someone seeking equitable relief may be denied a remedy if she is not prepared to act in a way which is equitable in the popular sense of the word.

He who comes to equity must come with clean hands. This maxim embodies the idea of reciprocity of equity which also underlies the previous maxim, but where the previous maxim looks to the future, this maxim looks to the past.

Delay defeats equity (which is sometimes given as *equity aids the vigilant but not the tardy*). In either form, this maxim may be illustrated by the equitable doctrine of LACHES.

Equality is equity. Where equity is called upon to divide interests between two or more people, it will divide them on an equal basis, unless there is some other clear and quantifiable basis for division.

Equity looks to the intention rather than to the form. For example, where A is selling her legal estate in land to B, as soon as an enforceable contract comes into being B will be the owner in the eyes of equity, even though the formalities for the transfer of title have not yet been completed.

Equity looks on that as done which ought to be done. This maxim may be illustrated with the same example as the previous one.

Equity imputes an intention to fulfil an obligation. Although this maxim is obviously very closely related to the previous two, a different example may be useful. If A agrees to pay a sum of money to the trustees of a family trust so that they can buy land in a particular county which will become subject to the trust, and then she herself buys land to that value in that county but gives no money to the trustees, equity will presume that she has merely bypassed the trustees and will, therefore, consider the land to be held under the family trusts.

Equity acts IN PERSONAM. For example, in the case of unregistered land (see TITLE TO LAND), a legal interest is good against the whole world (except anyone having a superior *legal* title), but an equitable interest may be defeated by a *bona fide* PURCHASER for value without notice. (Such a purchaser is sometimes known as EQUITY'S DARLING.)

Equity, like nature, does nothing in vain. For example, an equitable remedy will not be granted if its effect would be to compel someone to do something which is impossible.

Mediation

Mediation is a form of ALTERNATIVE DISPUTE RESOLUTION in which a mediator explores each party's side to a dispute with a view to clarifying the true point (or points) of deadlock between them, before seeking to find a way of resolving the dispute. The mediator has no powers of compulsion: her role is simply to assist the parties to resolve their dispute.

Memorandum of association

See ARTICLES OF ASSOCIATION.

Mens rea

A defendant can be convicted of a criminal offence (see CRIME) at COMMON LAW if, and only if, she commits the relevant *ACTUS REUS* (which may be pronounced *act-us ray-us* and which means *guilty act*) while also having the appropriate *mens rea* (which may be pronounced *mens ray-a* and which means *guilty mind*).

Whether *mens rea* is an essential element of an offence created by statute (see ACT OF PARLIAMENT) depends on the statutory wording in each case. In addition to the obvious *intentionally*, words such as *knowingly* and *wilfully* indicate the necessity for *mens rea*. On the other hand, where the statutory wording is not explicit, the court will consider whether it is appropriate to apply the PRESUMPTION OF STATUTORY INTERPRETATION, according to which Parliament is presumed to have intended *mens rea* to be an essential element of all statutory offences, unless there are good grounds for coming to the contrary conclusion in any particular case.

There are three states of mind which can constitute *mens rea*, namely, *intention*, *recklessness* and *negligence*.

Intention must be distinguished from *motive*. If A kills her husband, intending to do so in order that she can marry her lover, the intentional killing provides both the *actus reus* and the *mens rea* of MURDER, while the overall objective of marrying her lover will be merely the motive. (Motive may be relevant to sentencing – either to increase or reduce the seriousness of the offence – but it cannot be relevant to the fundamental question of innocence or guilt.)

In the example given in the previous paragraph, the intention to kill the husband (the *mens rea*) and the act of killing him (the *actus reus*) are clearly linked to each other as part of a single enterprise. However, there are situations in which, as a matter of fact, this is not so, but the policy of the law nevertheless requires a conviction. For example, if A shoots at B

M

with the intention of killing her, but the shot misses B and kills C, the court will treat A's intention in respect of B as if it were directed towards C. This *transfer* of A's intention from B to C means that there is still an *actus reus* and a *mens rea* which can be treated as part of a single enterprise, so A can properly be convicted of murdering C. (This example illustrates the doctrine known as *transferred malice.*)

Another problem arises in some cases where the defendant causes two kinds of harm but claims that she intended only one kind. For example, A pushes B off the top of a high building, intending to kill her, and does in fact do so. However, before hitting the ground, B falls through the glass roof of a ground floor extension to the building. A is plainly guilty of murdering B but the question is whether she is also guilty of causing criminal damage to the roof. The answer to this question depends on whether (granted that A did not intend to break the glass roof), the fact that it would be broken was a virtually certain consequence of pushing B off the building *and* A knew that it was a virtually certain consequence. If the court concludes that the damage was a virtually certain consequence which was known to A, it will convict A of criminal damage to the roof, on the basis that she had an *indirect*, or *oblique*, intention to cause the damage.

Although the hypothetical scenario given above clearly illustrates the nature of the doctrine of *oblique intention*, in reality, there are two reasons why this doctrine may not be relevant.

First, where the evidence clearly supports a charge in respect of a very serious offence such as murder, and the doctrine of *oblique intention* could be used to support an additional, relatively minor, charge such as small-scale criminal damage, the prosecution would be unlikely to charge the relatively minor offence.

Secondly, however, there may be no need to rely on the doctrine even where the prosecution does wish to proceed with both charges (where, for example, the seriousness of the two offences is more equal). Adapting the murder scenario which is discussed above, suppose that A had not pushed B off the top of the tall building but had intended to smash an object by throwing it off the building. Suppose also that the falling object had smashed not only itself but also the glass roof of the extension. If A is able to advance a potentially plausible argument that she was, as a matter of law, the owner of the object (and, therefore entitled to smash it if she wished to do), the prosecution may regard a charge in respect of the glass roof as being in the nature of an insurance policy to increase its chances of securing at least one conviction. On this variation of the scenario, the prosecution would not need to rely on the doctrine of oblique intention in respect of the damage to the glass roof if the circumstances as a whole were such that the case could be presented on the basis of recklessness with regard to the damage to the glassroof (the *mens rea* required for criminal damage being either *intention* or *recklessness*).

Recklessness requires that the defendant took an unreasonable risk of causing a kind of harm which she foresaw as a possible consequence of her action. The question of foresight is answered subjectively (or, in other words, *what did that particular defendant actually foresee?*) rather than *what would a reasonable person in that defendant's position have foreseen?* So, for example, when dealing with a fifteen-year-old defendant with learning difficulties, the court cannot apply a normal adult's standard of foresight. (However, leaving aside special cases such as this, the more obvious the risk would be in the eyes of a reasonable person, the less likely the court will be to believe a defendant who asserts that it was not obvious to her. But this is a purely practical question which is quite distinct from the nature of the test to be applied.) On the other hand, the question of whether the risk is *unreasonable* will be answered objectively.

There are a few offences for which *negligence* (which in the context of criminal law means falling below the standard of an ordinary and reasonably prudent person) is sufficient to constitute *mens rea*. Apart from the obvious one of driving without due care and attention, the main exceptions are the statutory offences of harassment, and causing or allowing the death of a child or vulnerable adult.

For the purposes of the offence of *harassment*, a defendant is guilty if she either knows or ought to know that her conduct amounts to harassment. The question of what she ought to know is determined by reference to what a reasonable person, in possession of the same information as the defendant, would know.

For the purposes of the offence of *allowing the death of a child or vulnerable adult*, a defendant (D) has the necessary *mens rea* if (i) the victim (V) died as the result of an unlawful act which occurred while they were living in the same household (and within which they had frequent contact with each other); (ii) D was, or ought to have been, aware that there was a significant risk that someone else living in the household would cause physical harm to V; (iii) D failed to take such steps as she could reasonably have been expected to take to protect V from that risk; and (iv) the fatal act occurred in the sort of circumstances of which D either was, or ought to have been, aware.

In the context of MANSLAUGHTER, one form of *mens rea* exists where the defendant is *grossly negligent*. In this context, however, the meaning of the word *negligence* differs from that which it has in the context of the

M

statutory offences mentioned above, because it requires negligence of the kind which is necessary in the law of TORT. In other words, in this context, it requires breach of a duty of care, causing damage (which, in this case, must be death), with the additional requirement that the defendant's conduct must be such that the court is satisfied that it can be properly classified as criminal. This degree of gross negligence may also be categorised as a form of *recklessness*.

Mental Health Review Tribunals

See TRIBUNALS.

Mere equity

The best way to approach the meaning of the phrase *mere equity* is by way of drawing a distinction with the meaning of the phrase equitable interest (see INTERESTS IN LAND). Equitable interests (such as interests under TRUSTS) are interests in land, and are, therefore, property rights. Mere equities, on the other hand, fall into a different category, being rights which are ancillary to property rights, rather than actually being such rights.

Mere equities include

- the right to have a CONVEYANCE set aside for UNDUE INFLUENCE;

and

- the right to have a document rectified for mistake (for example, where the rent is stated to be £130 when it should be £230, or a repairing COVENANT has been inadvertently omitted from a LEASE).

Mesne profits

Mesne profits (the first word of which is pronounced *mean*) are the rents and profits which a trespasser has either received or ought to have received while she has been in possession of land. The rightful occupier of the land can sue the trespasser for the appropriate sum of money.

Mining lease

A *mining lease* is a lease under which the lessee is allowed to extract minerals from the land. The rent payable will usually vary according to the value of the minerals which are extracted.

Minister of the Crown

In constitutional law and practice, a *Minister of the Crown* is a member of the government who will either head, or have specific responsibilities within, a government department. By convention (see CONSTITUTIONAL CONVENTIONS), a minister must belong to either the House of Commons or the House of Lords. The official titles vary and include not only *Minister* but also *Secretary of State*, *Minister of State*, and *Parliamentary Under-Secretary*. The Queen may, by ORDER IN COUNCIL, transfer responsibilities from one minister to another and dissolve, merge and create government departments.

Ministerial responsibility

The CONSTITUTIONAL CONVENTION of *ministerial responsibility* consists of two sub-doctrines, namely *collective responsibility* and *individual responsibility*.

Collective responsibility requires that ministers must either support government policy or resign from the government.

Individual responsibility requires that ministers must accept responsibility for significant errors perpetrated by their departments.

Minor

A *minor* is a person under the age of 18. To put it another way, 18 is now the age of majority. (Before the Family Law Reform Act 1969, the age of majority was 21 and a person under that age was known as an *infant*. The word *infant* will, therefore, be encountered in pre-1969 cases.)

Minor interests

Although the phrase *minor interests*, which was introduced by the Land Registration Act 1925, is no longer used under the regime established by the Land Registration Act 2002, there remains a category of interests which are not OVERRIDING INTERESTS but are not capable of being registered as titles in their own right.

Such interests are now capable of being protected by entering a *restriction* or a *notice* on the register, and may still be conveniently called *minor interests*, even if only as a matter of usage rather than of law.

Restrictions are commonly used, for example, in order to protect beneficiaries under a trust of land by requiring the purchase money on any sale of the land to be paid to at least two trustees.

M

Notices are used for matters such as equitable EASEMENTS which would be registrable as LAND CHARGES in the case of land with unregistered title.

Misdemeanour

See FELONY.

Misfeasance

See MISFEASANCE IN PUBLIC OFFICE and MALFEASANCE.

Misfeasance in public office

The TORT of *misfeasance in a public office* is committed where a public officer acts either

- maliciously with the intention of harming the claimant; or
- knowing both that she has no power to do the act in question and that that act will probably injure the claimant; and
- in either case, the act does harm the claimant.

Misrepresentation

A *misrepresentation* is an untrue statement of fact (or, perhaps, of law) which induces a person to enter into a contract with the person making the misrepresentation. A contract entered into as a result of a misrepresentation is voidable (see VOID).

Mistake

It is fundamental to the concept of a CONTRACT that there is an agreement between two or more parties, but it may happen that an apparent agreement is flawed as the result of a *mistake* made by one or more of the parties. However, it is by no means an easy task to distinguish between those mistakes which will, and those which will not, render a contract VOID. For example, where the parties to a contract for the sale of a painting both wrongly believed it to be by a specific artist, the contract was not void because they were both agreed about the physical object which formed the subject-matter of their contract. On the other hand, the court held that a separation agreement between a couple who were apparently married was void when it transpired that the apparent husband's first wife (whom he had assumed to be dead), was, in fact, still alive. It followed that the

M

couple who had entered into the agreement were not legally married, and therefore there was no basis for their separation agreement.

Equity (see COMMON LAW) may take a more characteristically flexible approach than the common law, with the remedy of RESCISSION being available. Additionally, even where the common law holds a contract to be valid notwithstanding some element of mistake, equity might withhold the remedy of SPECIFIC PERFORMANCE.

Mitigation

1 In the context of DAMAGES, a potential claimant has a duty to *mitigate* her loss, and thus reduce the amount of her claim. For example, if A negligently drives her car so that it crashes into B's house, B should make the damage weather-proof (rather than leaving the house to deteriorate) until it can be repaired properly.

2 In the context of *sentencing*, a defendant may present *mitigation* which, if successful, will reduce the severity of the sentence which would otherwise have been imposed.

M'Naghten Rules

The *M'Naghten Rules*, which were formulated in the case of *M'Naghten* [1843–60] All ER Rep 229, are the classic statement of the meaning of insanity for the purposes of the criminal law. They are discussed in the entry for AUTOMATISM. (*M'Naghten* is pronounced *MacNorton*.)

Money Bill

A *Money Bill* is a Bill which exclusively concerns public financial matters. If the House of Lords does not pass a Money Bill within one month, it may proceed to the Royal Assent without the Lords' approval. In practice, however, the Lords' consideration of Money Bills is even more perfunctory than this time-scale suggests.

See also the PARLIAMENT ACTS 1911 AND 1949.

M

Monism

See DUALISM.

Mortgage

A *mortgage* (which is pronounced with a silent 't') is a means of providing security, in the form of land, for a loan. The borrower (who mortgages the land) is the *mortgagor*, and the lender (who takes the security for the loan) is the *mortgagee*.

Before the Law of Property Act 1925, a borrower who gave security in the form of land would convey the land to the lender, who would then convey it back to the borrower when the loan was paid off. The 1925 Act replaced the expensive and time-consuming double conveyance which this form of mortgage inevitably required, with two new versions.

Under the basic version, the borrower grants the lender a long LEASE (often 3,000 years, but the exact length is immaterial), subject to a proviso that the lease shall terminate when the loan is paid off (or, to put it more technically, *when the mortgage is redeemed*). In conveyancing terminology, this form of mortgage is known as a *demise for a long term of years subject to a proviso for cesser on redemption*. Of course, logic (not to mention the rule of *NEMO DAT QUOD NON HABET*) dictates that someone who holds no more than a leasehold interest cannot sell the freehold. Clearly, therefore, this would present a serious problem where a borrower defaulted on payment and the lender wished to sell the land in order to recover her money. Accordingly, the 1925 Act gives the lender power to sell the freehold, even though the mortgage gives her only a leasehold. However, another problem with a mortgage in the form of a demise for a long term of years with a proviso for cesser on redemption, is that many leases contain restrictions on sub-letting. It follows, therefore, that property held under a lease containing such a term would be effectively unmortgageable under the 1925 regime if the only available form of mortgage required the borrower to grant a lease to the lender. In order to cope with this difficulty, the 1925 Act introduced an alternative form of mortgage, in the shape of the wholly new conception of a *charge by way of legal mortgage*.

As a matter of *form*, a charge by way of legal mortgage is, as its name suggests, merely a CHARGE on the land; and, therefore, the question of the borrower (or chargor) granting a lease to the lender (or chargee) does not arise. However, although the charge by way of legal mortgage solves this problem, it creates another.

A chargee of land has no more than an interest in the proceeds of sale of the land; and, because she is only a chargee, no sale can take place without an order of the court, which leaves her in a significantly weaker position than a *mortgagee* (whose remedies include a power of sale). It is for this reason that although the new concept introduced by the 1925 Act is, in form, simply a charge, it is expressed to be *by way of legal mortgage*, in order to provide a lender who takes such a charge with the same remedies as a lender who has taken a mortgage by demise by way of security for the loan. For many years, charges by way of legal mortgage have been much more common than mortgages by demise; and, since the Land Registration Act 2002, they have been the only form of mortgage available in respect of REGISTERED LAND.

The remedies available to a mortgagee (including a chargee by way of legal mortgage) are to take possession of the land (which may require an order of the court, depending on the circumstances); to sell the land; to foreclose (which means applying to the court for an order of foreclosure which will vest ownership of the land in the lender); to appoint a receiver (who will then manage the land on behalf of the borrower); and, of course, to sue the lender for the amount of the outstanding loan. As a matter of form, the sum secured is usually repayable after six months (on a date which is known as the *legal date for redemption*), but provided the borrower keeps up with her repayments (and performs her other covenants under the mortgage, such as to keep the property in good repair), equity (see COMMON LAW) will not allow the lender to exercise her remedies merely because the legal date for redemption (or, in other words, the date for redemption at common law) has passed. Thus, even after the legal date for redemption has passed, the borrower retains an *equitable right to redeem*, and is said to have an *equity of redemption*.

Motive

See MENS REA.

Motor Insurers' Bureau

The *Motor Insurers' Bureau* compensates the victims of negligent motorists who cannot be traced or who are uninsured. Every insurer who underwrites compulsory motor insurance is legally obliged to be a member of the MIB and to contribute to its funding.

M

MP

The abbreviation *MP* means *Member of Parliament* and appears after the name of a Member of the House of Commons (see PARLIAMENT): for example, Joan White MP. Although the House of Lords is one of the Houses of Parliament, and therefore its members are, literally Members of Parliament, they do not take the abbreviation *MP* after their names.

MR

The letters MR after a judge's name indicate that he (or she) is the MASTER OF THE ROLLS (although there has never been a female Master of the Rolls so it must remain a matter for speculation whether *Master* would be converted to *Mistress*).

Murder

Murder is a COMMON LAW offence and consists of the unlawful killing of a human being under the Queen's peace with malice aforethought. (The requirement that the victim must be *under the Queen's peace* explains why killing the enemy in time of war is not murder.)

For these purposes, the law considers an unborn child to be not yet a human being, which explains why killing an unborn child is not murder (but see CHILD DESTRUCTION). However, if a child who is born alive after suffering pre-natal injuries subsequently dies from those injuries, the killing will be murder if the infliction of the injuries was accompanied by the appropriate *mens rea*.

Although *malice aforethought* is the traditional formulation of the *mens rea* of murder, the phrase is misleading. More particularly, the word *malice* in this context does not reflect the way in which it is used elsewhere in the law (see, for example, DEFAMATION and INJURIOUS FALSEHOOD), nor does *malice aforethought* require the kind of deliberation, or premeditation, which the word *aforethought* implies. In reality, the *mens rea* of murder is an intention either to kill or to cause grievous bodily harm.

SELF-DEFENCE is a complete defence to murder. DIMINISHED RESPONSIBILITY and PROVOCATION may be regarded as partial defences in the sense that, if accepted or proved, they reduce murder to MANSLAUGHTER.

M

National Assembly of Wales

The *National Assembly of Wales* (commonly known simply as *the Welsh Assembly*) was originally (under the Government of Wales Act 1998) the transferee of the legislative powers which were previously allocated to the Secretary of State for Wales. Those powers were limited to the making of DELEGATED LEGISLATION, but the Government of Wales Act 2006 removed this limitation so that (subject to a great many detailed exceptions) the Assembly has power to do anything that the United Kingdom Parliament could have done in relation to Wales. In addition to complying with the detailed exceptions set out in the 2006 Act, Assembly Measures must, of course, comply with the law of the EUROPEAN COMMUNITY and EUROPEAN UNION, as well as with the CONVENTION RIGHTS under the HUMAN RIGHTS ACT 1998.

Natural justice

See PROCEDURAL FAIRNESS.

Natural law

The phrase *natural law* describes one of the major groups of legal theories, which is contrasted with another major group, namely *positivist theories of law*.

The essential difference between the two schools of thought is that natural law emphasises the link between law and morality, while positivism, by emphasising the law as laid down (or *posited*), regards law and morality as two distinct subjects. This is not to say that positivists are uninterested in whether laws are just or unjust, but simply that they see the question of what the law *is* as being a separate question from the question of what the law *ought to be*.

When both schools of thought are considered in more detail, the distinction between the two becomes less clear cut. At that stage, rather than being seen as watertight compartments, natural law and positivism can be seen as constituting a whole spectrum of thought, with the purest forms of each occupying opposite ends, while the more subtle forms occupy a substantial grey area around the middle.

Natural person

A *natural person* is a human being. This form of *legal personality* contrasts with CORPORATIONS, which are artificial legal persons.

Necessary in a democratic society

The EUROPEAN CONVENTION ON HUMAN RIGHTS (ECHR) provides that (for the reasons set out in each of the articles) all the rights protected by arts. 8 to 11 may be restricted by law to such extent as is *necessary in a democratic society*. (For the full text of the articles, see Appendix 3.)

Although the ECHR itself does not specify what is meant by the phrase *necessary in a democratic society*, the EUROPEAN COURT OF HUMAN RIGHTS has identified 'tolerance and broad-mindedness' as two of the 'hallmarks' of a democratic society. The Court has also said that *necessary* means something between *indispensable* on the one hand and *reasonable* or *desirable* on the other; and, more particularly, a restriction will not be necessary unless it corresponds with a *pressing social need* and is *proportionate* to the legitimate aim pursued.

Negligence

Broadly speaking, the TORT of *negligence* is committed by a defendant who

- owes the claimant a duty of care; and who
- breaches that duty; thus
- causing harm to the claimant.

Originally, the question of whether or not a duty existed was answered by applying the *neighbour principle*, according to which A owes a duty of care to B if (but only if) B is so closely and directly affected by A's conduct that A ought reasonably to foresee that B will be affected by A's action or inaction. This emphasises the *objective* nature of the test. In other words, the question is not whether A *actually* foresaw that B would be sufficiently closely and directly affected by his action or inaction, but whether a *reasonable* person *ought* to have foreseen this relationship. In the days before the use of gender-neutral language became the norm, this hypothetical reasonable person was often characterised as being *the man on the Clapham omnibus* (which can easily be modernised by substituting *passenger* for *man*). By way of a practical example, on the basis of this objective test, a manufacturer ought reasonably to foresee that consumers may well be harmed where deficiencies in the manufacture or packaging of his product result in contaminated products being put on sale.

As the court continued to work its way through cases on this basis, it developed a scheme of types of cases in which liability would (or would not) arise. For example, it was by no means obvious whether liability in negligence, which clearly applied to physical harm, should also extend to cases where the harm took the form of psychiatric illness (caused, for example, by witnessing a road traffic accident, or its bloody aftermath); or where the loss was purely economic (as a result, for example, of making a bad investment on the basis of professional advice).

The court came to the view that cases such as these imported a different element beyond simple objective foreseeability. It came to see this element in terms of the closeness of the relationship, and, therefore, it came to call this element *proximity*. Furthermore, the court came to add to this requirement of proximity another requirement, namely that, in all the circumstances of the case, it must be *just and reasonable* to impose liability on the defendant. In other words, the test for establishing whether or not the defendant owed the claimant a duty of care (of the kind that would be sufficient to ground a claim in negligence) came to be the *reasonable foreseeability of harm to a person (the claimant) who was in a sufficiently proximate relationship to the defendant that it would be just and reasonable to impose liability on the defendant.* Clearly, these elements would overlap in many cases, but they may nevertheless provide a useful framework for thinking about the question of whether or not there was a duty of care, in order to decide whether the threshold of liability for negligence has been crossed.

Assuming that the defendant did owe a duty of care in all the circumstances of a particular case (and that, therefore, the threshold of liability has been crossed) there remain the questions of

- whether the defendant was in breach of that duty;
- whether the claimant has suffered harm of a kind in respect of which the court is willing to provide a remedy; and (assuming that the claimant receives a favourable answer to this question) whether that harm was caused by the potential defendant's action or inaction.

Once again, there are overlaps both

- between these questions (taken collectively) and the threshold question which has already been discussed; and
- between these questions as against each other.

N

For example, questions of reasonableness may arise again, but this time in relation to the question of whether the defendant has breached his duty of care. In absolute terms, the level of expertise required of a chiropodist is lower than that required of a surgeon, but both are required to possess and exercise that level of skill which a reasonable member of their respective professions would possess and exercise.

Similarly, in deciding whether the harm suffered by the claimant is within a category of harm for which the court is willing to award compensation, the court has to turn its mind again to arguments surrounding compensation for physical injury, psychiatric injury and pure economic loss. Having done so, it must again consider whether, in all the circumstances of the case, the harm sustained by the claimant was *caused* by the defendant.

The last of these issues may, in effect, overlap entirely with the question of whether the defendant was in breach of his duty of care. However, more complex issues may arise where there are arguments based on *causation*, or *remoteness of damage*.

One classic issue, which is usually expressed in terms of *causation*, concerns liability where A injures B to the extent that B seeks medical attention. If that medical attention causes further injury, is A responsible for the whole of B's injury, or only for the injury sustained up to the point where B received medical attention?

Another classic issue, which this time is usually expressed in terms of *remoteness of damage*, arises where a reasonable defendant would have reasonably foreseen the occurrence of some harm, but would not have foreseen the harm which the claimant actually suffered. This, in turn, can be broken down into possibilities.

The first possibility is that the harm actually suffered was not of the same type as that which could reasonably have been foreseen.

The second possibility is that the harm actually suffered was of the *same type* as that which could reasonably have been foreseen, but was significantly *more severe*.

Again, these questions are not necessarily as clear cut as they might appear to be at first sight. Suppose an industrial accident injures two employees, both of whom are badly burned. Also suppose that the burns suffered by one of them heal with no particular complications beyond residual scarring, while the burns suffered by the other are followed by skin cancer. Are these two medical outcomes to be classified as different types of harm (because a burn is clearly different from cancer) or are they the same type of harm (because they are both physical injuries)?

For a full defence to a claim in negligence, see ASSUMPTION OF RISK; and for a partial defence, see CONTRIBUTORY NEGLIGENCE. Although an occupier of land may well be liable in negligence to people who come onto that land, a specific additional scheme has been enacted to deal with OCCUPIERS' LIABILITY.

See also RES IPSA LOQUITUR.

Nemo dat quod non habet

The Latin phrase *nemo dat quod non habet* (which may be pronounced *nay-moh dat quod nohn habet*) means *no one can give what he has not got*. It is used to describe the situation in which someone who does not have title to property nevertheless purports to transfer title to someone else. Despite the obvious logic of the phrase, there are several exceptional cases in which someone who receives property may acquire good title to it, even though the person from whom it is received did not have good title.

Nemo iudex in sua causa potest

The Latin phrase *nemo iudex in sua causa potest* (which may be pronounced *nay-moh yew-dex in soo-a cowsa pot-est* and which often appears simply as *nemo iudex in sua causa*), can be translated literally as *no one can be a judge in his own cause*. It is also known as the *rule against bias*.

See also PROCEDURAL FAIRNESS.

Nervous shock

The term *nervous shock*, which was formerly used in the law of NEGLIGENCE, has now been replaced by terms such as *psychiatric harm* and *post traumatic stress disorder*.

Neutral citation of cases

Where cases are reported in several series of law reports, the fact that they appear at different page numbers in each series makes it difficult to cite passages from the judgments with pinpoint accuracy. In order to overcome this problem, and to facilitate the citation of cases reported on the internet, the courts have introduced a system known as *neutral citation*, under which each case is given a reference which is independent of the system of law reporting, and within each case the paragraphs are numbered. Thus any passage can be the subject of a pinpoint citation which will be the same in all full-transcript reports of the case. (For the difference between *full-transcript* and *short reports*, see LAW REPORTS.) The *Practice Direction (Judgments: Form and Citation)* [2001] 1 WLR 194, introduced the system of neutral citation into the ADMINISTRATIVE COURT and both divisions of the COURT OF APPEAL. Each case is numbered sequentially, as the following forms show:

- High Court (Administrative Court) [2001] EWHC Admin 1 (or 2 or 3, and so on);
- Court of Appeal (Civil Division) [2001]EWCACiv 1 (or 2 or 3, and so on);
- Court of Appeal (Criminal Division) [2001] EWCA Crim 1 (or 2 or 3, and so on).

The *Practice Direction (Judgments: Neutral Citation)* [2002] 1 WLR 346, extended the system to the other Divisions of the High Court, in the following forms:

- High Court (Queen's Bench Division) [2002] EWHC 1 (or 2 or 3, and so on) (QB);
- High Court (Family Division) [2002] EWHC 1 (or 2 or 3, and so on) (Fam);
- High Court (Chancery Division) [2002] EWHC 1 (or 2 or 3, and so on) (Ch).

In practice, the High Court (Administrative Court) has adopted the form used by the High Court in other cases, producing, for example, [2004] EWHC 1 (Admin). The House of Lords also adopted neutral citation (in the form of [2002] UKHL 1 (or 2 or 3, and so on)), and the SUPREME COURT continues to use it.

Nisi

The Latin word *nisi* (pronounced *nye-sye*) means *unless*. With the general abandonment of Latin, the word has fallen into disuse, but an *order nisi* was a provisional order which would take effect after a set period of time unless something happened to prevent it from doing so.

Nolle prosequi

The Latin phrase *nolle prosequi* (pronounced *noll-eh pro-sec-wee*), which literally means *I refuse to prosecute*, is the name given to the document which the Attorney-General (see LAW OFFICERS OF THE CROWN) issues when he intervenes in order to prevent a prosecution being continued.

Nonfeasance

See MALFEASANCE.

Northern Ireland Assembly

The *Northern Ireland Assembly*, which was created following the Good Friday Agreement of 1998, has power to pass Acts in respect of *transferred* matters. Certain other matters are *reserved*, which means that they remain outside the scope of the Northern Ireland Assembly altogether, but there is an intermediate category of *excepted* matters, which begin by being *reserved* but may subsequently be *transferred* by an Order made by the Secretary of State for Northern Ireland.

The validity of an Act of the Assembly is not affected by any invalidity in the Assembly proceedings leading to its enactment; but no provision contained in an Act of the Assembly is law if it is incompatible with COMMUNITY LAW or a Convention right under the HUMAN RIGHTS ACT 1998.

Notice

1 In various legal contexts, the word *notice* may have its everyday meaning of something such as a document or display which contains information. (Obvious examples include notice given by an employee before leaving a job, and a notice in the form of a sign setting out parking restrictions.)
2 In the context of land law it is often important to know whether a particular person *has notice of* interests which adversely affect their land. This topic is explained in the context of purchasers of land (see PURCHASER).

Nuisance

Nuisance can be either a TORT or one of two CRIMES.

The tort of *private nuisance* consists of unreasonable interference with the use or enjoyment of the claimant's land. Typically, the interference emanates from the use or enjoyment of the defendant's land. However, this is not an essential element of the tort, which may also be committed by, for example, flying over the defendant's land. The interference with the use or enjoyment of the defendant's land may fall within any of the following three categories:

- indirect physical interference (for example, by overhanging vegetation);
- physical damage caused by activities (such as those causing vibration); and
- things such as noise and smell.

The scope of the criminal offence of *public nuisance* is rather ill-defined, but can be broadly defined as *any conduct which annoys a substantial portion of the public*, such as bomb hoaxes or badly organised popular music festivals. Alongside its criminal consequences, public nuisance may also give rise to tortious liability to any individual who suffers special harm, over and above that suffered by the populace at large.

Another way in which nuisance can be a crime is in the form of *statutory nuisance*. This arises where premises are prejudicial to health or a nuisance. The utility of this form of nuisance as a means of protecting health is apparent from the fact that it was originally contained in Public Health legislation, although it is now contained in the Environmental Protection Act 1990.

N

Oo

Obiter dictum
See BINDING PRECEDENT.

Obligations
The law relating to CONTRACT and TORT (and sometimes including RESTITUTION) is often known collectively as the law of *obligations.*

Obstruction of the highway
See HIGHWAY.

Obstruction of a police officer in the execution of his duty
It is one of the oddities of the COMMON LAW that many of the cases which establish the extent of a police officer's duty have arisen where people have allegedly either *obstructed or assaulted police officers in the execution of their duty,* and the only point at issue has been whether the officers were, as a matter of law, acting in the execution of their duty at the relevant time.

Obtaining by deception
See FRAUD and OBTAINING SERVICES DISHONESTLY

Obtaining services dishonestly
The offence (see CRIME) of *obtaining services DISHONESTLY* is committed where

- a person obtains services (whether for herself or for someone else) by a dishonest act;
- knowing that the services were, or might be, provided on the basis that they were or would be, paid for; but nevertheless

- intends that payment will not be made or will be made only in part; and
- the services are not paid for in full.

Occupiers' liability

An occupier of land has many duties towards people who come onto her land, particularly under the TORT of NEGLIGENCE. Additionally, however, there is a discrete area of law, known as *occupiers' liability* and governed by the Occupiers' Liability Acts of 1957 and 1984.

The Occupiers' Liability Act 1957 provides that an occupier of land owes what it calls a *common duty of care* to anyone who is lawfully on the premises. The Act calls such people *visitors,* and they include not only those who have been expressly invited to enter (such as the occupier's friends), but also those with implied permission to enter (such as postal delivery workers) and those who may have a lawful power of entry even against the will of the occupier (such as, in certain circumstances, police officers).

The common duty of care is a duty to take such care as is reasonable, in all the circumstances, to see that visitors will be reasonably safe in using the premises for the purposes for which they are invited or permitted to be there. The Act requires an occupier to take into account the fact that children will often be less careful for their own safety than adults are for theirs (unless the circumstances are such that the occupier could reasonably expect children to be accompanied by adults). It also provides that an occupier is entitled to expect that visitors who are pursuing their trade will take their own precautions against any special risks which are reasonably incidental to their trade. (For example, where specialised cleaning contractors are overcome by noxious fumes generated by the chemicals they use in their cleaning processes, the occupier of the premises will not be liable for failing to take precautions for their safety.)

An occupier may avoid or restrict liability by displaying appropriate notices; and, where the visitor is present under a CONTRACT, by inserting an appropriate exclusion clause in the contract. There is a full defence of ASSUMPTION OF RISK and a partial defence of CONTRIBUTORY NEGLIGENCE.

The Occupiers' Liability Act 1984 provides a substantial degree of protection to people who are not visitors within the meaning of the 1957 Act. More particularly, it includes not only trespassers but also people exercising *private* (but not *public*) rights of way, and people exercising their rights under the National Parks and Access to the Countryside Act 1949 and the Countryside and Rights of Way Act 2000.

The 1984 Act imposes on an occupier (O) a duty of reasonable care to anyone (C) who is not a visitor, in respect of dangers which O knows, or has reasonable grounds to believe, exist, provided that two conditions are satisfied. The first condition is that O must also know (or have reasonable grounds to believe), that C is in (or may come into) the vicinity of the danger. The second condition is that the circumstances must be such that it is reasonable to expect O to offer some protection to C.

Generally speaking, the comments made on the exclusion and restriction of liability and on defences that apply in relation to visitors apply equally to non-visitors. However, while the 1984 Act makes provision for the occupier's duty of care to be discharged by giving adequate warning of any dangers, there is no provision permitting exclusion of liability.

Offences against the person

The phrase *offences against the person* is often used as shorthand for all offences of ASSAULT, BATTERY and HOMICIDE. Curiously, however, the offence of bigamy is contained in the Offences Against the Person Act 1861.

Offences triable either way

Offences which may be tried by either a MAGISTRATES' COURT or the CROWN COURT are said to be *triable either way.*

Offences triable only on indictment

Offences triable only by the CROWN COURT are said to be *triable only on indictment* (the last word of which is pronounced *indite-ment*).

Offences triable only summarily

Offences triable only by a MAGISTRATES' COURT are said to be *triable only summarily.*

Offer

See CONTRACT.

Office copy

An *office copy* of an official document (for example, from the LAND REGISTRY) is authenticated by a stamp or seal, and is, for most practical purposes, as good evidence of its contents as the original document would be.

Official Journal of the European Union

The *Official Journal of the European Union* (or *OJEU*), which was previously known as the *Official Journal of the European Communities* (or *OJEC*), and which is commonly referred to as the *OJ*, is the official organ of the European Union. It is published daily in each of the official languages of the EU and appears in several parts.

The *L series* contains the text of legislation; the *C series* carries a very wide range of information and notices, including the opinions of the *Economic and Social Committee* and the *Committee of the Regions*, and the judgments of the COURT OF FIRST INSTANCE (which is now, after the Treaty of Lisbon, the *General Court*) and the EUROPEAN COURT OF JUSTICE.

The *Official Journal* is available online, free of charge, at http://www.europa.eu.int/.

Ombudsman

The first *ombudsman* in the English legal system was the Parliamentary Commissioner for Administration, whose jurisdiction covered central government departments and some other public bodies. The Parliamentary Commissioner was the model for ombudsmen dealing with the National Health Service (the *Health Service Commissioner*) and LOCAL GOVERNMENT (the *Commissioners for Local Administration*). In practice, the offices of the Parliamentary Commissioner and the Health Service Commissioner were held by the same person (although there was no legal requirement that this should be so) and this practice has been formalised by merging the two offices into the single office of the *Parliamentary Commissioner for Administration and the Health Service Commissioner*. In Wales, merger has gone further, with a single ombudsman dealing with local government, as well as the National Health Service and administration under the NATIONAL ASSEMBLY OF WALES.

The function of an ombudsman is to investigate complaints of *maladministration causing injustice*. Neither of the key terms has any statutory definition, but Richard Crossman (the Minister responsible for piloting the Bill which became the Parliamentary Commissioner Act 1967) gave the classic indication of the meaning of *maladministration* as 'bias, neglect, inattention, delay, incompetence, ineptitude, perversity, turpitude, arbitrariness and so on'. It is generally accepted that *injustice* includes not only financial loss but also less measurable matters such as frustration. It is important to notice that an ombudsman cannot uphold a complaint unless the maladministration *caused* the injustice: simply finding the existence of both maladministration and injustice is not enough without the presence of a causal link as well.

The European Ombudsman (who is based in Strasbourg, with a branch office in Brussels) deals with complaints of maladministration by any of the Community institutions, except the Court of Justice and the General Court (which was, before the TREATY OF LISBON 2007, the *Court of First Instance*). In this context, *maladministration* means administrative irregularities, administrative omissions, abuse of power, negligence, unlawful procedures, unfairness, malfunction or incompetence, discrimination, avoidable delay, and lack or refusal of information.

Omnia praesumuntur rite esse acta

See PRESUMPTION OF LEGALITY.

Option to purchase

An *option to purchase* something is the right to purchase it on whatever terms (for example, as to price, or the period of time after which the option will lapse if it has not been exercised) as may be agreed. An option to purchase REAL PROPERTY is registrable as a NOTICE if the land is registered and as a class C(iv) LAND CHARGE if the land is unregistered.

Order in Council

The Council referred to in the phrase *Order in Council* is the PRIVY COUNCIL, and, technically, they are made by the Queen on the advice of the Privy Council. Orders in Council may be PRIMARY LEGISLATION, made under the ROYAL PREROGATIVE, or DELEGATED LEGISLATION, made under statutory powers, in which case they are STATUTORY INSTRUMENTS.

Orders *in* Council are distinct from Orders *of* Council. The latter are made by the Privy Council itself, rather than by the Queen on the advice of the Privy Council. They usually involve the regulatory affairs of various professional bodies.

O

Order of Council

See ORDER IN COUNCIL.

Ouster clause

An *ouster clause* is a statutory provision which purports either to exclude access to the courts altogether or to impose a very short time limit after which access will not be allowed. The first type (a *strict ouster clause*) is ineffective to prevent a claim for JUDICIAL REVIEW on the ground that the decision which is being challenged is *ultra vires* (because a decision which is *ultra vires* is VOID and is not, therefore, as a matter of law, a decision at all). The other type of ouster clause (a *time-limited ouster clause*) is effective.

Although the logic which leads to strict ouster clauses being ineffective might seem to apply with equal logic to their time-limited counterparts, another way of looking at it is simply to say that a time-limited ouster clause merely imposes a very short LIMITATION PERIOD; and the concept of limitation periods is very deeply entrenched.

Overreaching

Equitable interests in land which is subject to a strict settlement (see SETTLE-MENTS OF LAND) or a TRUST OF LAND may be *overreached* when the land is sold.

Overreaching means that the equitable interest is extinguished in relation to the land, and becomes converted into an interest in the purchase money. However, overreaching will not take place unless the purchase money was paid to at least two trustees (see TRUST) or a TRUST CORPORATION.

Assuming that overreaching has occurred in a particular case, it follows that the beneficiaries who have lost their beneficial interests must look to the trustees (or trust corporation) to make good their losses. Where overreaching does not occur, the purchaser will be bound by the equitable interests which would have been overreached if he had been prudent enough to pay the purchase money to at least two trustees or a trust corporation.

O

Overriding interests

Overriding interests are interests in land which bind purchasers of land with registered title (see REGISTERED LAND), even though the interests themselves cannot be registered. The most important examples of such interests include

- leases for seven years or less (except that those which take effect more than three months after they are granted are registrable and are, therefore, outside the scheme of overriding interests);

- in certain circumstances,
    - the rights of people who are occupying the land;
    - legal EASEMENTS and PROFITS À PRENDRE; and
- the rights of people in ADVERSE POSSESSION of the land.

Overruling

See BINDING PRECEDENT.

O

P

The letter P after a judge's name indicates that he is the *President* of the Family Division of the HIGH COURT. It is said as if the word *President* appeared in full. It is also similarly used to identify the President of the SUPREME COURT.

PACE

PACE is an acronym formed from the initial letters of the *Police and Criminal Evidence Act* 1984.

Parliament

Since there are two Houses of Parliament (namely the House of Commons and the HOUSE OF LORDS), many people proceed on the basis that these two Houses, taken together, constitute *Parliament*. On the other hand, one of the basic principles of the British constitution is that (subject only to the exceptional procedure contained in the PARLIAMENT ACTS 1911 AND 1949), a Bill cannot become an Act *of Parliament* unless it has been approved not only by the Commons and the Lords but also by the Queen. The tri-partite analysis seems to indicate that the Queen is part of the Parliament which enacts legislation.

In practice, however, nothing turns on whether the Queen is technically one of the constituent elements of Parliament.

The House of Commons consists of members who represent 646 constituencies, each of which returns one member. (The number of constituencies varies from time to time, to take account of shifts in the population.)

The House of Lords consists of approximately 750 peers, made up of about 620 life peers, together with all former Law Lords (including those who became Justices of the SUPREME COURT in 2009, when that court came into being), the Archbishops of Canterbury and York and 24 senior diocesan bishops of the Church of England, 90 hereditary peers elected by the hereditary peerage as a whole, and two royal office-holders (namely the

Lord Great Chamberlain and the Earl Marshal). (The composition of the House of Lords is likely to be reformed within the foreseeable future, but the current position can be checked at any time at http://www.parliament.uk/.)

Parliament Acts 1911 and 1949

The *Parliament Act 1911* was passed to enable the Liberal government to get its legislative programme through, despite the opposition of the House of Lords. The effect of the Act was to remove the House of Lords' power of veto over BILLS (except for Bills to prolong the life of Parliament, in respect of which it remained) and to substitute for it a power to delay Bills for two years (except for Bills certified by the Speaker of the House of Commons as Money Bills, in respect of which the delaying power was only one month, in order to give that House the opportunity to consider such Bills and suggest amendments).

The *Parliament Act 1949* was passed in order to reduce the House of Lords' delaying power to one year, but without affecting the provisions of the 1911 Act relating to Bills to prolong the life of Parliament and Money Bills. The House of Lords did not pass the 1949 Act, which accordingly received the Royal Assent without the Lords' approval.

After many years of academic debate as to whether Bills passed under the Parliament Acts procedure are PRIMARY LEGISLATION or DELEGATED LEGISLATION, the Appellate Committee of the House of Lords held that they are primary legislation.

Parliamentary Commissioner for Administration

See OMBUDSMAN.

Parliamentary Commissioner for Standards

The Office of the *Parliamentary Commissioner for Standards* was created by the House of Commons in 1995.

The Commissioner's main responsibilities are:

- maintaining and monitoring the operation of the Register of Members' Interests, under which Members are required to declare relevant pecuniary interests or benefits of any nature, whether they are direct or indirect, and whether they existed in the past, exist in the present, or are expected to exist in the future;

P

- providing advice on a confidential basis to individual Members and to the Select Committee on Standards and Privileges about the interpretation of the *Code of Conduct and Guide to the Rules relating to the Conduct of Members*;
- preparing guidance and providing training for Members on matters of conduct, propriety and ethics;
- monitoring the operation of the *Code of Conduct and Guide to the Rules* and, where appropriate, proposing possible modifications of it to the Select Committee;
- investigating complaints about Members who are allegedly in breach of the *Code of Conduct and Guide to the Rules*, and reporting his findings to the Committee.

The Commissioner's office also maintains and monitors the operation of the Register of All-Party Groups; the Approved List of All-Party Parliamentary Groups and Associate Parliamentary Groups; the Register of Interests of Members' Secretaries and Research Assistants; and Register of Journalists' Interests.

The Register of Lords' Interests is maintained by the Lords' Registrar, under the authority of the Clerk of the Parliaments, and is not within the jurisdiction of the Parliamentary Commissioner for Standards.

The Parliamentary Commissioner for Standards is subject to the exclusive control of Parliament, and the court cannot intervene by way of JUDICIAL REVIEW.

Parliamentary Counsel

Parliamentary Counsel are lawyers who are employed on a full-time basis to draft government legislation.

The head of the Office of the Parliamentary Counsel is known as *First Parliamentary Counsel*.

Parliamentary Privilege

Parliamentary privilege is the name given to the rights enjoyed by each House of PARLIAMENT, and their members (and which are not shared by anybody else), without which (it is said) they could not perform their functions. Furthermore, Parliament claims to have exclusive jurisdiction in relation to such matters (with the exclusivity of this jurisdiction meaning that it is the courts which are excluded).

The principal examples of Parliamentary privilege are:

- freedom of speech (for example, members of either House are not liable in the law of defamation for statements made in the course of proceedings in Parliament; and before the decision in *Pepper v Hart* [1993] 1 All ER 42 this aspect of Parliamentary privilege was sometimes advanced as a reason for not allowing the courts to refer to HANSARD for the purposes of statutory interpretation); and
- Parliament's control of its own composition (for example, except where there are any statutory provisions to the contrary – as there are, for example, in relation to Election Courts under the Representation of the People Act 1983 – each House has the exclusive right to determine its own membership).

Additionally, most textbooks still list freedom from *civil* arrest as an example of Parliamentary privilege. While this privilege does still exist, it is also (since the abolition of imprisonment for debt) of little real importance.

There is no Parliamentary privilege of freedom from *criminal* arrest, which is, of course, far more important than its civil equivalent.

Parliamentary privilege is very closely related to *contempt of Parliament*, which is the name given to any act or omission which obstructs or impedes (or tends to obstruct or impede) either House (or its members or officers) in the performance of their duties. Although, strictly speaking, every breach of Parliamentary privilege is also a contempt of Parliament, in practice the latter phrase is usually reserved for the following kinds of conduct:

- misconduct in the presence of the House (for example, interrupting its proceedings);
- disobedience to Rules or Orders of the House (for example refusing to withdraw from the House when required to do so);
- presenting forged or falsified documents to the House (for example, forging signatures to petitions);
- misconduct by members or officers in their capacities as such (for example, deliberately misleading the House);
- constructive contempts (for example, using the name or the crest of either House in connection with unofficial business; or making offensive comments about either House or its members and thus diminishing the respect in which the House or its members would otherwise be held);
- obstructing members or officers of either House in the performance of their functions; and
- obstructing witnesses who give evidence to committees of either House.

P

The punitive powers available to Parliament in respect of breaches of privilege and contempts are committal to prison; the imposition of a fine (although this power is available to the House of Commons only); admonishment (*sic*) and reprimand; suspension and expulsion.

Parol evidence rule

The *parol evidence rule* states that where a contract is in writing, the parties cannot produce additional evidence as to the terms of their agreement. The rule is, however, subject to many exceptions. Among the more commonly encountered exceptions are cases where the written agreement was not intended to contain the whole of the agreement, and those where the extrinsic evidence is to be used in order to prove the content of terms which are to be implied into a written contract.

Although in some legal contexts the word *parol* means *oral*, its meaning in the present context is not limited in this way, and where an exception to the parol evidence rule applies, the court may receive both written and oral evidence.

Partnership

The statutory definition of *partnership* is 'the relationship which subsists between persons carrying on business in common with a view of (*sic*) profit'.

Generally speaking (but, for the exceptional case, see the part of this entry dealing with *limited liability partnerships*):

- no formalities are necessary for the creation of a partnership (although, in practice, the agreement which creates a partnership is commonly contained in a partnership DEED);
- a partnership is not a CORPORATION; and, therefore, the name of a partnership is, in effect, simply a form of shorthand for the names of all the partners for the time being (and the fact that the names of many partnerships end in '& Co' is simply a matter of convention and has no legal effect);
- each partner is individually liable for the whole of the debts and other obligations of the partnership (unless he is a limited partner, in which case his liability is limited to the amount of capital he has contributed to the firm, but there must be at least one partner – known as a *general partner* – whose personal liability is unlimited).

In the case of a *limited liability partnership*, the partnership is a corporation, and the debts and other obligations of the partnership are those of the partnership itself and not of the individual partners. In other words, the personal liability of each partner is limited to the extent of his investment in the partnership.

Unlike traditional partnerships, limited liability partnerships cannot be created informally, but require an *incorporation document* which must be registered by the Registrar of Companies (even though it is not a company). Its name must end with either the words *limited liability partnership* or the letters *LLP*.

Part performance

See CONTRACT.

Passing off

The TORT of *passing off* originated as a specific form of INJURIOUS FALSE-HOOD, but in substance it is a form of what would now be regarded as unfair competition. It is committed by a person who carries on a business under such a name, or in such a manner, as to mislead the public into thinking that it is someone else's business.

PCA

PCA is a common abbreviation for the PARLIAMENTARY COMMISSIONER FOR ADMINISTRATION.

Penalty clause

See LIQUIDATED DAMAGES.

P

Per curiam

Where more than one judge sits in court, they may each give individual judgments. When this occurs, difficult questions of interpretation may arise before it is possible to identify the extent to which the judges agree (or disagree) with each other. However, propositions of law on which all the judges agree are said to be made *per curiam* (pronounced *per kewree-am*). This Latin phrase literally means *by the court*, but when used in the context of English Law, it means *by the court as a whole*.

Per incuriam

The Latin phrase *per incuriam* (pronounced *per in-kew-ree-am*) literally means *through lack of care*. However, in the context of the doctrine of BINDING PRECEDENT, the phrase has a more technical meaning, and is applied to a decision which is made in ignorance of a relevant, binding statute or previous decision. A court cannot declare that a decision which is binding on it was made *per incuriam*; but a court which is not bound by a decision can proceed not to follow that decision. (A court which does decide not to follow a decision in these circumstances will do so on the basis that the usual interests of JUDICIAL COMITY should give way to the fact that it was made *per incuriam*.)

Perjury

A person commits the criminal offence (see CRIME) of *perjury* if, having been lawfully sworn as a witness in judicial proceedings, he wilfully (or, in other words, not by mistake or carelessness) makes a statement which is false, provided that he either knew it was false or did not believe it to be true. Where the falsity or otherwise of the statement is in question, the judge (and not the jury) must decide the issue on an objective basis.

The requirement that the defendant must have been sworn is satisfied if he has affirmed or made a solemn declaration, instead of swearing an oath. The offence extends to making sworn statements which are preliminary to the hearing of the judicial proceedings themselves.

Personal property

Personal property (which is sometimes contracted to *personalty*) is any property which is not REAL PROPERTY.

Personal representative

A *personal representative* is responsible for administering the estate of someone who has died. Personal representatives are either executors or ADMINISTRATORS. A personal representative who obtains a grant of probate in respect of a WILL is an executor. A personal representative who obtains letters of administration on an INTESTACY (or letters of administration with the will annexed on a partial intestacy) is an administrator.

Personalty

See PERSONAL PROPERTY.

Persuasive authority

Courts which are aware of, but are not bound by, decisions of other courts (including those from other common law jurisdictions) may nevertheless treat those decisions as having *persuasive authority*.

See also BINDING PRECEDENT.

Petition of Right

See BILL OF RIGHTS 1689.

Plaintiff

Before the introduction of the CIVIL PROCEDURE RULES, someone who would now be called a CLAIMANT in a COUNTY COURT or the HIGH COURT would have been called a *plaintiff*.

Planning permission

Planning permission is required for *development*, which is defined as building, mining, engineering or other operations in, on, over, or under land; or the making of a material change of use in any land. When judging the materiality of a change of use, the test is whether it is material from a *planning* point of view.

Police and Judicial Co-operation in Criminal Matters

See EUROPEAN COMMUNITY AND EUROPEAN UNION.

Portion

A *portion* is property settled on the children (or the ISSUE) of the settlor, under a strict settlement (see SETTLEMENTS OF LAND).

Positivist theories of law

See NATURAL LAW.

P

Possession

The word *possession* has different shades of meaning in different contexts, but generally speaking it indicates both physical control of the thing possessed and the intention to exercise that control. In the case of land, it has an extended meaning under the Law of Property Act 1925, as a result of which a person is in possession of land if he receives, or is entitled to receive, rents and profits from it.

Possessory title

See ADVERSE POSSESSION and REGISTERED LAND.

Preliminary reference procedure

See EUROPEAN COURT OF JUSTICE.

Presumption of legality

Under the *presumption of legality*, it is assumed that people have acted lawfully unless and until the contrary is admitted, or proved to the satisfaction of a competent court, in accordance with the appropriate STANDARD OF PROOF. For example, anyone charged with a criminal offence (see CRIME) is presumed to be innocent until their guilt is proved beyond reasonable doubt.

The presumption is sometimes expressed in the form of the Latin maxim *omnia praesumuntur rite esse acta* (which may be pronounced *omnee- a pry-zoo-mun-tur ree-teh ess-eh ac-ta*). This may be translated as 'everything is presumed to have been done properly'.

Presumptions of statutory interpretation

The COMMON LAW has developed various principles which are usually gathered together under the heading of *presumptions of statutory interpretation*. There is no universally agreed list of these presumptions, but the following would typically be included:

- presumption against *injustice*;
- presumption against *absurdity*;
- presumption against *retrospectivity*;
- presumption of *strict interpretation of penal provisions*, with a particular sub-presumption that where Parliament creates a criminal offence which is silent as to MENS REA, there is a presumption that *mens rea* is an essential element of the offence;
- presumption against excluding access to the courts;
- presumption against interfering with fundamental rights;
- presumptions that CONSOLIDATING ACTS do not change the law (but there is no corresponding presumption in relation to codifying Acts);

- presumption that Parliament intends to comply with international law;
- presumption that Parliament intends to comply with EUROPEAN UNION law;
- presumption that a wrongdoer should not be allowed to gain an advantage from his wrongdoing;
- presumption that a statute does not bind the CROWN;
- presumption that a statute does not interfere with existing rights.

Primary legislation

The validity of *primary legislation* does not depend on any previous enactment. Legislation which does depend for its validity on some previous enactment, must, by definition, be *secondary legislation* (which is also known as *subordinate legislation* or DELEGATED LEGISLATION).

Privacy

Historically, English law has approached the protection of privacy indirectly, especially through the torts of libel and slander (see DEFAMATION) and BREACH OF CONFIDENCE.

Since the enactment of the HUMAN RIGHTS ACT 1998, however, English courts have been developing a right to *privacy* as such, based on art. 8 of the EUROPEAN CONVENTION ON HUMAN RIGHTS, which protects the right to respect for family and private life, one's home and one's correspondence. (For the full text of art. 8, see Appendix 3.)

Private Act

A *Private Act* is an ACT OF PARLIAMENT which relates to either specific localities (a local Act) or specific people (a personal Act).

Local authorities are among the most common promoters of local Acts. The purpose of a local authority Act will be to give that local authority powers which it would not otherwise have under the general law. Personal Acts are very rare, but a typical example would be an Act to permit two named people to marry each other, even though they are within the prohibited degrees of affinity.

Either kind of private Act will contain a preamble reciting the reasons for its enactment (even though such preambles are very seldom found in the context of a modern PUBLIC GENERAL ACT).

P

Private international law

See INTERNATIONAL LAW.

Private law

See PUBLIC LAW.

Privilege

The word *privilege* occurs in many legal contexts, but it always indicates some kind of immunity which would not exist if the privilege did not exist. For example, the law of EVIDENCE recognises a privilege against self-incrimination (which means that nobody who is giving evidence can be required to answer any question which may incriminate himself). Similarly, legal professional privilege protects solicitors and barristers from having to disclose information provided to them by their clients.

See also DEFAMATION, INJURIOUS FALSEHOOD; and PARLIAMENTARY PRIVILEGE.

Privity of contract

At common law (and leaving aside for the moment a relatively recent statutory intervention) the general doctrine was that only a party to a contract could sue, or be sued, on the contract. Using rather old-fashioned language, this idea can be expressed by saying that only those who are *privy to a contract* can sue on it, and it is this form of words which gives rise to the standard label for the doctrine, namely *privity of contract*.

Privity of contract, which is very closely connected with the rule that CONSIDERATION *must move from the promisee*, is eminently sensible to the extent that it stops busybodies interfering in other people's affairs; but it is also capable of working substantial injustice in some cases. Suppose, for example, that A promises to pay a sum of money to B in return for B's promise to look after A's children after A's death. Suppose that when A dies, B fails to honour his promise to look after the children. The children were not party to the contract (and therefore the doctrine of privity of contract says that they cannot sue to enforce the contract between A and B); and this conclusion is reinforced by the fact that they have given no consideration for A's promise.

The Contracts (Rights of Third Parties) Act 1999 made some inroads into the doctrine of privity of contract by providing that (subject to exceptions in relation to certain types of contract), a third party can enforce a contract which either expressly confers a benefit on, or purports to give a legally enforceable right to, the third party (provided, in the latter case that, on the proper construction of the contract, it actually has that effect).

Privity of estate

See LEASEHOLD COVENANTS.

Privy Council

The *Privy Council* is an ancient body whose functions are, in practice, almost entirely formal, being limited to approving decisions which have already been made elsewhere. It normally meets in the presence of the Queen. The formal nature of the Privy Council's business is reflected in the fact that only a handful of members attend the vast majority of meetings, and the presence of the Queen is reflected in the fact that the members remain standing throughout the proceedings.

There is no closed category of potential members, but, in practice, Privy Councillors (who are appointed for life) are drawn principally from the ranks of senior politicians. Additionally, however, and by convention, the Archbishops of Canterbury and York, together with the judges who head each of the divisions of the COURT OF APPEAL and of the HIGH COURT, also become members.

The *Judicial Committee of the Privy Council* functions as the final court of appeal from United Kingdom overseas territories and Crown dependencies, and from those Commonwealth countries which have chosen to retain the possibility of appeal to either the Queen in Council or (in the case of Republics) to the Judicial Committee in its own name. It also has jurisdiction over certain appeals which arise, for example, from the ecclesiastical courts of the Church of England, and from the Royal College of Veterinary Surgeons' disciplinary procedure.

The Judicial Committee originally had jurisdiction in respect of disputes arising from DEVOLUTION to Northern Ireland, Scotland and Wales. In October 2009, however, this jurisdiction was transferred to the newly established SUPREME COURT.

The Committee consists of the Justices of the SUPREME COURT together with retired LORDS OF APPEAL IN ORDINARY and some senior judges from those jurisdictions from which it remains the final court of appeal. It normally functions through panels of three members, who do not remain standing during the proceedings (which may, of course, occupy several days).

P

Probate

A grant of *probate* is the document, obtained from the PROBATE REGISTRY, which authorises an executor (see PERSONAL REPRESENTATIVE) to administer the estate of someone who has died having left a WILL.

Probate, Divorce and Admiralty Division

See HIGH COURT.

Probate Registry

The *Probate Registry* is that part of Her Majesty's Courts Service which deals with grants of PROBATE and letters of administration (see ADMINISTRATOR).

Procedural fairness

Procedural fairness (or *procedural propriety*) embraces the two doctrines previously known as *natural justice* and *procedural ultra vires*.

Natural justice (which is not at all the same thing as NATURAL LAW) has three elements, namely

- the right to a hearing;
- the rule against bias; and
- the right to be given reasons for a decision.

The *right to a hearing* means the right to present one's case and does not necessarily involve the right to be heard orally. In many situations, the right to make written representations will be sufficient. However, an oral hearing will be appropriate where there is conflicting evidence on matters of fact (because the demeanour of witnesses when they give evidence and the way they cope with cross-examination may both be useful indicators of their credibility).

A person who is being given a hearing must be given adequate notice of both

- the date, place and time of the hearing (or the last date and time for the submission of written representations), so that he can prepare his case; and
- the case which he will have to answer (and the decision which is made must be based on this information).

The *rule against bias* is breached if a fair-minded and informed observer, having considered the facts, would conclude that there was a *real possibility* that the tribunal was biased.

The *right to be given reasons* after a decision has been made is the weakest of the three rules, because the court accepts that sometimes a decision may be based on matters such as experience and professional judgment. Nevertheless, wherever it is possible to do so, a person affected by a decision should be given sufficient information to allow him to assess the legality of the decision-making process and, where an appeal is available, decide whether there are grounds for appeal. Additionally, the duty to give reasons concentrates the decision-maker's mind on precisely what the reasons are.

The doctrine of procedural ULTRA VIRES states that a decision-maker who fails to comply with specific procedural requirements laid down by STATUTE or DELEGATED LEGISLATION, is acting unlawfully. However, whether the resulting decision is VOID or merely voidable (see VOID) depends on whether the requirement which has been breached is *mandatory* (or, in other words, compulsory) or merely *directory* (or, in other words, *advisory* or *optional*).

Procedural law

Although many areas of law are concerned with matters of *substance* (for example, what the prosecution must prove in order to secure a conviction for MURDER) and so are called SUBSTANTIVE LAW, many other areas are concerned with *procedural* matters (for example, what EVIDENCE will the court be willing to admit when deciding whether the prosecution has proved that the DEFENDANT has committed murder), and so are often called *procedural law*. An older term for *procedural law* is *adjectival law*.

Profit à prendre

The French phrase *profit à prendre* (which is often pronounced in a hybrid way with the first two words being given an English pronunciation and the final word being pronounced *prond-ruh*) means the right to take something from another person's land. Typical examples of profits include profits of *piscary* (to take fish), of *estovers* (to take wood) and of *pasture* (whose meaning is self-evident).

Although profits have obvious similarities with EASEMENTS, they are a distinct legal concept. More particularly, an easement must always serve a dominant tenement, whereas profits may – but do not have to – do so.

P

A profit that does benefit another piece of land is called a *profit appurtenant* (with both words usually being pronounced as if they were English).

A profit that does not benefit another piece of land is called a *profit in gross* (again, with an English pronunciation). For example, A can have a profit of pasture against B's land whether or not A owns any land.

Where the owner of the land which is subject to the profit can also take whatever it is that the owner of the profit can take, the profit is said to be *in common*. Where only the owner of the profit has the right, the profit is said to be *sole*.

Prohibiting order

A *prohibiting order* is available by way of JUDICIAL REVIEW to prohibit the respondent from acting unlawfully in the future. (Before the introduction of the CIVIL PROCEDURE RULES, a prohibiting order was known as *prohibition*.)

Prohibition

See PROHIBITING ORDER.

Proper law of a contract

The phrase *proper law of a contract* refers to the legal system under which any disputes arising from the contract will be resolved. In most cases there will, of course, be little or no doubt as to the proper law of a contract. However, where such a doubt does arise, it will usually be resolved by reference to either whatever the parties to the contract agreed, or the legal system with which the contract has its closest and most real connection.

Property

The word *property* is applied to anything which can be owned. Some legal systems classify property into that which is movable and that which is immovable. In English Law, however, the major division is into REAL PROPERTY and PERSONAL PROPERTY.

Proportionality

The doctrine of *proportionality* is part of the Roman Law tradition, and therefore features prominently in both EUROPEAN UNION law and the law of the EUROPEAN CONVENTION ON HUMAN RIGHTS. The doctrine of proportionality is often used as a weapon with which to attack governmental action on the basis that less severe action would have achieved the desired objective and therefore the action which has actually been taken is disproportionate.

So, for example, the EUROPEAN COURT OF JUSTICE held that the principle of proportionality was breached by a scheme which required people to offer security to ensure they performed a particular obligation but also required them to forfeit the whole security, irrespective of the scale of their breach.

Similarly, the EUROPEAN COURT OF HUMAN RIGHTS held that although the United Kingdom government's relaxation of restrictions on night flights at London's Heathrow airport had some beneficial effect on the national economy, this was not sufficient to outweigh the rights (under art. 8 of the European Convention on Human Rights) of those people whose sleep was disturbed by the resulting increase in aircraft noise.

Prosecution

The word *prosecution* almost always refers to criminal (see CRIME) proceedings. However, there are a few situations in which it can properly be used in relation to CIVIL LAW proceedings. For example, where a CLAIMANT begins civil proceedings but is very slow in pursuing them, they may be struck out *for want of prosecution*; and the TORT of MALICIOUS PROSECUTION may be available in respect of some civil proceedings.

Provocation

Provocation is available as a defence to MURDER and to no other charge. Where the plea succeeds, it has the effect of reducing the charge to MAN-SLAUGHTER, to which it is then a guilty plea.

Provocation arises where the defendant loses his self-control as a result of things done or things said, or a combination of the two. In any case, the things that were done or said (or both done and said) must have been such that they would cause a reasonable man or woman to lose his or her self-control. Age and sex are the only personal characteristics of the defendant which the jury are allowed to take into account. This restriction prevents defendants from relying on their personal defects of character (such as racial prejudice and homophobia) in order to excuse their conduct.

Public general Act

A *public general Act* is an ACT OF PARLIAMENT which is of importance to the whole community. However, it need not affect everyone within the community. For example, an Act authorising a professional body to regulate entry to a profession will be a public general Act even though only a very small number of people will be seeking entry to that profession.

There is a presumption that a public general Act forms part of the law of the whole United Kingdom (which comprises three separate legal systems, namely those of England and Wales, Scotland and Northern Ireland). It is, therefore, standard drafting practice to include an express provision excluding Scotland or Northern Ireland (or both), where it is appropriate to do so. This exclusion will be found towards the end of an Act, under the heading of *Application* or *Application and Extent*. Although it is not necessary to do so, some drafters include express statements when an Act *does* extend to Scotland or Northern Ireland or both.

The *extent* of an Act is not the same thing as its *application*, with the latter governing the activities to which the Act applies. For example, the Sexual Offences Act 2003 provides that certain conduct will constitute criminal offences in both England and Wales, and Northern Ireland, provided that (a) it constitutes an offence under the law of the country where the conduct occurs; and (b) it would also constitute a sexual offence if it occurred in England and Wales, or Northern Ireland. (Broadly speaking, the relevant conduct involves sexual offences against children and young people.) A provision of this kind deals with *application* rather than *extent*.

Public interest immunity

The doctrine of *public interest immunity* (which is often abbreviated to *PII* and which used to be called *Crown privilege*) permits evidence to be withheld under certain circumstances.

More particularly, PII may arise in cases where the DEFENDANT is the CROWN (in the sense of the EXECUTIVE or CENTRAL GOVERNMENT) or some other body which operates in the public interest. Such defendants may claim that the public interest requires certain evidence to be withheld from the court, even though this would breach the basic principle that the best available evidence should always be put before the court.

At one time there were two grounds on which such a claim could be made. One was that the evidence belonged to a class of evidence which was of such a nature that it should not be put into the public domain by being produced in court, while the other was that the nature of the evidence itself was such that it should not be produced. Furthermore, the courts' deference to the executive used to be such that they would accept without question a certificate, signed by a MINISTER OF THE CROWN, to the effect that the evidence should not be produced.

However, attitudes to Crown privilege changed, partly because the doctrine came to be applied to other defendants (including non-governmental bodies such as the National Society for the Prevention of Cruelty to Children) and partly because the use of the word *privilege* conveyed a rather dated impression of the doctrine. Additionally, the courts became much less happy to accept Ministerial certificates.

The modern practice is for PII not to be claimed on class grounds, and, in other cases, for the court itself to consider the evidence in question (rather than simply accepting the view of the Crown) before deciding whether it should be put into the public domain by being used in the case.

Public international law

See INTERNATIONAL LAW.

Public law

Public law is that part of the law which deals with the structure, powers, duties and activities of the state. All other areas of law are *private law*.

Puisne judge

The old French word *puisne* (pronounced as if it were the English word *puny*), simply means *junior*. Curiously, however, judges of the HIGH COURT are called *puisne judges*. A puisne judge's formal style is *Mr* (or *Mrs*) *Justice Black*, which is written in either case as *Black J*. However, the correct oral style when speaking *about* a puisne judge is *Mr (or Mrs) Justice Black*, or *His Lordship* (or *Her Ladyship*) and when speaking *to* a judge it is *My Lord* (or *My Lady*) or *Your Lordship* (or *Your Ladyship*), depending on the grammatical requirements of the sentence.

It is simply wrong to describe a High Court judge as either *Judge Black* (because this is the correct style for a CIRCUIT JUDGE) or as *Justice Black* (because this is the correct style for a judge of the SUPREME COURT).

Punitive damages

See DAMAGES.

Pur autre vie

The old French expression *pur autre vie* (the anglicised pronunciation of which is *poor oh-ter-vye*, although some lawyers prefer the original French pronunciation) may be translated as *for the life of another*. So, for example, if A has an interest in land which will terminate when B dies, A's interest is *pur autre vie*. An interest *pur autre vie* can be only an equitable interest (see INTERESTS IN LAND).

Purchaser

Although the word *purchaser* can be used in a legal context with its every-day meaning of *buyer*, it can also have a more technical meaning in the context of REAL PROPERTY law.

More particularly, in this context, a purchaser is someone who obtains ownership of property as the result of someone else's action, rather than by operation of law. For example, if A inherits property under the WILL of T, he obtains the property as a result of T having made his will so as to achieve that result. In other words, he obtains the property by *purchase*, or he is a *purchaser*.

On the other hand, if A inherits property from X when X has died without leaving a will, he obtains the property because he comes within the rules governing INTESTACY contained in the Administration of Estates Act 1925. In other words, he obtains the property *by operation of law* and is not, therefore, a purchaser.

Applying the same underlying approach, someone who lends money on a MORTGAGE (a *mortgagee*) acquires his interest in the property as a result of the borrower (or *mortgagor*) executing the mortgage by way of providing security for the loan, and so he is a purchaser.

Of course, in the vast majority of cases, a purchaser in the technical sense is also be a purchaser in the everyday sense.

The principal significance of being a purchaser in the technical sense is that it can trigger the operation of the doctrine of the *bona fide purchaser of the legal estate for value without notice of an equitable interest*. And this is important because such a purchaser takes the legal estate without being bound by any equitable interest of which he has no notice.

Notice of an equitable interest can be obtained in various ways. First, a purchaser of a legal estate will be bound by an equitable interest if

- the interest is registrable (whether at the Land Registry or the Land Charges Registry, depending on whether title to the land is registered or unregistered); and
- it is actually registered.

This principle is absolute. It therefore has the effect of placing very firmly on the purchaser the burden of searching the relevant Register.

Furthermore, a purchaser will not be bound by an equitable interest which is registrable but not registered, *even if he does know about it*. This principle is also absolute.

Where interests are not registrable, there are three ways in which a purchaser can acquire notice of an equitable interest.

First, he may have *actual knowledge* of the equitable interest.

Secondly, he may have *constructive knowledge* of the equitable interest. Constructive knowledge arises where the purchaser does not actually know of the equitable interest but ought to have done so. For example, it may be something he would have discovered if he had investigated title to the land properly, whereas in fact he did so carelessly by accepting a root of title which did not meet the requirement of being at least 15 years old (and so was not a GOOD ROOT OF TITLE).

Thirdly he may have *imputed knowledge* of the equitable interest. The classic case of imputed knowledge is where the purchaser's solicitor has knowledge of an equitable interest but fails to communicate this knowledge to the purchaser. The solicitor's knowledge will, nevertheless, be imputed to the purchaser. In this situation, the purchaser may well have an action in professional negligence against his solicitor, but this merely serves to reinforce – and certainly does not detract from – what is being said here about the doctrine of notice.

A purchaser of a legal estate who does not have either actual, constructive or imputed notice of an equitable interest which is not registrable will not be bound by that interest provided he acts *bona fide* (which may be pronounced *boh-na fy-dee* and means, literally, *in good faith*, or, in other words, *honestly*).

Unfortunately, the word *value* has no fixed meaning in the context of property law. Sometimes it has its obvious meaning of *money or money's worth*, but sometimes it also includes marriage.

P

QB (or QBD)

QB was originally the abbreviation for the court of *Queen's Bench*. However, since the Judicature Act 1873, it (or its variant in the form of *QBD*) has been the abbreviation for the Queen's Bench Division of the HIGH COURT.

QC

See QUEEN'S COUNSEL.

Qualified privilege

See DEFAMATION.

Qualified title

See REGISTERED LAND.

Quantum

Quantum (pronounced *kwon-tum*) is Latin for *amount* and is most commonly used in relation to damages, in sentences such as: 'The defendant having admitted liability, the only dispute was as to quantum'.

Quantum meruit

The Latin phrase *quantum meruit* (pronounced *kwon-tum mehr-oo-it*) means *as much as is deserved*. So, for example, where the parties have entered into a contract for the painting of a house but the contractual relationship breaks down before the job is finished, the decorator will clearly not have earned the full payment due under the contract. She may, however, claim on a *quantum meruit* basis, for the value of the work she has already done.

Quarter days

The standard *quarter days* (on which tenancies often begin and end, and on which rents – especially in respect of commercial properties – are often payable) are

- 25 March (Lady Day);
- 24 June (Midsummer Day);
- 29 September (Michaelmas Day); and
- 25 December (Christmas Day),

although there are some local variations in different parts of the country with regard to Lady Day and Michaelmas Day.

Since most readers of this book (whether or not they come from the Christian tradition) will have no difficulty in remembering that Christmas Day falls on 25 December, all that is necessary in order to remember the other three standard dates is the knowledge that they all fall on the twenty-something of the month at three monthly intervals. The precise date is then given by the number of letters in the name of the relevant month: *25* for Lady Day in M a r c h; *24* for Midsummer's Day in J u n e; and *29* for Michaelmas Day in S e p t e m b e r.

Quarter Sessions

The court of *Quarter Sessions* (which as the name implies had to be held at least four times a year, although in practice it was commonly held more frequently) was abolished by the Courts Act 1971, along with the *Assize courts*. The jurisdictions of both were merged and transferred to the newly-created CROWN COURT.

Quashing order

Where the court wishes to quash a decision or order as a result of a successful claim for JUDICIAL REVIEW, it will make a *quashing order*. Before the introduction of the CIVIL PROCEDURE RULES, the same result was achieved by an order called *certiorari*, which may be pronounced *sur-shore-air-eye*.

Q

Quasi-contract

See OBLIGATIONS and RESTITUTION.

Quasi-judicial decision-making

See ADMINISTRATIVE DECISION-MAKING.

Queen's Bench Division

See HIGH COURT.

Queen's Counsel

The rank of *Queen's Counsel* (or QC) may be awarded to barristers and solicitors who have demonstrated excellence in a specified range of competencies, as demonstrated by their experience of advocacy in the higher courts.

Applications are considered by an independent panel consisting of both lawyers and non-lawyers. The panel makes its decisions on the basis of evidence which has been gathered from those who have seen the applicant 'in action', and which it then assesses against the competencies. The recommendations of the panel go to the Queen (*via* the Secretary of State for Justice) for the issue of letters patent.

There are few formal advantages to being a QC, although the holder of this rank may expect to receive better quality work for which she can expect to be able to charge higher fees.

Solicitors and academic lawyers may also be appointed as honorary QCs, but these appointments are entirely matters for the Secretary of State for Justice and do not involve the panel which considers applications from practising lawyers.

QCs wear gowns made of silk rather than ordinary cloth (or *stuff*) and are, therefore, often called *silks*. The process of becoming a QC is called *taking silk*.

Barristers, but not solicitors, who do not take silk are called *juniors*, however old or experienced (or both) they are.

Naturally, when the monarch is male, the terminology changes to *King's Counsel* and *KC*.

Quia timet **injunction**

The Latin phrase *quia timet* (which may be pronounced *kwee-a tim-et*) means *because he fears*. A *quia timet injunction* is, therefore, granted to someone who has not yet suffered harm but is in fear of doing so imminently.

Because no harm has yet been suffered, it is very difficult to persuade the court to grant a *quia timet* injunction.

Quorum

The Latin word *quorum* (pronounced *kwor-um*) means *of whom*, and refers to the number of members who must be present at a meeting of a committee or similar body for the meeting to be able to transact its business validly (or, in other words, to be *quorate* – pronounced *kwor-ate*). If the rules governing a specific committee or similar body do not specify the number of members who will constitute a quorum, the default position at COMMON LAW is that a majority of members must be present.

Q

R

R as the first element in a case name is an abbreviation for one of two Latin words, namely *Rex* (pronounced in the obvious way, and meaning *the King*) or *Regina* (pronounced *redge-eye-na* and meaning *the Queen*), according to the sex of the monarch who was reigning at the time of the case.

Rack rent

The *rack rent* of a property is the full commercial rent which could be obtained for it on the open market.

Rape

This entry deals not only with *rape*, but also with *assault by penetration*, and *sexual assault*.

A person commits *rape* if (a) he intentionally penetrates the vagina, anus or mouth of another person (who, in the case of anal or oral penetration, may be either male or female) with his penis; and (b) the complainant does not consent to the penetration and the accused does not reasonably believe that the complainant consents. Both the elements of (b) must be present, so there is no offence if the complainant does not actually consent but the accused reasonably believes that he or she did so. The reasonableness of the accused's belief is determined by having regard to all the circumstances, including any steps which the accused undertook to ascertain whether the complainant consented.

Consent means agreement by choice, given by someone who has the freedom and capacity to make that choice. Thus, for example, the fact that the complainant agreed by mistake, or under DURESS, will not constitute a defence.

There are two sets of circumstances giving rise to presumptions relating to consent. The presumptions arising in one set can be rebutted by evidence, while those arising in the other are conclusive (or, in other words, cannot be rebutted).

The rebuttable presumptions arise where the accused did the relevant act when, to the knowledge of the accused, any of the following circumstances existed:

- at the time of (or immediately before) the relevant act, anyone was using violence against either the complainant or another person;
- at the time of (or immediately before) the relevant act, the complainant had cause to believe, and did in fact believe, that violence was being, or would be, used by anyone against another person;
- at the time of the relevant act, the complainant was, but the accused was not, unlawfully detained;
- at the time of the relevant act, the complainant was asleep, or otherwise unconscious;
- at the time of the relevant act, the complainant was unable, by reason of physical disability, to communicate to the accused whether or not he or she was consenting;
- at the time of the relevant act, any person had administered to (or caused to be taken by) the complainant, any substance which was capable of causing or enabling the complainant to be stupefied or overcome.

The presumptions are that (a) the complainant did not consent, unless sufficient evidence is adduced to raise an issue as to whether he or she did so; and (b) the accused did not reasonably believe that the complainant was consenting unless sufficient evidence is adduced to raise an issue as to whether he or she did so.

The conclusive presumptions arise when it is proved that the accused did the relevant act and he either (a) intentionally deceived the complainant as to the nature or purpose of that act, or (b) intentionally induced the complainant to consent to the relevant act by impersonating someone whom the complainant knew personally. Under these circumstances it is irrebuttably presumed that the complainant did not consent to the relevant act.

A person commits the offence of *assault by penetration* if he penetrates the vagina or anus of another person with part of his body (other than his penis – which would, of course, make the offence one of rape – but including, for example, a finger) or by anything else (or, in other words, any object), and the penetration is *sexual*. For these purposes, penetration is *sexual* where either a reasonable person would consider either (a) that it is, in its nature, sexual; or (b) that it may or may not be, in its nature, sexual, but either the circumstances or the purpose of the person doing the touching, (or both) show(s) that it is sexual.

R

In accordance with first principles of ASSAULT, there will be no liability if the person who is touched has consented to the touching, so it is relevant to notice that the provisions relating to consent in relation to *rape* are equally applicable here.

There is another, lesser, offence of *sexual assault*, which occurs where a person (a) intentionally touches another person and (b) the touching is sexual. The issue of whether touching is *sexual* is determined in the same way as the issue of whether penetration is sexual for the purposes of the offence of *assault by penetration*.

As with *assault by penetration*, it is relevant to notice that the provisions relating to consent for *rape* are equally applicable here.

There are specific provisions relating to sexual offences against people below the age of 16, and people suffering from mental disorder. There are also specific provisions relating to sexual offences committed by members of a complainant's family or by people (such as care workers) who are in a position of trust in relation to complainants.

Ratification

1 In English domestic law, where someone who has no power to make a decision nevertheless purports to do so, a person who did have power to make the decision may subsequently *ratify* (or in other words, *adopt*), the purported decision, thus making it effective.

One classic example of ratification in this sense arises where an AGENT enters into a CONTRACT which is beyond the scope of his authority. His principal will become bound by the contract if he subsequently *ratifies* it.

Another relatively common situation arises where a committee which is *inquorate* (for the meaning of *inquorate*, see QUORUM) nevertheless proceeds to deal with its agenda. A subsequent meeting of the committee which *is* quorate may ratify the decisions of the previous meeting (although, of course, no executive action may lawfully be taken in respect of those decisions in the meantime).

2 In Public international law (see INTERNATIONAL LAW), the formal adoption of treaties involves a two-stage process. The first stage is for the representatives of the contracting states to sign a treaty as soon as the negotiations leading to the treaty are concluded and the treaty (as a document) has come into existence. The second stage is for the contracting states to go through whatever process is prescribed by their own constitutions in order to decide whether or not they wish to ratify the treaty. A treaty does not usually become legally effective

unless and until it is ratified, although some treaties provide that they shall come into effect when a specified number of contracting states have ratified them.

Ratio decidendi

See BINDING PRECEDENT.

Real consent

Many medical and surgical procedures involve conduct which, apart from the patient's consent, would be unlawful (as constituting ASSAULT or BATTERY or both).

Historically, the courts approached this problem in terms of *informed consent*, on the basis that a patient who is not informed of the risks which attach to the procedure he is to undergo cannot be truly said to have consented.

However, the House of Lords has rejected the doctrine of *informed consent*, saying that the issue in each case was whether the patient's consent was *real*. More particularly, a doctor is not required to advise his patient of all the risks. Provided there is a respectable body of medical opinion to the effect that it is proper to withhold information relating to a specific risk (typically, because the risk is so remote that advice as to its existence can properly be withheld) the patient's consent will still be regarded as being *real*.

Real property

Originally, the common law divided all property into *real property* (which is sometimes contracted to *realty*) and *personal property* (which is sometimes elided to *personalty*). The essence of the distinction was that where a claim (for example, in trespass) related to *real* property the court could make an order restoring the property to the claimant, but if it related only to *personal* property, the court could do no more than award damages.

The origin of the word *real* in this context lies in the fact that the Latin word for *thing* is *res* (pronounced *rays*) which became the English word *real*, so restoring a claimant to the thing itself was achieved by a *real* remedy. Admittedly, over time this simple distinction became somewhat blurred, with *real remedies* becoming available in respect of leasehold property (despite the fact that the essence of a LEASE is a contract); and equity making the remedy of SPECIFIC PERFORMANCE available in some contractual disputes, even though they dealt only with personal property.

Nevertheless, the origin of the distinction continues to provide a useful explanation of the meaning of the word *real*.

Realty

See REAL PROPERTY.

Reasonable man

The phrase *reasonable man* (which came into use long before the requirements of gender neutrality came to prominence) indicates an *objective* test. So, for example, where the law of NEGLIGENCE tests the requirement of *foreseeability* by the standards of the reasonable man, the extent of what the defendant actually did (or did not) foresee is irrelevant, because the key question is what a reasonable person in the defendant's position should have foreseen.

The *man on the Clapham omnibus* is the classic alternative phrase for the *reasonable man*, but the *passenger on the Clapham omnibus* provides a gender-neutral version. However, it is difficult to see what is wrong with simply talking about the *reasonable person*.

Recitals

Legal documents, and particularly DEEDS, may begin with *recitals*, which form an introductory narrative, explaining why the parties consider the document to be necessary. However, recitals are not essential to any category of documents, and they are often omitted where there is nothing to justify their inclusion. Each paragraph of the recitals will commonly, but not necessarily, begin with the word *whereas*.

The effect of recitals is very similar to that of preambles to statutes. More particularly, they cannot prevail over the clear meanings of words contained in the body of the document, but can be used to resolve ambiguities created by those words.

R

Recklessness

See MENS REA.

Recognisance

A *recognisance* is an undertaking to pay a specified sum of money if some specified thing does (or does not) happen within (or at) a specified time.

One example is given in the entry for BAIL. Another one arises where a court binds someone over to keep the peace. Part of this process involves the person concerned *entering into a recognisance*, so that (taking a figure and a period at random) they agree to be bound over in the sum of £200 for 12 months.

Recorder

A *recorder* is the lowest rank of part-time judge in the Crown Court.

Registered land

Strictly speaking, the phrase *registered land* is inaccurate, since it is the *title* to land, and not the land itself, which is either *registered* or *unregistered*. However, the phrase is firmly established as shorthand for *land with registered title*. Similarly, land to which the title is *unregistered* is very often called *unregistered land*.

Title to land may be registered with different grades. The main grades are *absolute title*, *possessory title* and *qualified title*, with the additional possibility of *good leasehold title*.

Absolute title is such that the Registrar is sufficiently confident as to ownership at first registration that he is prepared to guarantee title.

Possessory title is such that the owner at first registration had nothing other than the fact of possession to prove his ownership, and accordingly the Registrar is not willing to guarantee anything before first registration.

Qualified title is such that the Registrar has a specific reason to doubt ownership at first registration.

In the case of leasehold title (see LEASE), the additional possibility of *good leasehold* arises where the leasehold was granted out of a freehold (see ESTATES IN LAND) which was neither registered nor proved, but the Registrar nevertheless takes the view that the leasehold is such that a competent professional could advise a willing buyer to accept it.

Registered title

See REGISTERED LAND.

Regulations (European Community and European Union law)

Regulations are the form of Community law that most closely resembles STATUTES within the English legal system, but Community Regulations nevertheless differ from English statutes in one important respect. Under the doctrine of the LEGISLATIVE SUPREMACY OF PARLIAMENT, the English courts have no power to quash Acts of Parliament (because it is Parliament and not the courts which are supreme). Under Community law, on the other hand, the EUROPEAN COURT OF JUSTICE does have power to quash Community Regulations which fail to comply with Community law.

See DIRECT APPLICABILITY AND DIRECT EFFECT OF EUROPEAN COMMUNITY AND EUROPEAN UNION LAW and SOURCES OF EUROPEAN COMMUNITY AND EUROPEAN UNION LAW.

Rehabilitation of Offenders Act 1974

The purpose of the *Rehabilitation of Offenders Act 1974* is to allow people with relatively minor criminal convictions to be treated, for most purposes, as if they do not have a criminal record, once a specified period of time has elapsed.

More particularly, all criminal convictions, except those resulting in a sentence of imprisonment of more than 30 months, become *spent* at the end of the *rehabilitation period.*

The length of the rehabilitation period depends upon the sentence, with the longest period being 10 years (for sentences of imprisonment of more than 6 months but not more than 30 months) down to 6 months for an absolute discharge and, where an order of disqualification of any kind is imposed, the duration of the order. Some rehabilitation periods are reduced where the offender is a MINOR.

The effect of a conviction becoming spent is commonly misunderstood. The conviction is *not* expunged from the record, but the circumstances in which it can be legitimately referred to are strictly limited. More particularly, in most CIVIL LAW proceedings, neither a party nor a witness may be asked any question where the answer would involve disclosing that he has a spent conviction; and, if such a question is asked, he may refuse to answer it. Similarly, an applicant for a job who is asked whether he has any criminal convictions, may, generally speaking, answer the question without referring to spent convictions.

There are, however, several sensitive areas (such as certain judicial proceedings relating to children, employment within the legal profession and the administration of justice, and employment which brings the offender into close contact with children and other vulnerable people) which are excluded from the scope of the Act.

When a convicted defendant's previous convictions are read out in court, it is common practice to present only those convictions which are *not* spent, unless the court feels the public interest requires that spent convictions should also be mentioned.

Remainder

An interest in *remainder* is one which comes into possession only on the expiry of some prior interest. For example, if property is given to A for life and then to B absolutely, B's interest is in remainder while A is alive (and B, to use a term which originated before the days of gender neutral language, is the *remainderman*).

Remand

See BAIL.

Remoteness of damage

Where A's unlawful conduct harms B, the question will sometimes arise as to whether the harm is too remote for the law to take it into account. The rules as to *remoteness of damage* vary according to the context, but the positions in both TORT and CONTRACT can be outlined quite briefly. In the context of torts, such as NEGLIGENCE, where liability does not depend on the intention of the defendant, the test is whether the harm was a *reasonably foreseeable* consequence of the defendant's conduct. In the case of torts, such as DECEIT, where liability does depend on the intention of the defendant, the test is whether the harm is a *direct* result of the defendant's conduct.

In the context of contract, there are alternative tests. The first is whether the harm is such as may be fairly and reasonably considered as arising in the ordinary course of things from the defendant's breach of contract. The second is whether the harm is such as may be reasonably supposed to have been within the contemplation of the parties (when they entered into the contract) as being a probable result of it being breached.

Rent

Rent comes in two forms. The first, and most obvious, is the money paid by a tenant to his landlord, which is technically called *rent service* but which is commonly called simply *rent*.

Secondly, however, there is the possibility of a *rentcharge*, which is a sum of money payable (usually annually) by the current owner of land.

Creating rentcharges was one way in which landowners could provide for their dependants, by selling land subject to the purchaser accepting an obligation to pay a specified and recurrent sum either for a fixed period or in perpetuity. Furthermore, this obligation would take the form of a charge on the land, so that payment would be secured against anyone who was the owner of the land for the time being. Obviously, the existence of a rentcharge is likely to mean that anyone buying the land will pay a reduced price for it, with the amount of the reduction reflecting the amount of the rentcharge

The Rentcharges Act 1977 prohibited the creation of new rentcharges but did not affect the existence or enforceability of existing ones.

Rentcharge

See RENT.

Rescind

See RESCISSION.

Rescission

A CONTRACT which has been entered into as a result of either a misrepresentation or a mistake may be subject to *rescission* by either one of the parties or the court.

Rescission has the effect of setting aside the contract altogether, with regard to both the past and the future. This means that both parties must return to the other any benefit which they have obtained under the contract up to the date of rescission. It follows from this that there can be no rescission where such restitution is impossible (for example, because one party has received property which he no longer owns).

Res ipsa loquitur

The Latin phrase *res ipsa loquitur* (which may be pronounced *rays (or reez) ip-sa lock-wit-ur*) means *the thing speaks for itself*. It is used in the TORT of NEGLIGENCE where an accident has happened in a situation which is under the management of the defendant, and the accident is of a kind which does not happen in the ordinary course of things – for example, where scaffolding collapses – unless someone has failed to exercise proper care. In situations of this kind, it is open to the court to find negligence on the part of the defendant even though there is no precise evidence as to the exact conduct which constitutes that negligence.

Res judicata

The Latin phrase *res judicata* (which may be pronounced *rays jew-di-carta*) is the name of the COMMON LAW doctrine which prevents cases from being reopened once they have been finally dealt with by the courts. The doctrine states that once a court has made a decision which disposes of a case, and, where there is the possibility of an appeal, the time within which notice of appeal must be given has expired, the decision is final and binding.

The doctrine of *res judicata* must not be confused with the doctrine of *binding precedent*, which is concerned with striking a balance between promoting certainty as to the law on the one hand, and allowing individual courts sufficient flexibility to deal sensibly with cases on the other.

Restitution

Towards the end of the 20th century, the name of *restitution* came to be applied to an area of law which provides remedies in cases where one party has unjustly enriched himself to the detriment of another, but where there was no contract.

Many cases which now come within the scope of restitution would previously have been classified as *quasi-contract* and would have been called, more particularly, *claims for money had and received*.

Restorative justice

Restorative justice takes place within the context of the criminal justice system. It functions by bringing together everyone who has a stake in a particular conflict or offence in order to identify both the most appropriate way to deal with its aftermath and any implications it may have for the future.

More particularly, offenders are confronted with the impact that their conduct has had on their victims and given the opportunity to make reparation, while victims gain the opportunity to have the impact on their lives acknowledged, as well as receiving any amends which offenders are able to make. By promoting interpersonal contact between offenders and their victims, restorative justice seeks to break down 'them and us' mindsets.

R

Restrictive covenants relating to freehold land

A *restrictive COVENANT* is negative (in the sense that it restricts the use of land) while a positive covenant requires someone to do something. An initial difficulty arises from the fact that the way a covenant is expressed does not necessarily reveal its true nature. For example, a covenant to maintain a piece of land as an open space is positive in form but negative in substance, since its effect is to prevent building on the land. In other words it is a *restrictive* covenant, despite its *positive* form.

Restrictive covenants cause no problems while the original parties retain ownership of the pieces of land concerned (because they are both bound in accordance with the ordinary principles of contract), but the position is more complicated where either or both of the original parties are no longer the owners.

Some, but not all, of the rules require a distinction to be drawn between the land which has the benefit of the covenant and the land which has the burden of the covenant. (In the example given above, the land which cannot be built upon has the burden, while its neighbour has the benefit.) Additionally, the position differs in some respects between COMMON LAW and equity.

The basic rules may be outlined as follows.

- At common law
    - the *benefit* of a covenant passes with (or as it is usually said, *runs with*) the land when ownership passes to a successor-in-title of the party who entered into the covenant, provided the covenant relates to (or, as it is usually said, *touches and concerns*) the land (rather than being merely a personal obligation as between the original parties); but
    - the *burden* of a covenant does not run with the land in any case, and
    - both principles apply equally to both positive and negative covenants.
- In equity
    - the *benefit* of a *restrictive* covenant runs with the land, provided that
        - it was expressed to do so when it was created (or, in other words, it is *expressly annexed* to the land); or
        - it is *impliedly annexed* to the land either under s. 78 of the Law of Property Act 1925, or perhaps because the land which was intended to be benefited can be identified with reasonable certainty; or
        - it is *expressly* transferred with the land at the same time as the title to the land itself is transferred; or
        - there is a building scheme (such as a housing estate); but
    - the *burden* of a covenant, whether it is positive or restrictive, runs with the land in any case.

Where reliance is placed on the equitable rules (as it must be where, for example, an equitable remedy such as an INJUNCTION is sought), it follows that the general principles of equity must be complied with (see, for example, the MAXIMS OF EQUITY), as must the doctrine of NOTICE (although the importance of the latter point is significantly reduced by the fact that restrictive covenants created after 1925 are registrable as LAND CHARGES).

See also LEASEHOLD COVENANTS.

Resulting trust

A *resulting trust* arises where the legal ownership of property is transferred in circumstances which make it appropriate for the beneficial interest to go back (or revert) to the transferor. The use of the word *resulting* may seem odd because in modern English a *result* is usually an *outcome*. However, in the present context, the word *result* derives from a Latin word meaning *to jump back*, and refers to the beneficial ownership (see BENEFICIAL OWNER) *jumping back* to the transferor.

Resulting trusts arise in a variety of circumstances. However, by way of a single example, a resulting trust will arise where property is transferred for a purpose which ceases to exist. Pursuing a precise version of the same example, if A transfers property to B for life but fails to make any provision as to what is to happen when B dies, on B's death the legal estate will pass according to the appropriate rules of inheritance but the beneficial ownership will revert (or *result*) to A (or A's estate if A is also dead by that time).

Retrospectivity

See PRESUMPTIONS OF STATUTORY INTERPRETATION.

Reversing

See BINDING PRECEDENT.

Reversion

See LEASE.

Revocation

See CONTRACT.

Right of audience

A *right of audience* is a right to be heard as an advocate in court.

R

Right to a fair hearing

The Latin phrase *audi alteram partem* (which may be pronounced *ow-dee al-ter-am part-em* and is translated literally as *hear the other side*) is still sometimes used to mean the *right to a hearing*. This right is one of the traditional principles of natural justice (see PROCEDURAL FAIRNESS).

Once it has been established that the right to a hearing exists in all the circumstances of the case (see PROCEDURAL FAIRNESS for when this will be so), the next question is whether

- the *hearing* needs to be *oral* (or, in other words, a *hearing* in the strict sense of the word) or whether
- the opportunity to make written representations will be enough to enable people to make their cases.

Written representations will usually be enough, unless there is likely to be a need to cross-examine witnesses (which may be the case where, for example, conflicting evidence is being given on matters of fact and it is, therefore, essential to know who is telling the truth).

In all cases, the notice of the hearing

- must accurately identify the issues which are to be decided, and
- where written representations are being used, it must identify
  - the place at which, and the date and time by which all representations must be received, or
- where an oral hearing is to be held, it must identify
  - the place, date and time at which the hearing will be held;

and

- whether there is an oral hearing or written representations, it must
  - allow a reasonable time for people to prepare their cases.

The right to a hearing does not necessarily include the right to be legally represented.

There is a substantial overlap between the right to a hearing in English law and the RIGHT TO A FAIR TRIAL under the EUROPEAN CONVENTION ON HUMAN RIGHTS.

Right to a fair trial

Article 6 of the EUROPEAN CONVENTION ON HUMAN RIGHTS protects the right to a fair and public trial, within a reasonable time and before an independent and impartial tribunal established by law, whenever civil rights and obligations or criminal charges are involved. The right extends to the whole process and not only to the hearing itself (so, for example, anyone who is charged with a criminal offence has the right to be told, in detail and in a language which he understands, what is alleged against him).

The *right to a fair trial* is a Convention right under the HUMAN RIGHTS ACT 1998.

For the full text of art. 6, see Appendix 3.

Right to education

Article 2 of the First Protocol to the EUROPEAN CONVENTION ON HUMAN RIGHTS provides that

- no one shall be denied the *right to education*, and
- the state shall (in relation to the education which it provides) respect the right of parents to ensure that such education and teaching is in conformity with their own religious and philosophical convictions.

The right to education is a Convention right under the HUMAN RIGHTS ACT 1998. However, it exists only in relation to access to existing educational facilities: it does not impose any obligation on states to provide education. Furthermore, it does *not* include vocational training,

The United Kingdom has made a reservation accepting art. 2 only to the extent that it is compatible with 'the provision of efficient instruction and training, and the avoidance of unreasonable public expenditure'. This makes it clear that admissions policies based on school catchment areas prevail over parental freedom of choice.

Another restriction on parental rights extends to limiting freedom of conscience. More particularly, the statutory prohibition on corporal punishment is not incompatible with the Convention right under art. 2 of the protocol and therefore parents cannot insist on their children being subjected to corporal punishment in circumstances where their (Christian) religious convictions tell them that such punishment is appropriate.

For the full text of art. 2 of the First Protocol, see Appendix 3.

R

Right to life

Article 2 of the EUROPEAN CONVENTION ON HUMAN RIGHTS protects the *right to life*. This precludes capital punishment but not abortion.

For the full text of art. 2, see Appendix 3.

Right to marry and found a family

See RIGHT TO RESPECT FOR FAMILY AND PRIVATE LIFE, ONE'S HOME AND ONE'S CORRESPONDENCE.

Right to respect for one's family and private life, one's home and one's correspondence

Article 8 of the ECHR protects the *right to respect for one's family and private life, one's home and one's correspondence.*

The European Commission on Human Rights (a body which has now been abolished but which conducted preliminary inquiries before cases reached the Court) drew a distinction between art. 8 and art. 12 (which protects the right to marry and found a family) on the ground that art. 8 relates to a continuing state of affairs, while art. 12 relates to a one-off event. Therefore denying prisoners the right to cohabit was not a breach of art. 8, but denying them the right to marry was a breach of art. 12. An important aspect of the right to respect for correspondence is that prisoners have the right to confidential and uncensored correspondence with their lawyers.

For the full text of arts. 8 and 12, see Appendix 3.

Right of pre-emption

A *right of pre-emption* is the right to buy specified property before it is offered for sale to anyone else.

Right of way

See EASEMENT.

Robbery

A person commits *robbery* if he steals anything and, either immediately before, or during the stealing, he either uses force on anyone or seeks to put anyone in fear of being, then and there, subject to force.

Root of title

See GOOD ROOT OF TITLE.

Royal assent

See BILL.

Royal charter

A *royal charter* is a document in the form of LETTERS PATENT, issued by the Queen (or King as the case may be) conferring specified rights and privileges.

The inclusion of the word *royal* in the names of many learned societies and professional bodies (for example, the Royal Photographic Society and the Royal Town Planning Institute) indicates the fact that they have been granted royal charters.

Royal prerogative

Historically, the royal prerogative consisted of a bundle of powers which were exercised by the monarch personally. Over many centuries, the range of these powers was reduced, with the largest single reduction coming with the enactment of the BILL OF RIGHTS 1689. Since 1689, the range of prerogative powers has continued to dwindle as legislation has become by far the more important source of governmental power. Moreover, almost all those prerogative powers that do remain are now exercised by the government, albeit in the name of the Crown.

Beyond the fact that it is *residual*, the nature of the royal prerogative is not beyond dispute. Some commentators content themselves with simply saying that it is the residue of the Crown's former executive powers, while others adopt a more restrictive meaning, saying that to qualify as part of the royal prerogative, a power must be unique to the Crown. For example, according to the first definition, when the government (or the royal household) buys office equipment, the contract is entered into under the royal prerogative; but according to the second definition this is not the case since anyone can enter into such contracts. The court has generally preferred the second definition, even though, as a matter of logic, the first one has much to commend it, because it gives real meaning to the *royal* aspect of the royal prerogative.

Historically, the precise definition of the royal prerogative was more important than it is now, since the courts used to take the view that all they could do was identify its limits. However, the court now asserts its power to go beyond mere identification and is willing to intervene in the exercise of prerogative powers (unless there is some overwhelming reason, such as the interests of national security, why it should leave such control to the political process).

Significant examples of the royal prerogative include the appointment and dismissal of Ministers; the movement and deployment of the armed forces; the award of honours; decisions to summon, prorogue and dissolve Parliament; and the power to pardon convicted criminals.

R

Ruat coelum, fiat justitia

The Latin maxim *ruat coelum, fiat justitia,* (which may be pronounced *rooat ky-lum, fee-at jus-tit-ee-a*) may be translated as 'let the heavens fall, but let justice be done'. Advocates (and judges) may rely on this maxim when they wish to oppose (or reject) an argument that the long-term uncertainties and practical problems (or both) which would flow from making a particular decision are so great that some other decision should be made instead. More particularly, the maxim offers a useful way of resisting arguments based on the FLOODGATES PRINCIPLE.

Rule against bias

See BIAS and PROCEDURAL FAIRNESS.

Rule of law

The doctrine of the *rule of law* states what is essentially a political ideal, namely that government should be conducted according to law, rather than discretion. In practice, of course, this ideal is unattainable, since the exercise of discretion is inevitable. However, the rule of law may nevertheless identify the limits of that discretion and provide remedies where those limits are breached.

Theories of the rule of law may be divided into two categories, namely *formal versions* and *substantive versions*.

Formal versions require only that the law should conform with whatever formal requirements each legal system may impose. (For example, in the English legal system, an ACT OF PARLIAMENT is defined simply in terms of compliance with the appropriate Parliamentary procedure.) Substantive versions, however, go one stage further and require also that the content of the law must conform to certain standards. (For example, the system of Community law contains the principle of PROPORTIONALITY against which the legality of individual laws – and executive and administrative actions – are judged.)

Rules of the Supreme Court

Before they were replaced by the CIVIL PROCEDURE RULES (CPR) in 1998, the *Rules of the Supreme Court* (*RSC*) governed procedure in the High Court and the Court of Appeal. (In this context the expression *supreme court* refers to the collective which is now called the *superior courts of England and Wales* – see SUPREME COURT.)

The only aspect of the RSC which is likely to have any real current relevance for Law students is Order 53 (O. 53, RSC), which was central to the procedural aspects of JUDICIAL REVIEW when many cases which are still leading authorities were decided, and which was carried forward with only minor changes to become Part 54 of the Civil Procedure Rules (Pt 54, CPR).

Rylands v Fletcher

The rule in *Rylands v Fletcher* (1866) LR 1 Exch 265, (1868) LR 3 HL 330, which is an aspect of *private* NUISANCE, imposes strict liability in TORT on any person who brings onto his land, and keeps there, anything which is likely to do harm if it escapes (assuming, of course, that it does escape and does cause harm). The word *anything* is interpreted widely in this context, to include not only (and fairly obviously) water, gas and fairground swings, but also (and less obviously) fire and explosions.

Although liability is strict in the sense that no intention to cause harm is necessary, it nevertheless extends only to harm which is reasonably foreseeable.

The liability arises only in respect of *non-natural* uses of land. Historically, this was taken to mean something which is artificial, but now it means something extraordinary or abnormal. So, for example, *Rylands v Fletcher* will not now create liability where a water main bursts and the escaping water washes away the earth which supports someone else's property. (There may, of course, be some other cause of action – such as NEGLIGENCE – depending on all the facts of the case.)

R

Sanction

The word *sanction* has two meanings which are so different as to be almost opposites.

One meaning is *adverse consequence*, or *punishment*. This meaning is used in certain positivist theories of law (see NATURAL LAW) which argue that a rule cannot have the status of law unless there is the possibility of a sanction when it is breached.

The alternative meaning is *approval*, as where someone in authority *sanctions* a particular action or course of conduct.

Saunders v Vautier

The rule in *Saunders v Vautier* (1841) 10 LJ Ch 354, states that the BENEFI-CIARIES under a TRUST can put an end to the trust by compelling the trustees to transfer the trust property to themselves or to anyone else they may nominate. In order to invoke this rule, the beneficiaries must all be (a) agreed; (b) of full age (currently 18) and sound mind: and (c) together entitled to the whole of the beneficial interest in the trust property.

Scottish Parliament

The *Scottish Parliament* has power to pass Acts of the Scottish Parliament (known as ASPs to distinguish them from APSs, which are Acts of the Parliament of Scotland, which ceased to exist when the Act of Union 1706 was passed). The validity of an ASP is not affected by any invalidity in the Parliamentary proceedings leading to its enactment, but no provision contained in an ASP is law if it is incompatible with COMMUNITY LAW or a *Convention right* under the HUMAN RIGHTS ACT 1998.

Search order

Search orders under the Civil Procedure Act 1997 (previously known as *Anton Piller orders* after the case of *Anton Piller KG v Manufacturing Processes Ltd* [1976] 1 All ER 779) are orders of the court which require someone to allow someone else to enter their premises for the purposes of inspecting, removing or making copies of, evidence which might otherwise be destroyed or taken out of the jurisdiction of the court.

Search orders are usually made on an interim basis (see INTERIM RELIEF), but may be issued at the final stage of the proceedings if they relate to evidence which a successful claimant needs in order to be able to enforce the judgment of the court.

Secondary legislation

See DELEGATED LEGISLATION and PRIMARY LEGISLATION.

Secretary of State

The title of *Secretary of State* is generally given to the most senior members of the GOVERNMENT. The Ministerial Salaries Act 1975 provides that no more than 21 ministers may hold the post of *Secretary of State*.

Secret trust

A *secret trust* may be either *fully secret* or *half secret*. Fully secret trusts may be created where property passes either in accordance with a WILL or on an INTESTACY. Half secret trusts may arise only where property passes in accordance with a will.

A *fully secret trust* arises under a will where property is left to someone who has been given instructions by the testator as to how the property is to be used for the benefit of someone else and has agreed to accept the property on that basis. For example, a married woman may have a long-term lover for whom she wishes to make provision under her will, but without the relationship becoming known to the world at large. (Following a grant of PROBATE or letters of administration with the will annexed (see ADMINISTRATOR), wills become public documents which anyone can inspect at the relevant Probate Registry.) In this sort of situation, therefore, the testator may leave property to a trusted friend or professional adviser (such as a solicitor), to whom she has given (and who has accepted) instructions as to how the property is to be used.

Following the same logic, a fully secret trust may also arise where the donor has been content to rely on the rules governing inheritance on intestacy, rather than making express provision by will (although in this case the person acquiring the property as a trustee must necessarily be a member of the donor's family).

S

In both the situations outlined in the previous paragraphs the trust is *fully secret* because not even the fact of its existence is in the public domain.

A *half secret trust* arises under a will which states that property is being left on trust, and that the testator has given instructions as to the terms of the trust, but the will does not specify either the identity of the beneficiary under the trust or the terms of the trust. (A trust of this kind is *half secret* because only the fact of its *existence* – but nothing more – is in the public domain.)

In the case of an intestacy, there is, by definition, no will in which the creation of the trust can be disclosed. It follows, therefore, that a *half secret* trust cannot arise on an intestacy.

Secured creditor

In many situations, creditors are willing to rely on their rights of action to sue for the money they are owed if the creditor does not pay voluntarily. However, in some situations a prudent creditor will wish to take security (or, in other words, be a *secured creditor*). Two of the most common forms of security are MORTGAGES of, and CHARGES on, land.

Sedition

The CRIME of *sedition* consists of incitement to violence against the laws and institutions of the state.

Self-defence

In both criminal law and the law of tort, it is lawful to use reasonable force in *self-defence*.

Sending for trial

See MAGISTRATES' COURT.

Separation of powers

The constitutional doctrine of the *separation of powers* begins by classifying all powers exercised by the state under one of *three* headings, namely:

- legislative (or *law-making*) power;
- executive (or *law-applying* power, in the sense in which the EXECUTIVE applies the law); and

- judicial (or *law-interpreting* and *applying* power, in the sense in which the *courts* apply the law);

and then goes on to say that

- no more than one type of power should be exercised by any one decision-maker.

The idea behind the doctrine is that freedom flourishes best in a system where the exercise of state power is spread across a number of different state agencies and officials, rather than all being concentrated in a small number of hands. However, the strict form of this doctrine has never categorised the British constitution. For example, the courts perform both the judicial function of deciding cases and, to some extent (through the doctrine of BINDING PRECEDENT) the legislative function of making law, while the GOVERNMENT (provided it has a substantial majority in the House of Commons – see PARLIAMENT) effectively dominates the LEGISLATURE.

Servient tenement

An EASEMENT (for example a *right of way*) is a right which benefits one piece of land (known as the *dominant tenement*) and burdens another (known as the *servient tenement*).

In the case of a *PROFIT À PRENDRE* (which is a right to take something from someone else's land, such as a right of pasture), there will also always be a *servient tenement*, but there may, or may not, be a dominant tenement.

Servitude

See SLAVERY.

Settlement of land

Although the Trusts of Land and Appointment of Trustees Act 1996 (which is commonly abbreviated to TOLATA) prohibits the creation of any new *settlements of land*, it allows existing settlements to continue. It remains necessary, therefore, to have some knowledge of the concept.

A settlement of land exists where ownership of land was limited in succession – for example, where A transferred land to B for her lifetime and, on her death, to C. Strict settlements (as settlements of land were often called) were widely used by the great landed families as a means of ensuring that the family's wealth was kept within the family. Additionally, however, many examples were created by accident when one spouse left property to the other, with the proviso that, on the death of the survivor, it should pass to their child or children. This kind of accidental settlement was most likely to occur when a WILL was made without the benefit of legal advice. (The work which solicitors gained from administering accidental settlements is one of the reasons why the formal part of the annual dinners of some local law societies include a toast 'to people who make their own wills'.)

The essence of a strict settlement is that the legal estate is vested in the person who is entitled to ownership for the time being (in the example given above, that is B), who is known as the *tenant for life*. (Those who come after the tenant for life are known as *remaindermen*, the terminology applicable to settled land having become established long before there was any expectation of gender neutrality in language.)

The tenant for life has extensive powers over the settled land (including, for example, selling, mortgaging and, in some circumstances, leasing it). However, any money which is received goes to the *trustees of the settlement*, who will use it for the benefit of the beneficiaries as a whole, either by spending it on improving the land itself or by investing it. Later beneficiaries who are deprived of their interests in the land as the result of a disposal by an earlier tenant for life are protected by the doctrine of OVERREACHING, under which their interests in the land itself are converted into interests in the money into which the interests of land have been converted.

Severance

The word *severance* has different meanings depending on whether it is used in the context of PUBLIC LAW or LAND LAW.

1 In *public law* the word *severance* means cutting up a decision, or a piece of DELEGATED LEGISLATION, into its component parts, as a preliminary to deciding whether one defective part will make the whole decision, or piece of delegated legislation, unlawful. The basic test is to ask whether, once the offending part has been cut out, what remains is substantially the same as the original. If this question is answered in the affirmative, the remainder will be upheld; but if it is in the negative, the whole thing will be quashed. In the event of quashing, it will then be a matter for the decision-maker or legislator to decide whether to remake the decision or piece of delegated legislation without the unlawful component, or to proceed either altogether differently or not at all.

A common example of a situation giving rise to issues of severability is a decision which is subject to conditions. If the conditions are unlawful, must the court quash the whole decision, or can it quash the condition alone, leaving the decision standing, free from the conditions? (The answer, briefly, is that if the court thinks the decision-maker regarded the condition as being fundamental to the whole decision, the whole decision will be quashed; but where the court thinks the decision-maker regarded the condition as being merely desirable, the substance of the decision will be left standing, free from the condition.)

2 In land law, the word *severance* relates to the termination of *joint tenancies* (see CO-OWNERSHIP).

Sexual assault

See RAPE.

Sic utere tuo ut non alienum laedas

The Latin maxim *sic utere tuo ut non alienum laedas* (pronounced *seek ooterr-eh too-oh ut noan al-ee-ay-num lye-das*) is the basis of the TORT of NUISANCE. It may be translated as *use your own property in such a way that you do not harm anyone else's*.

Slander

See DEFAMATION.

Slavery

Article 4 of the EUROPEAN CONVENTION ON HUMAN RIGHTS prohibits *slavery* and *servitude*. The Convention does not define either *slavery* or *servitude*. However, art. 1(1) of the Slavery Convention 1926 defines slavery as 'the status or condition of a person over whom any or all of the powers attaching to the right of ownership are exercised', and the EUROPEAN COURT OF HUMAN RIGHTS has defined *servitude* as 'the obligation to provide another with certain services, [and] the obligation on the part of the "serf" to live on another's property and the impossibility of changing his condition'.

The right protected by art. 4 is a CONVENTION RIGHT under the HUMAN RIGHTS ACT 1998.

Solicitor-General

See LAW OFFICERS OF THE CROWN.

Solicitor-General for Scotland

See LAW OFFICERS OF THE CROWN.

Solicitors

Solicitors work in many contexts, including private practice, CENTRAL GOVERNMENT, LOCAL GOVERNMENT and industry and commerce. They provide legal advice and conduct legal proceedings. All solicitors have the right of audience (or, in other words, the right to appear as advocates) in magistrates' courts and county courts. (They also appear in TRIBUNALS and STATUTORY INQUIRIES but since anyone can appear in these contexts, no right of audience is involved.) Solicitors can also gain the right of audience in the higher courts, but only a few choose to do so. Generally speaking, therefore, solicitors instruct barristers to appear in the higher courts.

Barristers have much the same range of working contexts as solicitors, but barristers in private practice are much more likely to devote most of their time to advising on, and when necessary conducting, legal proceedings. However, some barristers – especially some of the most senior ones practising in CIVIL LAW – devote very significant proportions of their time to giving advice (rather than providing advocacy services) in the hope that litigation can be either settled without a hearing or (better still) avoided altogether.

For many years, barristers were not allowed to deal directly with members of the public, but had to be instructed by solicitors in even the simplest cases. Although this rule no longer applies, in practice very few barristers are willing to deal directly with members of the public.

Sources of European Community and European Union law

The principal *sources of European Community law* were, and the sources of *European Union law* are

- the *Community Treaties* (namely the TREATY OF ROME 1957, the TREATY OF MAASTRICHT 1992; the TREATY OF AMSTERDAM 1997, the TREATY OF NICE 2001 and the TREATY OF LISBON 2007);
- *regulations*, which are the form of Community law that most closely resembles statute law within the English legal system;

- *directives*, which require member states to achieve (by a specified date) certain legal results within their national legal systems, while leaving it for each member state to decide how this should be done; and
- *decisions*, which are addressed to member states or to individuals (for example, where a member state has breached European Union (EU) law when giving state aid to a particular company or industry) and are binding upon those to whom they are addressed.

Decisions of the EUROPEAN COURT OF JUSTICE are also commonly included among the sources of EU law. While this appears to be obviously correct – and, indeed, is so – at a purely practical level, it carries with it a conceptual danger. The point is simply that EU law has no doctrine of *binding* precedent. Since the decisions of the Court are not binding in later cases, it is the provisions of the treaties, regulations and other forms of EU law which the Court is interpreting which are truly binding and which are, therefore, strictly speaking, the sources of EU law. However, it is a convenient form of shorthand to describe decisions of the Court as being sources of EU law.

See also DIRECT APPLICABILITY AND DIRECT EFFECT.

Sovereignty

1 A state which is described as *sovereign* is fully independent.
2 The phrase *the sovereignty of Parliament* is sometimes encountered in the context of the British constitution. In this context, the phrase is meant to convey that no person or body can override Parliament. While this is true, it is more accurately conveyed by the phrase the LEGISLATIVE SUPREMACY OF PARLIAMENT, which locates the essence of Parliament's independence in its legislative (that is, law-making) function.

Special damages

See DAMAGES.

Specific performance

A court which grants *specific performance* is ordering someone to perform her contractual obligations. Specific performance will not be granted where damages would be an adequate remedy, and may be withheld in

any case in accordance with equitable principles, as summarised in the
MAXIMS OF EQUITY.

Spent conviction

See REHABILITATION OF OFFENDERS ACT 1976.

Standard of proof

It is inherent in any legal system where litigation is based on ADVERSARIAL
PROCEDURE that a party who is required to prove something must know
what *standard of proof* is required.

For the varying standards of proof in English Law, see CRIME.

It is important to note the distinction between *standard of proof* and
BURDEN OF PROOF and *standard of proof*.

Standing

An applicant for judicial review must establish that she has *standing* to
make the application. In essence, this means that she must have a sufficient interest in the subject-matter of the application, rather than being a
mere busybody. However, the courts now take a somewhat more relaxed
view of standing of the matter and are willing to recognise interest groups
(such as Friends of the Earth) as having standing in appropriate cases.

Before the CIVIL PROCEDURE RULES, standing was known by the Latin
name of *locus standi* (which may be pronounced *lock-us stand-eye*).

Stare decisis

Stare decisis (which may be pronounced *star-ray day-kysis*) means *to stand
by decisions*. The doctrine of *stare decisis* is an alternative name for the
doctrine of BINDING PRECEDENT.

Statement of compatibility

See HUMAN RIGHTS ACT 1998.

Statute

Within the English legal system, *statute* simply means ACT OF PARLIAMENT.
In other contexts, however, the word will have other meanings. For
example, the Rome Statute of the International Criminal Court is, despite

its name, really a TREATY establishing, and making provision for the proceedings of, the INTERNATIONAL CRIMINAL COURT.

Statute law

See COMMON LAW.

Statutory inquiries

See TRIBUNALS.

Statutory instrument

Statutory instruments are the most common form of DELEGATED LEGISLATION.

Stipendiary magistrate

See DISTRICT JUDGE (MAGISTRATES' COURT).

Strasbourg jurisprudence

The phrase *Strasbourg jurisprudence* means the law of the EUROPEAN CONVENTION ON HUMAN RIGHTS (ECHR) as interpreted by the EUROPEAN COURT OF HUMAN RIGHTS (ECtHR) and is derived from the fact that the COUNCIL OF EUROPE (which is the body responsible for administering the ECHR) is based in Strasbourg and the ECtHR sits there.

The ECtHR applies the following principles when interpreting the ECHR.

- The doctrine of *proportionality* requires the court to ask itself whether
  - the legislative or administrative objective is sufficiently important to justify interfering with a right protected by the ECHR; and
  - the means adopted to meet the objective are
    - rationally connected with it; and
    - no more than is necessary to attain the objective.

The ECHR itself acknowledges that the rights protected by arts 8 to 11 (see Appendix 3) may be subject to such restrictions as are *necessary in a democratic society*, while the ECtHR has

- identified *tolerance* and *broad-mindedness* as two of the *hallmarks* of a *democratic society*;

and has held that

S

- *necessary* means less than *indispensable* but more than *reasonable* or *desirable*; and
- *necessity* implies a *pressing and social need* and that, even so, action cannot be justified on the ground of necessity unless it is *proportionate* to the objective which is being pursued.

The concept of *the margin of appreciation* recognises that the membership of the Council of Europe spans a range of cultural traditions which will respond to the protection of fundamental rights in different ways; and such a range of responses is acceptable provided that each individual response is compatible with the protection of the rights which the ECHR seeks to protect.

Strict liability

In the law of TORT, *strict liability* means that a claimant can recover damages without having to prove any fault (in the sense of intention, recklessness or carelessness) on the part of the defendant.

In criminal law (see CRIME), an offence of strict liability is one in respect of which no MENS REA is required.

Strict settlement

See SETTLEMENTS OF LAND.

Subordinate legislation

See DELEGATED LEGISLATION and PRIMARY LEGISLATION.

Substantive law

Substantive law is that part of the law which deals with rights, duties, powers, liabilities and status. It is contrasted with ADJECTIVAL LAW, which is also known as procedural law.

Suicide pact

A *suicide pact* is an agreement between two or more people to bring about their own deaths, whether or not each is to kill herself.

Sui generis

The Latin phrase *sui generis* (pronounced *soo-eye jen-er-iss*) means *in a class of its own*. Where a thing or a concept is *sui generis*, therefore, it cannot be used for the purposes of argument by comparison or analogy.

Sui juris

The Latin phrase *sui juris* (pronounced *soo-eye jew-ris*) means *of full age and sound mind*. *Full age* means at least 18 years old.

Summary trial

Summary trial means trial in a MAGISTRATES' COURT rather than by the CROWN COURT.

Summons

A *summons* is a document requiring the recipient to attend court. A person who receives a summons is *summoned*, not *summonsed*.

Superior court

See INFERIOR COURT.

Superior courts of England and Wales

See SUPREME COURT.

Supervisory jurisdiction

The *supervisory jurisdiction* of the HIGH COURT is exercised by way of JUDICIAL REVIEW.

Supreme Court

Between the Supreme Court Act 1981 and the creation of the new Supreme Court under the provisions of the Constitutional Reform Act 2005, the *Supreme Court* consisted of the *Court of Appeal*, the *High Court* and the *Crown Court*. The two most startling things to notice about the Supreme Court in that manifestation were that (a) the doctrine of the LEGISLATIVE SUPREMACY OF PARLIAMENT means that no court can be supreme under the British constitution; and (b) it did not include the Appellate Committee of the HOUSE OF LORDS which (while admittedly not technically a court) was effectively the highest court of appeal in the English and Northern Irish legal systems (and to some extent the Scottish legal system).

The difficulties arising from the title of the Supreme Court as constituted by the 1981 Act, were in part preserved and in part resolved by the provisions of the Constitutional Reform Act 2005 which created what is (since October 2009) the Supreme Court of the United Kingdom. The difficulty which is preserved is that the creation of the new Supreme Court makes absolutely no difference to the doctrine of the legislative supremacy of Parliament.

The difficulty which is resolved is that the new court is at least supreme within the context of the judicial hierarchy, having taken over the jurisdiction of the Appellate Committee of the House of Lords (as well as the jurisdiction of the Judicial Committee of the Privy Council in relation to devolution cases relating to Northern Ireland, Scotland and Wales). However, even now its jurisdiction, while covering both civil and criminal cases arising in England, Wales and Northern Ireland, extends only to civil cases arising in Scotland. (For the meaning of *civil* and *criminal*, see CIVIL LAW and CRIME.)

The judges of the Supreme Court are called *Justices*, with one of them being designated as the *President of the Supreme Court*.

The courts which collectively made up the former *Supreme Court* are now known as the *Superior Courts of England and Wales*. By way of contrast, the new Supreme Court is the Supreme Court *of the United Kingdom* (forgetting, for the moment, criminal law in Scotland). One consequence of this is that the LORD CHIEF JUSTICE, as head of the judiciary of England and Wales, has no responsibility for the Supreme Court.

S

Tail

See ESTATES IN LAND.

Tenancy

Under a *tenancy*, a landlord lets LAND to a tenant, who acquires the right to exclusive occupation of the land while the tenancy continues. The parties may agree that a tenancy shall terminate on the expiry of a fixed period, or that it shall be renewable after the date on which it would otherwise expire.

Tenant for life

See SETTLEMENTS OF LAND.

Term of years

A *term of years* is another name for a LEASE.

Terrorism

The criminal offence of *terrorism* consists of using, or threatening to use, action which

- involves serious violence against people; or
- involves serious damage to property; or
- endangers human life, other than that of the person committing the action; or
- creates a serious risk to the health or safety of the public, or a section of the public; or
- is designed seriously to interfere with, or seriously to disrupt, an electronic system;

provided that in any case the action which is used or threatened, is designed to

- influence the government; or

- intimidate the public or a section of the public;

and in either case

- the use or threat is intended to advance a political, religious or ideological cause.

Neither the action which is used or threatened, nor the target of that action, nor the government it is designed to influence, nor the public it is designed to intimidate, need be in the United Kingdom.

Using or threatening to use firearms or explosives with the intention of advancing a political, religious or ideological cause constitutes the offence of terrorism, even if it is not intended to influence the government or to intimidate the public or a section of the public.

Finally, actions taken for the purposes of terrorism include actions taken for the benefit of a proscribed organisation (such as the Irish Republican Army or the Loyalist Volunteer Force).

Testament

The word *testament* is often used loosely to mean the same as a WILL or in conjunction with the word *will* (as in the phrase *last will and testament*), but strictly speaking a testament disposes only of PERSONAL PROPERTY.

Testate

A person who dies leaving a valid WILL is said to die *testate* (rather than *intestate* (see INTESTACY).

The rules governing succession to property which is left by will are called the rules of *testate succession*.

T

Testator

A person who makes a valid WILL is called a *testator* (or, if female, *testatrix*, which is the Latin feminine form of *testator*).

Theft

The offence (see CRIME) of *theft* consists of the dishonest appropriation of property belonging to another person with the intention of permanently depriving that other person of it.

Thin skull

See EGGSHELL SKULL.

Title to land

Title to land may be either *unregistered* or *registered*.

Unregistered title will be proved by producing documentary evidence in the form of conveyances and similar documents, going back at least 15 years in order to identify a GOOD ROOT OF TITLE. The only exceptional case, where unregistered title is not proved by documentary evidence, is where title has been gained by ADVERSE POSSESSION.

All *registered titles* are recorded at the Land Registry and are proved by producing authenticated copies (called *office copies*) of the relevant entries on the register.

TOLATA

TOLATA is an acronym formed from the *T*rusts *of L*and and *A*ppointment of *T*rustees *A*ct 1996.

See also TRUST OF LAND.

Tort

A *tort* is a CIVIL LAW wrong which is neither a breach of CONTRACT nor a breach of an equitable (see COMMON LAW) obligation. Important examples include DEFAMATION, NEGLIGENCE, NUISANCE and TRESPASS.

Tortfeasor

A *tortfeasor* is someone who commits a TORT.

Torture

1 Under English law, the offence of *torture* consists of
  - the intentional infliction of severe pain or suffering (which may be either physical or mental and may be caused by either an act or an omission) on another person; but
  - can be committed only by either
    - a public official or a person acting in an official capacity, or
    - a person who is not a public official or a person acting in an official capacity, but who is acting at the instigation, or with the consent, of such a person; provided that, in either case

– the public official, or the person acting in an official capacity, is performing or purporting to perform his official duties.

2 Article 3 of the EUROPEAN CONVENTION ON HUMAN RIGHTS prohibits *torture* and *inhuman or degrading treatment or punishment.*

The Convention does not define any of these terms but the EUROPEAN COURT OF HUMAN RIGHTS has held that

- *torture* means deliberate, inhuman treatment causing very serious and cruel suffering;
- *inhuman treatment or punishment* means the infliction of intense physical or mental suffering; while
- *degrading treatment* means ill-treatment which arouses in victims feelings of fear, anguish and inferiority capable of humiliating and debasing them; and, possibly, breaking their physical and moral resistance. Degrading treatment requires something which is more than merely disagreeable or uncomfortable; and the victim's age, sex and state of health are relevant; but the treatment need not take place in public.

The rights protected by art. 3 of the Convention are *Convention rights* for the purposes of the HUMAN RIGHTS ACT 1998.

For the full text of art. 3, see Appendix 3.

Transferred malice

See MENS REA.

Transsexual

See GENDER RECOGNITION CERTIFICATE.

Travaux préparatoires

The French phrase *travaux préparatoires* (which may be pronounced *travoh pray-para-twahr*) refers to documents such as official reports and minutes of meetings leading up to the enactment of legislation or the making of treaties.

Treason

Under the Treason Act 1351, the offence (see CRIME) of *treason* can be committed in the following ways: (a) plotting the death of the King, the Queen, or their eldest son; (b) raping or otherwise sexually assaulting either (i) the Queen; (ii) the King's eldest daughter while she is unmarried;

or (iii) the King's eldest son's wife; (c) levying war against the King; (d) actively supporting the King's (or when a Queen is reigning, the Queen's) enemies, either within the realm or elsewhere; (e) killing the Chancellor, the Treasurer, or the judges while they are acting in the execution of their duty.

The references to the Chancellor and the Treasurer would, presumably, now be interpreted as references to the LORD CHANCELLOR and the Chancellor of the Exchequer respectively.

Treasure

See CORONER.

Treasure trove

See CORONER.

Treasury Solicitor

The *Treasury Solicitor* (who, despite the job title, may be either a solicitor or a barrister) is the head of the Government Legal Service (GLS).

Treaty

A *treaty* is an agreement.

In English law, the expression *sale by private treaty* is sometimes used in the context of sales of land, where it contrasts with *sale by public auction*.

In INTERNATIONAL LAW, a treaty is an agreement between states. However, its title need not include the word *treaty*, with a variety of other words (such as *convention*) being used in some cases.

Treaty of Amsterdam 1997

The *Treaty of Amsterdam 1997* (commonly abbreviated to *ToA*), transferred *Co-operation in Justice and Home Affairs* from the TREATY OF MAASTRICHT to the TREATY OF ROME (commonly known as, and abbreviated to, the *EC Treaty*). It also re-numbered many of the articles of the EC Treaty. There are various ways of referring to the former numbering in conjunction with the current numbering, but the style adopted by the EU itself is, to take a single example, *art. 234 [ex177] EC*.

T

Treaty on European Union 1992

See TREATY OF MAASTRICHT.

Treaty on the Functioning of the European Union
See TREATY OF LISBON.

Treaty of Lisbon 2007

The *Treaty of Lisbon 2007* amended, but did not replace, the pre-existing treaties of the EUROPEAN COMMUNITY (EC) and EUROPEAN UNION (EU). It did, however, extinguish the individual identities of these pillars (see EURO-PEAN COMMUNITY and EUROPEAN UNION) of the EU as it existed before the Treaty, by merging them into the EU in its new form, as created by the Treaty. It also re-named the Treaty of Rome 1957 (which had been known as the *EC Treaty*) as the *Treaty of the Functioning of the European Union*.

The principal purposes of the Treaty are to improve the decision-making processes of the EU in terms of accountability and transparency and to give the EU LEGAL PERSONALITY. Although the Treaty contains many detailed provisions which are designed to achieve the first of these objectives, one of the most prominent aspects is the enhancement of the role of the EUROPEAN PARLIAMENT. The Treaty also creates the offices of *President of the European Council* and *High Representative for Foreign Affairs*, as well as providing for the CHARTER OF FUNDAMENTAL RIGHTS OF THE EUROPEAN UNION to become part of EU law.

The EU's acquisition of legal personality enables it to become a party to the EUROPEAN CONVENTION ON HUMAN RIGHTS; and the Treaty provides that it shall, in fact, do so.

The Treaty also acknowledges, for the first time, that a member state may withdraw from the EU. The formalities required for withdrawal are those required by the constitution of the member state concerned.

> *See also* EUROPEAN COMMUNITY AND EUROPEAN UNION; and EUROPEAN COURT OF JUSTICE; and for the con-solidated texts (subject to corrections) of the Treaty on European Union and the Treaty on the Functioning of the European Union, see http://eur-lex.europa.eu/en/treaties/.

Treaty of Maastricht 1992

The *Treaty of Maastricht*, which is also known as the *Treaty on European Union* or TEU, renamed the EUROPEAN ECONOMIC COMMUNITY as the EURO-PEAN COMMUNITY and created the EUROPEAN UNION.

Treaty of Nice 2001

The *Treaty of Nice 2001*, which was agreed at an Inter-Governmental Con-ference of the member states of the EUROPEAN COMMUNITY at the end of 2000, introduced certain institutional reforms in order to pave the way for enlargement of the EC, particularly by admitting certain states which were formerly part of the Communist bloc. By 2007, this process had resulted in the membership of the EC growing to 27 countries.

Treaty of Paris 1951

The *Treaty of Paris 1951* created the EUROPEAN COAL AND STEEL COMMUNITY. *See also* EUROPEAN COMMUNITY.

Treaty of Rome 1957

There are two *Treaties of Rome*, both signed in 1957. One created the EUROPEAN ECONOMIC COMMUNITY (which the TREATY OF MAASTRICHT re-named the EUROPEAN COMMUNITY) and the other created the EUROPEAN ATOMIC ENERGY COMMUNITY (also known as *Euratom*). The former is commonly known as, and abbreviated to, the *EC Treaty* until the Treaty of Lisbon 2007 re-named it as the *Treaty of the Functioning of the European Union* (or TFEU).

Trespass

The TORT of *trespass* takes three forms, namely trespass to *land*, trespass to *goods*, and trespass to the *person*.

Trespass to *land* consists of entering (or remaining on) land in the occupation of the claimant, without lawful justification. Since the claimant's principal objective will usually be to regain possession of the land, an injunction to prevent the continuation of the trespass is the remedy most likely to be sought, perhaps in conjunction with a claim for MESNE PROFITS. If the trespasser has caused physical damage, the claimant may also seek damages; but, curiously, these will be based on the reduction in value of the land as a result of the damage, rather than the cost of repair or reinstatement.

Trespass to *goods* consists of any unlawful interference with possession of the goods.

Trespass to the *person* falls under the entries for ASSAULT and FALSE IMPRISONMENT.

Trespasser

Although, in common usage, the word *trespasser* is applied only to someone who is present on someone else's land without his consent, as a matter of law it may be applied to anyone who commits any form of TRESPASS.

Tribunals

As the terminology itself suggests, the bodies which were previously generally known as *administrative tribunals* but which are now more often known simply as *tribunals*, are not courts. A major difference between tribunals and courts is that some members of each tribunal usually have extensive practical experience of the type of situations which come before that tribunal, although there is also a legally qualified chair.

The statutory framework of the tribunal system was radically overhauled by Part I of the Tribunals, Courts and Enforcement Act 2007. Very briefly, this framework has three pillars, namely (a) two new generic tribunals called the First-tier Tribunal and the Upper Tribunal; (b) Employment Tribunals together with the Employment Appeals Tribunal; and (c) the Asylum and Immigration Tribunal.

Over a period of time, the JURISDICTION of almost every existing tribunal will be transferred to one of the generic tribunals, following which the existing tribunal will be abolished. For example, in respect of England – there being separate Mental Health Review Tribunals for Scotland and Wales – the former *Mental Health Review Tribunal* has become the *First-tier Tribunal (Mental Health)*. Its principal function is to review the cases of patients detained under the Mental Health Act and to direct the discharge of any patients where the statutory criteria for discharge have been satisfied. It also has a discretion to discharge patients who do not meet the statutory criteria, where it considers this to be appropriate after making a balanced judgement between the freedom of the individual, the protection of the public and the best interests of the patient. Similarly, the former *Lands Tribunal* has become the *Lands Chamber of the Upper Tribunal*. Its functions include deciding certain disputes concerning land and, more particularly, the valuation of land, in a variety of contexts, including compensation in respect of land acquired by public bodies through the use of compulsory purchase orders. It also hears appeals from Valuation Tribunals, Leasehold Valuation Tribunals and Residential Property Tribunals, as well as deciding applications to discharge or modify restrictions on the use of land.

Broadly speaking, there is a right of APPEAL on a point of law from the First-tier Tribunal to the Upper Tribunal, which also has a jurisdiction by way of JUDICIAL REVIEW over the First-tier Tribunal. There is a further appeal on a point of law from the Upper Tribunal to the Court of Appeal.

As well as being distinguished from courts, tribunals must be compared and contrasted with *statutory inquiries* (which are often known simply as *inquiries*). In common with tribunals, inquiries are usually conducted by people with technical expertise. Examples of inquiries include appeals to the Secretary of State for the Environment, Food and Rural Affairs against the refusal of planning permission by a local planning authority. Also in common with tribunals, inquiries tend to be less formal, cheaper and more accessible than the courts.

The essential difference between tribunals and inquiries is that the former function independently of the GOVERNMENT (and indeed, under the 2007 Act, have the same independence as the traditional judiciary), while the latter are an integral of part of the government's decision-making processes.

Finally, in addition to the kinds of tribunals and inquiries outlined above, there is a third possibility. This arises where a MINISTER OF THE CROWN sets up a body for the specific purpose of inquiring into, and reporting on, a particular matter of public concern. Historically, the *ad hoc* nature of these inquiries led to a lack of consistency in their creation, but the Tribunals Act 2005 introduced a comprehensive framework for such inquiries.

The fact that a *Tribunals* Act deals with what are, essentially, *inquiries* creates a regrettable element of confusion. However, it does serve to emphasise the fact that, in addition to the meaning outlined above, the word *tribunal* is sometimes used in a general sense to mean *decision-maker* – for example, 'the meaning of an ordinary word of the English language is a question of fact to be decided by the tribunal of fact'. (The identity of the tribunal of fact will depend on the circumstances, with the main possibilities being a decision-maker such as a LOCAL AUTHORITY or a SECRETARY OF STATE, or, in the context of a court, the MAGISTRATES, the JURY or the JUDGE.)

Trust

A *trust* exists where someone (called a *trustee*) holds property either

- for the benefit of *someone else* or a *group of other people* (called the *beneficiary* or *beneficiaries*); or
- for some object permitted by law,

so that the benefit of the property goes to the beneficiary (or beneficiaries) or to the other objects of the trust.

The property may be either REAL PROPERTY or PERSONAL PROPERTY, and a trustee may also be a beneficiary.

See also SETTLEMENTS OF LAND, TRUST FOR SALE and TRUST OF LAND.

Trust corporation

A *trust corporation* which holds trust property may do anything which would normally require at least two trustees (for example, giving a good receipt for purchase when land held on trust is sold). Trust corporations are either the Public Trustee (who, as the title suggests, is a public official) or companies which fulfil certain criteria. (The clearing banks all qualify as trust corporations, which means that, for example, a testator can appoint one of these banks as an executor of his will and as trustee of his property which is disposed of by that will.)

Trustee

See TRUST.

Trust of land

The Trusts of Land and Appointment of Trustees Act 1996 (commonly known as TOLATA) introduced comprehensive reforms of the way in which land could be held on trust. More particularly, the Act abolished the old device of the TRUST FOR SALE altogether and converted existing examples into *trusts of land*. It also prohibited the creation of new SETTLEMENTS OF LAND, although by way of contrast with trusts for sale, it did allow existing examples to continue.

For the purposes of the Act, the expression 'trust of land' means 'any trust of property which includes land'. The trustees hold the legal estate in the land and have the powers of an absolute owner, but in exercising those powers they must generally give effect to the wishes of the beneficiaries to the extent that those wishes are consistent with the purposes of the trust. The trustees may delegate to the beneficiaries powers which are very similar to those of a tenant for life under a strict settlement (see SETTLEMENTS OF LAND).

Trust for sale

The *trust for sale* was a device under which TRUSTEES held the legal estate (see ESTATES IN LAND) in property subject to an obligation to sell the property and hold the proceeds of sale on trust for the BENEFICIARIES. However, there was a power to postpone sale, and in practice this power was almost always exercised. One very common situation in which trusts for sale operated was CO-OWNERSHIP of LAND.

Trusts for sale in respect of land were abolished by the Trusts of Land and Appointment of Trustees Act 1996 (commonly known as TOLATA), which replaced them with TRUSTS OF LAND.

T

Uberrimae fidei

The Latin phrase *uberrimae fidei* (which may be pronounced *you-berry-my-fid-ay-ee*) means *of the UTMOST GOOD FAITH*.

Ultra vires

The Latin phrase *ultra vires* (which may be pronounced *ultra vy-reez*) means *beyond the powers*. The doctrine of *ultra vires* applies to public sector CORPORATIONS (such as SECRETARIES OF STATE and LOCAL AUTHORITIES), who have only those powers which the law recognises them as having. It follows that anything which they purport to do which is *beyond those powers* will be VOID and of no legal effect.

Undivided shares

See CO-OWNERSHIP.

Undue influence

The equitable (see COMMON LAW) doctrine of *undue influence* applies where A's relationship with B is such that, in the eyes of equity, B is entitled to have confidence in A, but A abuses the relationship by taking advantage of B. There is no closed list of such relationships, but obvious examples include not only trustees and the beneficiaries under the trust, but also holders of religious office and followers of their faith, and family members. However, the doctrine is not intended to protect people from their own folly and it does not do so.

Unfitness to plead

See AUTOMATISM.

Unilateral contract

See CONTRACT.

Unitary authority

Some LOCAL AUTHORITIES exercise all local government functions in their areas. These are called *unitary authorities*, to distinguish them from other authorities which form part of a hierarchy of two or three local authorities (namely county councils and district councils, together with, in some cases, parish councils), each of which exercises only some of the local government functions for the relevant areas.

A local authority's name very seldom provides any indication as to whether it is unitary. For example, many unitary authorities are called *borough councils*; but so are many district councils which function beneath overarching county councils within a two- or three-tiered hierarchy.

Unliquidated damages

Unliquidated damages are assessed by the court, or agreed by the parties after the occurrence of the harm giving rise to the claim, in order to provide compensation.

See also LIQUIDATED DAMAGES.

Unregistered land

See TITLE TO LAND.

Unregistered title

See TITLE TO LAND.

Unsecured creditor

See SECURED CREDITOR.

U

Utmost good faith

A duty of the *utmost good faith* most frequently arises in certain types of contract. (For example, when making a proposal for a contract of insurance, the proposer must disclose anything which may influence a reasonable insurer in deciding whether to accept the risk, and if so, on what terms (including the amount of the premium).

The Latin phrase *uberrimae fidei* (which may be pronounced *you-berry-my-fid-ay-ee*) is still sometimes used instead of *of the utmost good faith*.

V v

Vacant possession

Where land is sold with *vacant possession*, the seller must move out no later than the date when the sale is completed, leaving the land vacant so that the purchaser can take possession immediately.

Valuable consideration

See CONSIDERATION.

Value

See PURCHASER.

V-C

The abbreviation *V-C* after someone's name means *Vice-Chancellor*. It is worth retaining the typographical convention of the hyphen in this abbreviation, in order to distinguish it from *VC*, which means that the person is the holder of the Victoria Cross.

Although the chief executives of most universities are called Vice-Chancellors (with the Chancellors themselves having largely formal and ceremonial roles), in a legal context the Vice-Chancellor is the Head of the CHANCERY DIVISION of the HIGH COURT.

Verdict

Except for a CORONER's court, a *verdict* is always a decision made by a JURY. It is, therefore, wrong to speak of *the judge's verdict*.

A jury in the CROWN COURT (or a jury in the HIGH COURT or a COUNTY COURT in the rare cases in which those courts sit with juries) is said to *return* a verdict.

A *coroner's court* (whether or not the coroner is sitting with a jury) is said to *record* (not *return*) a verdict.

Vertical direct effect

See DIRECT APPLICABILITY AND DIRECT EFFECT OF EUROPEAN COMMUNITY AND EUROPEAN UNION LAW

Vicarious liability

There is a general proposition in the law of TORT that an employer is *vicariously liable* for torts which his employees commit while they are acting within the scope of their employment, but he is not liable for the torts which his independent contractors commit while they are working for him. (Traditionally, people who would now be thought of as being *employees* were called *servants*.)

At the level of general principle, the doctrine of vicarious liability can be justified on three main grounds.

First, the law of tort exists in order to provide remedies for people who have been harmed. Therefore when those remedies take the form of DAM-AGES, it makes more sense to give judgment against an employer who will, generally speaking, be better placed than an employee to satisfy the judgment, whether from his own resources or as a result of having appropriate insurance cover. (This is sometimes called the *long pocket* – or the *deep pocket – principle*.) The traditional view is that there is no reason to suppose that this is necessarily true of an independent contractor.

Secondly, since the employer takes any profit which the business makes, it is only just and equitable that he should bear the costs when things go wrong on the way to the making of that profit. Again, an independent contractor will be making his own profit from his own business, and there is no obvious reason for saddling those who use his services with liability in respect of any torts he commits.

Thirdly, an employer who knows that he may be held vicariously liable will have a real incentive to be careful as to whom he employs, as well as doing all that he can to ensure that his employees perform their duties with reasonable care. On the other hand, although people who use the services of independent contractors will have the power of selection, they will not be in a position to tell their independent contractors how to do their jobs.

In practical terms, therefore, two questions will often arise: who is an *employee*; and what is meant by the *scope of an employee's employment*?

Employees must be distinguished from *independent contractors*. The law has not been able to formulate a simple test for drawing this distinction, but the basic idea may be easily illustrated by saying that a chauffeur is an employee while a taxi driver is an independent contractor.

V

Although the court will ultimately decide the question in the light of all the circumstances of each case, it has found one or other of the following two approaches to be useful in many situations.

- An employer can tell both an employee and an independent contractor *what to do*, but can tell only an employee *how to do it*. This is sometimes called the *control test*, and it works well in many circumstances. However, it is open to the objection that it fails to take account of the very real possibility that in many cases the employer lacks the necessary skill and knowledge to do the jobs of all his employees.
- An employee works as an integral part of the employer's business, whereas an independent contractor carries on business on his own account, performing tasks for other people under a separate contract for each job which he undertakes. This is more generally satisfactory than the *control test*, but in difficult cases the court will always look at all the circumstances when deciding the issue.

A finding that the TORTFEASOR is an employee does not necessarily determine the outcome of the case. The court must then proceed to determine whether the tort was committed *within the scope of the employee's employment*. Again, the basic idea may be easily illustrated by saying that the driver of a delivery van whose bad driving causes an accident while he is making his deliveries will be acting within the scope of his employment. However, if the accident occurs while he is having a break from his delivery duties and is using the van to go shopping, he will be 'on a frolic of his own' (as the standard expression goes). In other words, his employer will be vicariously liable in the first situation but not the second.

Although this distinction is basically sensible, it can be difficult to apply in practice. Suppose, for example, that the driver of a petrol tanker lights a cigarette while off-loading petrol, and an explosion ensues. Is the employer liable? The best approach which the court has developed is to ask how close is the connection between the tortious act and the work which the employee is employed to do? If the former takes place within the context of the latter, then the employer is vicariously liable. If the court decides that the facts do disclose vicarious liability, it must then proceed to decide how the damages should be apportioned between the employer and the employee. In most cases, bearing in mind the *long pocket* principle (see above), the full burden will fall on the employer, but the court will always have a discretion in the matter.

Finally, there is an exceptional case in which an employer can be liable for the torts of his independent contractors, but this arises only where the work of the independent contractor involves the performance of a duty which the law imposes on the employer. The existence of this exception can be justified as a matter of public policy on the basis that if it did not exist, employers would be able to avoid liability for breach of the duty by always using independent contractors to do the relevant work.

Void

Something which has the appearance of existing in the eyes of the law as being, for example, a CONTRACT, or a governmental decision, may nevertheless have some serious legal defect. In such cases it becomes necessary to identify the extent of the seriousness of the defect. If it is fundamentally serious, the contract or decision (or whatever else it may be) will be *void*. On the other hand, the defect may be less serious, while still being serious enough to prevent the contract or decision (or whatever else it may be) having full legal status. In cases of this sort, the law applies the label *voidable* (rather than *void*) which means that the person who is adversely affected must choose between accepting whatever it is as being legally effective or *avoiding* it (in which case it will cease to have legal effect).

Although something which is *void* is of no legal effect, the PRESUMPTION OF LEGALITY applies here as elsewhere, and someone who chooses to ignore something on the basis that it is void is adopting a high-risk strategy. It is only the court which can give authoritative decisions as to legality and illegality.

Voidable

See VOID.

Volenti non fit injuria

See ASSUMPTION OF RISK.

V

Warranty

See CONDITION.

Welsh Assembly

See NATIONAL ASSEMBLY OF WALES.

White paper

See GREEN PAPER.

Will

A *will* is a document which takes effect on the death of the person making it. The *testator* (who, if female, may be called the *testatrix*) usually appoints an *executor* or *executors* (who, if female, may be called an *executrix* or *executrices*) (see PERSONAL REPRESENTATIVE) and always directs how at least some of his or her property is to be dealt with. The role of executor or executrix may be undertaken by no more than four individuals or a TRUST CORPORATION (such as a bank). If some of the deceased's property is not disposed of by the will, it descends on INTESTACY according to the rules of intestate succession, and there is said to be a *partial intestacy*.

Without notice application

See EX PARTE.

Youth Courts

Youth Courts deal with criminal (see CRIME) cases where the defendants are less than 18 years old. They consist of magistrates who are on a *Youth Court Panel*.

Before the Criminal Justice Act 1991, the jurisdiction of Youth Courts was exercised by *Juvenile Courts*.

Appendix 1
Law reports and journals (some useful references)

AC (formerly App Cas)	*Appeal Cases (Law Reports)*
ACD	*Administrative Court Digest*
Admin LR	*Administrative Law Reports*
All ER	*All England Law Reports*
All ER (Comm)	*All England Law Reports (Commercial Cases)*
All ER (EC)	*All England Law Reports (European Cases)*
Anglo-Am	*Anglo-American Law Review*
BLR	*Building Law Reports*
Bus LR	*Business Law Reports*
CJQ	*Civil Justice Quarterly*
CLR	*Commonwealth Law Reports* (an Australian series)
CLWR	*Common Law World Review*
CLY	*Current Law Yearbook*
CMLR	*Common Market Law Reports*
CMLRev	*Common Market Law Review*
COD	*Crown Office Digest*
Ch (formerly ChD)	*Chancery (Law Reports)*
Co Law	*Company Lawyer*
Con LR	*Construction Law Reports*
Conv.(n.s.) (or Conv. or Conveyancer)	*Conveyancer and Property Lawyer (New Series)*
Cox CC	*Cox's Criminal Cases*
Cr App R (or CAR)	*Criminal Appeal Reports*
Cr App R (S) (or CAR(S))	*Criminal Appeal Reports (Sentencing)*
Crim LR	*Criminal Law Review*
DLR	*Dominion Law Reports* (a Canadian series)
EBLRev	*European Business Law Review*
ECR	*European Court Reports*
EG	*Estates Gazette*
EGLR	*Estates Gazette Law Reports*
EHRR	*European Human Rights Reports*
ELRev	*European Law Review*
ER	*English Reports*
FCR	*Family Court Reporter*

FLR	*Family Law Reports*
FSR	*Fleet Street Reports*
FTLR	*Financial Times Law Reports*
Fam	*Family Division (Law Reports)*
Fam Law	*Family Law*
Harv LR	*Harvard Law Review*
HLR	*Housing Law Reports*
ICLQ	*International and Comparative Law Quarterly*
ICR	*Industrial Cases Reports*
ILJ	*Industrial Law Journal*
Imm AR	*Immigration Appeals Reports*
IRLR	*Industrial Relations Law Reports*
ITR	*Industrial Tribunal Reports*
JBL	*Journal of Business Law*
JP	*Justice of the Peace Reports*
JPL	*Journal of Planning and Environment Law* (formerly *Journal of Planning Law*)
JPN	*Justice of the Peace Journal* (Abbreviating 'Journal' to 'N' may seem rather odd. The explanation is that this periodical was originally known as *Justice of the Peace Newspaper*, and the 'JPN' abbreviation has survived even though it is now commonly referred to as *Justice of the Peace Journal* by way of contradistinction to *Justice of the Peace Reports* – see 'JP'). This journal is now called *Criminal Law and Justice Weekly* as a result of which it is sometimes informally abbreviated to CL&JW, but it is frequently known by its old title and, in any case, its formal citation remains as JPN.
JR	*Juridical Review*
JSPTL	*Journal of the Society of Public Teachers of Law*
JSWL	*Journal of Social Welfare Law*
KB	*King's Bench (Law Reports)*
KIR	*Knight's Industrial Reports*
LGR	*Local Government Reports*

LG Rev	*Local Government Review* (renamed as *Local Government Review Reports* in November 1993, and absorbed into the *Justice of the Peace* in 1996)
LJ	*Law Journal*
Ll L Rep	*Lloyd's List Reports* (1919–1950)
Lloyd's Rep	*Lloyd's Reports* (1951 onwards)
LQR	*Law Quarterly Review*
LS	*Legal Studies*
LSGaz	*Law Society's Gazette*
LT	*Law Times*
MLR	*Modern Law Review*
Med LR	*Medical Law Reports*
NILQ	*Northern Ireland Legal Quarterly*
NZLR	*New Zealand Law Reports*
New LJ	*New Law Journal*
OJ	*Official Journal of the European Communities*
OJLS	*Oxford Journal of Legal Studies*
P (formerly PD)	*Probate (Law Reports)*
P & CR	*Property and Compensation Reports* (formerly *Planning and Compensation Reports*)
PL	*Public Law*
PTSR	*Public and Third Sector Reports*
QB (formerly QBD)	*Queen's Bench (Law Reports)*
RPC	*Reports of Patent, Design and Trade Mark Cases*
RTR	*Road Traffic Reports*
SJ (sometimes given as Sol Jo)	*Solicitors' Journal*
SLT	*Scots Law Times*
STC	*Simon's Tax Cases*
Stat LR	*Statute Law Review*
TLR	*Times Law Reports*
US	*United States Reports*
WLR	*Weekly Law Reports*
Yale LJ	*Yale Law Journal*

Appendix 2
Extracts from the Interpretation Act 1978

*The words appearing in **bold** type immediately after the section numbers are the marginal notes of the Queen's Printer's text.*

General provisions as to enactment and operation

3 Judicial notice Every Act is a public Act to be judicially noticed as such, unless the contrary is expressly provided by the Act.

4 Time of commencement An Act or provision of an Act comes into force –

(a) where provision is made for it to come into force on a particular day, at the beginning of that day;

(b) where no provision is made for its coming into force, at the beginning of the day on which the Act receives the Royal Assent.

Interpretation and construction

5 Definitions In any Act, unless the contrary intention appears, words and expressions listed in Schedule I to this Act are to be construed according to that Schedule.

6 Gender and number In any Act, unless the contrary intention appears

(a) words importing the masculine gender include the feminine;

(b) words importing the feminine gender include the masculine;

(c) words in the singular include the plural and words in the plural include the singular.

7 References to service by post Where an Act authorises or requires any document to be served by post (whether the expression' serve' or the expression 'give' or 'send' or any other expression is used) then, unless the contrary intention appears, the service is deemed to be effected by properly addressing, pre-paying and posting a letter containing the document and, unless the contrary is proved, to have been effected at the time at which the letter would be delivered in the ordinary course of post.

8 References to distance In the measurement of any distance for the purposes of an Act, that distance shall, unless the contrary intention appears, be measured in a straight line on a horizontal plane.

9 References to time of day Subject to section 3 of the Summer Time Act 1972 (construction of references to points of time during the period of summer time), whenever an expression of time occurs in an Act, the time referred to shall, unless it is otherwise specifically stated, be held to be Greenwich mean time.

11 Construction of subordinate legislation Where an Act confers power to make subordinate legislation, expressions used in that legislation have, unless the contrary intention appears, the meaning which they bear in the Act.

Statutory powers and duties

12 Continuity of powers and duties (1) Where an Act confers a power or imposes a duty it is implied, unless the contrary intention appears, that the power may be exercised, or the duty is to be performed, from time to time as occasion requires.

(2) Where an Act confers a power or imposes a duty on the holder of an office as such, it is implied, unless the contrary intention appears, that the power may be exercised, or the duty is to be performed, by the holder for the time being of the office.

13 Anticipatory exercise of powers Where an Act which (or any provision of which) does not come into force immediately on its passing confers powers to make subordinate legislation, or to make appointments, give notices, prescribe forms or do any other thing for the purposes of the Act, then, unless the contrary intention appears, the power may be exercised, and any instrument made thereunder may be made so as to come into force, at any time after the passing of the Act so far as may be necessary or expedient for the purpose –

(a) of bringing the Act or any provision of the Act into force; or

(b) of giving full effect to the Act or any such provision at or after the time when it comes into force.

14 Implied power to amend Where an Act confers power to make –

(a) rules, regulations or byelaws; or

(b) Orders in Council, orders or other subordinate legislation to be made by statutory instrument,

it implies, unless the contrary intention appears, a power, exercisable in the same manner and subject to the same conditions or limitations, to revoke, amend or re-enact any instrument made under the power.

Repealing enactments

15 Repeal of repeal Where an Act repeals a repealing enactment, the repeal does not revive any enactment previously repealed unless words are added reviving it.

16 General savings (1) Without prejudice to section 15, where an Act repeals an enactment, the repeal does not, unless the contrary intention appears –

(a) revive anything not in force or existing at the time at which the repeal takes effect;

(b) affect the previous operation of the enactment repealed or anything duly done or suffered under that enactment;

(c) affect any right, privilege, obligation or liability acquired, accrued or incurred under that enactment;

(d) affect any penalty, forfeiture or punishment incurred in respect of any offence committed against that enactment;

(e) affect any investigation, legal proceeding or remedy in respect of any such right, privilege, obligation, liability, penalty, forfeiture or punishment;

and any such investigation, legal proceeding or remedy may be instituted, continued or enforced, and any such penalty, forfeiture or punishment may be imposed, as if the repealing Act had not been passed.

(2) This section applies to the expiry of a temporary enactment as if it were repealed by an Act.

17 Repeal and re-enactment (1) Where an Act repeals a previous enactment and substitutes provisions for the enactment repealed, the repealed enactment remains in force until the substituted provisions come into force.

(2) Where an Act repeals and re-enacts, with or without modification, a previous enactment then, unless the contrary intention appears –

(a) any reference in any other enactment to the enactment so repealed shall be construed as a reference to the provision re-enacted;

(b) in so far as any subordinate legislation made or other thing done under the enactment so repealed, or having effect as if so made or done, could have been made or done under the provision re-enacted, it shall have effect as if made or done under that provision.

Miscellaneous

18 Duplicated offences Where an act or omission constitutes an offence under two or more Acts, or both under an Act and at common law, the offender shall, unless the contrary intention appears, be liable to be prosecuted and punished under either or any of those Acts or at common law, but shall not be liable to be punished more than once for the same offence.

...

Supplementary

21 Interpretation etc (1) In this Act 'Act' includes a local and personal or private Act; and 'subordinate legislation' means Orders in Council, orders, rules, regulations, schemes, warrants, byelaws and other instruments made or to be made under any Act.

(2) This Act binds the Crown.

Schedule I (extracts)

'Commencement', in relation to an Act or enactment, means the time when the Act or enactment comes into force.

'The Communities', 'the Treaties' or 'the Community Treaties' and other expressions defined by section 1 of and Schedule I to the European Communities Act 1972 have the meanings prescribed by that Act.

'Month' means calendar month.

'Person' includes a body of persons corporate or unincorporate.

'Secretary of State' means one of Her Majesty's Principal Secretaries of State.

'Writing' includes typing, printing, lithography, photography and other modes of representing or reproducing words in a visible form, and expressions referring to writing are to be construed accordingly.

Appendix 3
Extracts from the European Convention for the Protection of
Human Rights and Fundamental Freedoms

Articles 2–12 and 14 of, and Articles 1–3 of the First Protocol, and
Articles 1 & 2 of the Sixth Protocol to, the European Convention
for the Protection of Human Rights and Fundamental Freedoms
1950

Section 1

Article 2
1.   Everyone's right to life shall be protected by law. No one shall be
deprived of his life intentionally save in the execution of a sentence of a
court following his conviction of a crime for which this penalty is provided
by law.

2.   Deprivation of life shall not be regarded as inflicted in contravention
of this Article when it results from the use of force which is no more than
absolutely necessary:

(a)   in defence of any person from unlawful violence;

(b)   in order to effect a lawful arrest or to prevent the escape of a person
lawfully detained;

(c)   in action lawfully taken for the purpose of quelling a riot or
insurrection

Article 3
No one shall be subjected to torture or to inhuman or degrading treatment
or punishment.

Article 4
1.   No one shall be held in slavery or servitude.

2.   No one shall be required to perform forced or compulsory labour.

3.   For the purpose of this Article the term 'forced or compulsory labour'
shall not include:

(a) any work required to be done in the ordinary course of detention imposed according to the provisions of Article 5 of this Convention or during conditional release from such detention;

(b) any service of a military character or, in case of conscientious objectors in countries where they are recognized, service exacted instead of compulsory military service;

(c) any service exacted in case of an emergency or calamity threatening the life or well being of the community;

(d) any work or service which forms part of normal civic obligations.

Article 5
1. Everyone has the right to liberty and security of person. No one shall be deprived of his liberty save in the following cases and in accordance with a procedure prescribed by law:

(a) the lawful detention of a person after conviction by a competent court;

(b) the lawful arrest or detention of a person for non-compliance with the lawful order of a court or in order to secure the fulfilment of any obligation prescribed by law;

(c) the lawful arrest or detention of a person effected for the purpose of bringing him before the competent legal authority on reasonable suspicion of having committed an offence or when it is reasonably considered necessary to prevent his committing an offence or fleeing after having done so;

(d) the detention of a minor by lawful order for the purpose of educational supervision or his lawful detention for the purpose of bringing him before the competent legal authority;

(e) the lawful detention of persons for the prevention of the spreading of infectious diseases, of persons of unsound mind, alcoholics or drug addicts, or vagrants;

(f) the lawful arrest or detention of a person to prevent his effecting an unauthorized entry into the country or of a person against whom action is being taken with a view to deportation or extradition.

2. Everyone who is arrested shall be informed promptly, in a language which he understands, of the reasons for his arrest and of any charge against him.

3.   Everyone arrested or detained in accordance with the provisions of paragraph 1(c) of this Article shall be brought promptly before a judge or other officer authorized by law to exercise judicial power and shall be entitled to trial within a reasonable time or to release pending trial. Release may be conditioned by guarantees to appear for trial.

4.   Everyone who is deprived of his liberty by arrest or detention shall be entitled to take proceedings by which the lawfulness of his detention shall be decided speedily by a court and his release ordered if the detention is not lawful.

5.   Everyone who has been the victim of arrest or detention in contravention of the provisions of this Article shall have an enforceable right to compensation.

Article 6
1.   In the determination of his civil rights and obligations or of any criminal charge against him, everyone is entitled to a fair and public hearing within a reasonable time by an independent and impartial tribunal established by law. Judgment shall be pronounced publicly but the press and public may be excluded from all or part of the trial in the interest of morals, public order or national security in a democratic society, where the interest of juveniles or the protection of the private life of the parties so require, or to the extent strictly necessary in the opinion of the court in special circumstances where publicity would prejudice the interests of justice.

2.   Everyone charged with a criminal offence shall be presumed innocent until proved guilty according to law.

3.   Everyone charged with a criminal offence has the following minimum rights:

(a)   to be informed promptly, in a language which he understands and in detail, of the nature and cause of the accusation against him;

(b)   to have adequate time and facilities for the preparation of his defence;

(c)   to defend himself in person or through legal assistance of his own choosing or, if he has not sufficient means to pay for legal assistance, to be given it free when the interests of justice so require;

(d)   to examine or have examined witnesses against him and to obtain the attendance and examination of witnesses on his behalf under the same conditions as witnesses against him;

(e) to have the free assistance of an interpreter if he cannot understand or speak the language used in court.

Article 7
1. No one shall be held guilty of any criminal offence on account of any act or omission which did not constitute a criminal offence under national or international law at the time when it was committed. Nor shall a heavier penalty be imposed than the one that was applicable at the time the criminal offence was committed.

2. This Article shall not prejudice the trial and punishment of any person for any act or omission which, at the time when it was committed, was criminal according to the general principles of law recognized by civilized nations.

Article 8
1. Everyone has the right to respect for his private and family life, his home and his correspondence.

2. There shall be no interference by a public authority with the exercise of this right except such as is in accordance with the law and is necessary in a democratic society in the interests of national security, public safety or the economic well-being of the country, for the prevention of disorder or crime, for the protection of health or morals, or for the protection of the rights and freedoms of others.

Article 9
1. Everyone has the right to freedom of thought, conscience and religion; this right includes freedom to change his religion or belief, and freedom, either alone or in community with others and in public or private, to manifest his religion or belief, in worship, teaching, practice and observance.

2. Freedom to manifest one's religion or beliefs shall be subject only to such limitations as are prescribed by law and are necessary in a democratic society in the interests of public safety, for the protection of public order, health or morals, or for the protection of the rights and freedoms of others.

Article 10
1. Everyone has the right to freedom of expression. This right shall include freedom to hold opinions and to receive and impart information

and ideas without interference by public authority and regardless of frontiers. This Article shall not prevent States from requiring the licensing of broadcasting, television or cinema enterprises.

2.　The exercise of these freedoms, since it carries with it duties and responsibilities, may be subject to such formalities, conditions, restrictions or penalties as are prescribed by law and are necessary in a democratic society in the interests of national security, territorial integrity or public safety, for the prevention of disorder or crime, for the protection of health or morals, for the protection of the reputation or rights of others, for preventing the disclosure of information received in confidence, or for maintaining the authority and impartiality of the judiciary.

Article 11
1.　Everyone has the right to freedom of peaceful assembly and to freedom of association with others, including the right to form and to join trade unions for the protection of his interests.

2.　No restrictions shall be placed on the exercise of these rights other than such as are prescribed by law and are necessary in a democratic society in the interests of national security or public safety, for the prevention of disorder or crime, for the protection of health or morals or for the protection of the rights and freedoms of others. This Article shall not prevent the imposition of lawful restrictions on the exercise of these rights by members of the armed forces, of the police or of the administration of the State.

Article 12
Men and women of marriageable age have the right to marry and to found a family, according to the national laws governing the exercise of this right.

Article 14
The enjoyment of the rights and freedoms set forth in this Convention shall be secured without discrimination on any ground such as sex, race, colour, language, religion, political or other opinion, national or social origin, association with a national minority, property, birth or other status.

Note: Articles 16, 17 and 18 respectively provide that arts.10, 11 and 14 do not prohibit restrictions on the political activities of aliens; nothing in the Convention gives any right to do anything which would harm the rights which it protects; and the restrictions contained in the Convention may be applied only for the purposes for which they are prescribed.

Articles 1–3 of Protocol 1: Enforcement of Certain Rights and Freedoms not included in Section 1 of the Convention

Article 1

Every natural or legal person is entitled to the peaceful enjoyment of his possessions. No one shall be deprived of his possessions except in the public interest and subject to the conditions provided for by law and by the general principles of international law.

The preceding provisions shall not, however, in any way impair the right of a State to enforce such laws as it deems necessary to control the use of property in accordance with the general interest or to secure the payment of taxes or other contributions or penalties.

Article 2

No person shall be denied the right to education In the exercise of any functions which it assumes in relation to education and to teaching, the State shall respect the right of parents to ensure such education and teaching in conformity with their own religious and philosophical convictions.

Article 3

The High Contracting Parties undertake to hold free elections at reasonable intervals by secret ballot, under conditions which will ensure the free expression of the opinion of the people in the choice of the legislature.

Articles 1 and 2 of Protocol 6: Concerning the Abolition of the Death Penalty

Article 1

The death penalty shall be abolished. No one shall be condemned to such penalty or executed.

Article 2

A state may make provision in its law for the death penalty in respect of acts committed in time of war or of imminent threat of war; such penalty shall be applied only in the instance laid down in the law and in accordance with its provisions. The State shall communicate to the Secretary General of the Council of Europe the relevant provisions of that law.